AF554006

Kautilya

or

An Exposition of his Social Ideal and Political Theory

Narayan Chandra Bandyopadhyaya

LOW PRICE PUBLICATIONS

Delhi-110052

Distributed by
D.K. Publishers Distributors (P) Ltd.
4834/24, Ansari Road, Darya Ganj,
New Delhi-110002
Phones: 51562573, 51562574, 51562575
e-mail: dkpd@del3.vsnl.net.in
url: www.dkpd.com

First Published 1927 (R. Cambray & Co., Calcutta)

Reprinted in **LPP** 2005

ISBN 81-7536-386-X

Published by
Low Price Publications
A-6, Nimri Commercial Centre,
Near Ashok Vihar Phase-IV,
Delhi-110052
Phones: 27452453
e-mail: lpp@nde.vsnl.net.in
url: www.lppindia.com

Printed at
D K Fine Art Press P Ltd.
Delhi-110052

PRINTED IN INDIA

To the rising generation of
- - thoughtful Indians - -
is dedicated this humble
attempt at elucidation of
- the political and social -
principles of Kautilya, the
foremost political thinker of
- - Ancient Hindu India -

PREFACE

Ever since my appointment as a lecturer in the Post-graduate Department of the Calcutta University, I have been engaged in a study of the political thought and ideals of the ancient Hindus. As such, the Arthaśāstra of Kauṭilya claimed my special attention, for it was the handiwork of a remarkable personality, who, according to tradition, uprooted the unrighteous Nandas and laid the foundations of an Empire which called forth the admiration of the Greeks who had followed Alexander in his world-conquest.

It is unfortunate that nothing authentic has been preserved in regard to the life and work of Kauṭilya, and that his memory itself has been relegated to the faint recollections of tradition. In the absence of a reliable history, his Arthaśāstra remains the sole testimony of his greatness. The credit of its discovery is due to Dr. Shamasastry, whose ***editio princeps*** as well as English translation have been appreciated all over the world. The book carries us back to a glorious period of Hindu history, when India held her place among the great nations of the ancient world, and it unfolds to us the details of an art of government, which ensured peace at home and prestige abroad, which strengthened the foundations of political authority by making it devote its energies to the common good, and which fostered loyalty by making the ruler identify his interests with those of the ruled.

The object of the present volume is not so much to summarise the details of Kauṭiliyan administration as to present in a handy volume the guiding principles of the greatest Arthaśāstra teacher, to discuss his ideas as to the ends and functions of government, and to present the prospects of good government which he had before him. In attempting to do this, I have taken care to eliminate the unimportant details of an administration subsisting more or less in reality, in an age removed from us by more than two thousand years, and special attention has been paid to those topics which interest men of the modern age with their new angle of vision and modified objectives and ideals. In so doing, I have attempted to read ancient history with the altered vision of a moderner, taking precautions against reading modern institutions into our past history.

At the same time, I have laid emphasis on the evolutionary aspect of institutions and have tried to make my ideas clear by citing parallels from the history of other nations, more especially from the history of Medieval England. I have, moreover, done my best to note the peculiarities of Indian social and political evolution which would seem unique in their character. In India, we had a peculiar type of social organisation, based, apparently though, on narrow principles, yet presenting an outlook not only wide but sympathetic and humane in the highest degree. The diversity of ethnic elements stood indeed in the path of social homogeneity, and yet, the ends of society were not narrowed down to exclude heterogeneous elements in the interest of the ruling few. Thus arose a federative social organisation with heterogenous sections, which were all united in a common purpose like the different limbs of a living organism. The ends and functions of political authority, too, varied consequently. In spite of fundamental differences, radical diversities and traditional privileges of the different sections, the king became the defender of the rights of all irrespective of caste and creed, and centred his attention on the fruition of the material objectives of all classes of subjects. He was the protector of all and came to be conceived as the father of his subjects, though in many respects his authority was circumscribed.

In this volume, I have not only traced the peculiarities of the system and its germs in earliest antiquity but also their gradual elaboration in successive stages, till the system came to have its ablest and sincerest advocate in the person of the last and ablest of the Arthaśāstra writers.

I have, in these pages, confined myself more or less to the details and principles of good government, reserving for the next volume all other interesting topics like those relating to diplomacy, war, conquest and imperialistic consolidation. I have, however, not gone into questions about the date of the present work, nor allowed myself to be drawn into the vortex of a controversy prejudicial to an exposition of the real subject-matter. Personally, I find no reasons for rejecting the traditional date of the Arthaśāstra and I have accepted it. Furthermore, the arguments of those who dispute the date and authorship of the Kauṭilīya have been very ably answered by Mr. Jayaswal in his Hindu Polity. The arguments of Dr. Winternitz have been successfully refuted by my esteemed friend, Dr. Narendranath Law. I, too, have discussed the same question in my *Economic Life and progress* (Vol. I. pages 27 & 28), and whatever new points remain to be advanced will be mentioned in the appendix to the second volume, which is being printed.

For the publication of this volume, my best thanks are due to Srijut Taraknath Gupta, whose keen interest in the work made him do everything to arrange the preliminaries of publication. For help and encouragement, I am no less indebted to my old classfellow, Mr. P. C. Sen, M. Sc. and to Mr. S. C. Ghosh, M. A., my colleague in the Post-graduate Department and a Fellow of the Calcutta University. Finally, I express my sense of indebtedness to Messers. R. Cambray, who have taken over the publication of the work and have thus saved me much trouble.

Owing to unavoidable reasons, a number of mistakes and errors of print have crept in. The more serious of such errors have been corrected in the errata appended at the end. On my part, I crave the indulgence of generous readers for my own carelessness.

NARAYAN CHANDRA BANDYOPADHYAYA

30, Tarak Chatterjee's Lane.

June 1, 1927.

CONTENTS

BOOK I

Introductory.

BOOK II

Ideas about Society, State and Kingship.

BOOK III

The King, his duties and relation to the State.

BOOK IV

The Administration.

BOOK V

Retrospect and Criticism.

Bibliography.

The Yajurveda ... Bombay N. S. text
S'atapatha Brāhmaṇa... Trans by Eggeling
Aitareya Brāhmaṇa ... Haug's edition & Translation
The Dharma-sūtra of Apastamba (B. S, S. Edition)
" " Vaśiṣṭha (B. S. S. Edition)

The Dharma-sūtra of Gautama (Mysore edition)
Jātaka—Fausboll
Eng. Trans. by Cowell.
Beng. Trans. by I. C. Ghose
(Vols I, II, III.)
The Inscriptions of Aśoka.
Gupta Inscriptions by Fleet.
The Cāṇakya-kathā, C. O. S. edited by Dr. N. Law.
The Mudrā-rākṣasa—B. S. S. Edition by Telang.
The Kauṭilya Arthaśāstra—*Editio Princeps* and Eng. Trans. by Dr. R. Shamasastry.
The Vātsyāyana Kāma-sūtra
The Sarva siddhānta-saṅgraha ... M. G. S. S. edited by Kuppusvamy.
The Sarva-darśana-saṅgraha ... ... Edited by Jivānanda Vidyāsāgara.
The Saḍdarśana-samuccaya, Benares Sanskrit Series.
English Constitutional History—By Medlay, Tasswall Langmead and Feilden.
Decline and Fall of Roman Empire—by Gibbon
Maspero ... Struggle of Nations
MacLaren ... ... History of Japan during the Meiji Era.
Jastrow ... ... Civilization of Babylonia.
Seth ... ... Ethical Principles.
Haney ... ... History of Economic Thought

ERRATA

Page.	Line.	Incorrect.	Correct.
3	f. n.	भोचेाग्नि	भोच्याग्नि
14	,,	त्रिवर्ग	विवर्ग
17	,,	विधि	विधि:
32	14	अनुवन्ध	अनुबन्ध
,,	21	पुण:	पुन:
36	8	व्राह्मण	ब्राह्मण
37	26	व्यवहारम्	व्यवहारम्
42	10	वलीयान्	बलीयान्
44	44	वाणप्रस्थ	वानप्रस्थ
47	3	commonality	commonalty.
56	19	isolaton	isolation
58	8	वलीयानवल'	बलीयानबल'
60	5	hymus	hymns
63	6	theoritical	theoretical
65	20	strung	stung
68	13 & 17	Law	the law
81	2	राजस्व: स्रोतियस्व:	राजस्वं स्रोत्रियस्वं
85	1 & 2	व्राह्मण	ब्राह्मण
95	25	जाङ्गलीविद:	जाङ्गलीविद:
119	16	Vali	Bali
124	12	गुह्यमेको	गुह्यमेको
129	15	stand	stands
1?1	25	अभात्या	अमात्या
142	7	Vali	Bali
148	8	Vali	Bali
152	f. n.	Vāhya	Bāhya
189	25	वहु	बहु
202	8	capilalist	capitalist
223	27	पाढो	पाठो
241	2	वन्धु	बन्धु
270	13	Vrsata	Vrṣala
276	17	Yāgñavalkya	Yājñavalkya
241	13 & 20	वाल	बाल
293	14	Sāti-parva	S'ānti-parva

There have been some more unavoidable mistakes, especially with regard to ब. This is due to the inexperience of the press- workers, in an establishment mainly concerned with English work. Moreover, the difference between व and ब is hardly understood in Eastern India.

KAUTILYA

I

KAUTILYA OR CANAKYA

Next to the heroes of the Epics or the Purāṇas, no name is more familiar to Indians than that of Cāṇakya* or, as he is otherwise known, Kauṭilya or Viṣṇu-gupta. Throughout the whole of India, nītis or wise sayings attributed to him, are even now taught to beginners. This nīti literature is not confined to India, but has travelled to distant countries like Ceylon, Burma Tibet, Siam, and even to Persia and Arabia, and

* विष्णुगुप्तस्तु कौटिल्यश्चाणक्यो द्रामिलोऽङ्गुलः । (Trikāṇḍaśeṣa ; ब्रह्मवर्गः) The name Kauṭilya, by which the author of the Artha-śāstra designates himself, means "crookedness". Mahamahopadhyaya Gaṇapati Sastri makes this name Kauṭalya i e. one descended from the Kuṭala gotra.

has found place in the literatures of those countries. *

The very fact that this almost universal adoration is paid to his memory, shows that Kauṭilya was in his own days regarded as a master, whose worldy wisdom and foresight gained for him the veneration of his contemporaries. Their reverence was transmitted from one generation to another, and his real history having been forgotten, tradition surrounded his name with a halo of intellectual glow that marked him out for the spontaneous veneration of posterity, not only in his own country but in the world outside.

No authentic history of this remarkable man has reached us, except references to his success in diplomacy or proficiency in the Art of Government, of which he was a redoubtable exponent in the remote past Of this, again, we have no clear details, and even when such are obtainable, they clearly transport him from the region of history proper and make him the hero of a cycle of semi-mythical legends, of which we shall give some account later on.

* We have Cāṇakya *Nītis* in the various provinces of India, some comprising Sanskrit verses, while the rest are supposed to be the views of Cāṇakya rendered into the vernacular. We have such *nītis* attributed to Cāṇakya in Ceylon (the Pathyavākya), in Burma (the Lokanīti), and in Siam. Counterparts of these seem to exist even in Persian and Arabic. Mr. Van Manen, who is engaged in a collection of this literature, expects to place them before scholars very soon.

Among the Purāṇas, the Viṣṇu preserves the tradition that Kauṭilya destroyed the Nandas and through his diplomacy put Maurya Candragupta on the throne. The only detail we find in that Purāṇa is in the prophecy which runs as follows :—

"The nine Nanda brothers will rule the world for one hundred years. They shall then be ejected by the Brāhmaṇa Kauṭilya and on their fall, the Mauryas will rule the earth. Kauṭilya will establish Candra-gupta in the kingdom".

Next, we find Kauṭilya's name and his excellence as a writer on Polity* mentioned in Jain and Buddhist tradition. Cāṇakya's name is mentioned in the Mṛcchakaṭika, a drama written in the first century A. D.† In the introduction to the Kāmandaka Nītisāra, a work on Polity, we find a repetition of the tradition about the downfall of the Nandas. The author of this remarkable treatise, who utilised much of his material from the

---

* महापद्मः । ···तत्पुत्राश्चैकं वर्षशतमवनीपतयो भविष्यन्ति । नवैवतान्नन्दान् कौटिल्यो ब्राह्मणः समुद्धरिष्यति । तेषामभावेमौर्याश्चपृथिवीं भोक्ष्यन्ति । कौटिल्य एव चन्द्रगुप्तं राजेऽभिषेक्ष्यन्ति । V. P.—Cāṇakya's name occurs in the Jain Nandi sutra (समये अमच्चपुत्ते चाणक्के थूलबद्दय). *See* Shamasastry's Sanskrit introduction to the first edition of the Arthaśāstra. The Kauṭilīya is also enumerated in the list of false sciences.

† The Sakāra in the first Act prides upon his own valour and speaking of his determination to chastise Vasantasenā, compares himself to Cāṇakya, whom he describes as the ravisher of Draupadī.

Kauṭilīya, makes a reverential mention of him.* Later authors of nīti and romance repeatedly cite his name in connection with his mastery of the Science of Polity as does also the author of the Pañca-tantra. † In the sixth century A.D., the great romance-writer † and poet Daṇḍī refers to the importance of the great work on Daṇḍa-nīti, composed by Ācārya Viṣṇu-gupta for the benefit of the Maurya, comprising six thousand ślokas ‡. As pointed out by Dr. Shamasastry, Daṇḍī seems to have been acquainted with the principles and many of the details of the Kauṭilyan Art of Government and this is amply confirmed by the fine parallelism of some passages of his book with those of the Arthaśāstra. (See the English Introduction to Shamasastry's translation, first edition, pp. vii—ix)

---

* यस्याभिचारवज्रेण वज्रज्वलनतेजसः ।
पपात मूलतः श्रीमान् सुपर्वा नन्दपर्वतः ॥
एकाकी मन्त्रशक्त्या यः शक्त्या शक्तिधरोपमः ।
आजहार नृचन्द्राय चन्द्रगुप्ताय मेदिनीम् ॥
नीतिशास्त्रामृतं धीमानर्थशास्त्रमहोदधेः ।
समुद्दध्रे नमस्तस्मै विष्णुगुप्ताय वेधसे ॥
दर्शनात्तस्य सुदृशो विद्यानां पारदृश्वनः ।
यत्किञ्चिदुपदेक्ष्यामः राजविद्याविदां मतम् ॥

Kāmandaka, V. 4—8.

† ततो धर्मशास्त्रादीणि मन्वादीनि अर्थशास्त्राणि चाणक्यादीनि कामशास्त्राणि वात्स्यायनादीनि ।

‡ VIIIth Ucchāsa of the second part.

अधीष्वतावद्दण्डनीतिम् । इयमिदानीमाचार्यविष्णुगुप्तेन मौर्यार्थे षड्भिःश्लोकसहस्रैः संक्षिप्ता । सैवेयमधीत्य सम्यगनुष्ठीयमाना यथोक्तकार्यक्षमेति ॥

While Daṇḍī regarded Kauṭilya as the master of a science, the knowledge of which facilitated success in this world, his system, a century later, received a violent denunciation in the hands of Bāṇa, the biographer of king Harṣa, and well-known as the author of the romance Kādambarī.* But inspite of it, Kauṭilya's name finds mentioned in a large number of works. The name Viṣṇugupta occurs in the Bṛhat-saṃhitā of Varāhamihira, though it is more probable that some other Viṣṇu-gupta who was an astronomer, is meant. Kālidāsa, the great poet, seems to have been fairly acquainted with the principles of the Arthaśāstra and occasionally his language bears a close similarity to that of the latter work. (See Shamasastry's introduction, pp. xiv, xv).

It is needless to multiply references, but one fact appears clear *viz.* that Kauṭilya was universally looked upon as one of the greatest authorities on the science of Polity. Many later authorities regarded him as a great teacher and utilised materials drawn from his work. Not to speak of Kāmandaka, who

---

* किं वा तेषां साम्प्रतं येषामतिनृशंसप्रायोपदेशनिर्घृणं कौटिल्यशास्त्रं प्रमाणं, अभिचारक्रियाक्रूरैकप्रकृतयः पुरोधसो गुरवः, परातिसन्धानपरा मन्त्रिणः उपदेष्टारः, नरपतिसहस्रोज्झितायां लक्ष्म्यामासक्तिः, मरणात्मकेषु शास्त्रेष्वभियोगः, सहजप्रेमार्द्र-हृदयानुरक्ता भ्रातर उच्छेद्याः etc. ।

expressly regards himself as a disciple of Kauṭilya*, we find another, a Jain Somadeva-sūri, basing his shorter work on the Kauṭilīya. Many Smṛti writers borrowed their ideas and the principles they laid down in thir works directly from the Arthaśāstra. The fine parallelism between some chapters of the Arthaśāstra and the present Yāgñavalkya Smṛti has been very ably pointed out by Dr. Shamasastry in foot-notes appended to both his first edition and the translation. The author of the present volume has found out the indebtedness of the Kātyāyaṇa Smṛti to the Arthaśāstrā.† Kauṭilya's views, moreover, appear in the classical commentaries. Mallinātha refers to them, while in one place, Kulluka Bhaṭṭa, the commentator of the Manusaṃhitā, quotes a long passage from the present Arthaśāstra.

As we have already stated, most of the references and traditions connect Kauṭilya with the Nandas, whose downfall is attributed to his anger and his successful diplomacy. This, as

* Somadeva-sūri mentions the story of Cāṇakya's successful diplomacy, which put an end to the Nandas. For a comparison of parallel ideas and passages, see Shamasastry's introduction to the Eng. Tran., p. xxi.

† For a parallelism between some of the legal maxims and principles of Kātyāyana and those of the Arthaśāstra, we refer our readers to the Introduction to the Kātyāyana-mata-saṅgraha, edited by the present author and published by the Calcutta University.

shown already, appears from the Viṣṇupurāṇa, from the statements in the Daśakumāra-carita and in Soma-deva's Nītivākyāmṛta.

Details of this, however, appear only in some later works. Of these we may mention the following, *e.g.*

(*a*) The Kathā-sarit-sāgara.

(*b*) The drama of Mudrā-rākṣasa with its commentary by Ḍhuṇḍhirāja who seems to have been thoroughly acquainted with the Cāṇakya tradition.

(*c*) The Cāṇakya-kathā in verse, based on the prose version written by Ravinartaka (published by N. Law in the Calcutta Oriental Series and complete in 352 ślokas).

The version of the Kathā-sarit-sāgara may be summarised as follows :—(I. 5th Taraṅga).

"King Nanda (Yoga-nanda) had injured his minister Śakaṭāla, who consequently thought of ruining his master. One day, he found a Brahmin "digging the earth to root out a plant of *darbha* grass because it had pricked his foot." This stern determination of the Brahmin struck him and he made up his mind to make him his chief instrument in destroying Nanda. On behalf of the king, he invited the Brahmin to preside at the Śrāddha in Nanda's family. On the appointed day, he was led and placed at the head of the table, but this was disputed by another Brahmin,

Subandhu. The king deciding in favour of the latter, Cāṇakya had to leave the hall, but before doing so, he openly vowed to kill Nanda within seven days, and swore never to bind his śikhā, until and unless that was accomplished. He was given protection by Śakaṭāla and performed a magic rite, as the consequence of which Yoga-nanda caught a burning fever and died on the seventh day. After his death, his son Hiraṇya-gupta was killed by Śakaṭāla and Candra-gupta, a son of the previous Nanda, became king.

This account, which finds place in a story-book, borders more on myth when it attributes the death of Nanda to a magic rite. The two other accounts, which are substantially in agreement with each other as also to the prefatory verses in Ḍhuṇḍhirāja's commentary, give us more details, which though containing elements of myth, preserve some element which may be relied upon. They attribute Cāṇakya's anger to the insults of the Nandas in the assembly and repeat the story of his vow and the unbinding of his sacred tuft. While agreeing in this, they attribute the success of Cāṇakya to his successful diplomacy which roused up a confederacy against the Nandas and thereby brought about their downfall. This was followed by the destruction of the last surviving Nanda and of the princes of the confederacy who wished to oust or defeat Cāṇakya's *protege* Candra-gupta, the founder of the Maurya dynasty. This prince is mentioned in the Purāṇas and also in the Greek accounts under the name of Sandracottus. Here we give a summarised version of the account found in the Cāṇakya-kathā.

According to this story, Kauṭilya was a poor Brahmin who lived in the vicinity of the city of Pāṭaliputra, the capital of a powerful empire which embraced a large part of north-eastern India. There ruled the imperial Nandas, who according to the Viṣṇupurāṇa, were the last Kṣattriya kings to rule in the beginning of the Kali Age. One of these Nanda kings, Sarvārtha siddhi, had two wives, a Kṣattriyā named Sunandā and a Śūdrā named Murā, who being very beautiful and attached to her royal master, won his affection inspite of her low origin.

Being desirous of sons, the king entertained a powerful ascetic in his palace and having washed his feet with his own hands, sprinkled that water on his queens. Sunandā received nine drops while only one fell on Murā. The latter received it with great reverence for the sage who was also greatly pleased with her. Murā gave birth to a son who came to be known as Maurya. When this boy attained maturity, the king handed him over to an Ācārya who taught him all the Śāstras and the mode of using the various weapons.

The king was also much pleased with this prince, who had so many virtues and was so obedient to him. He thus enhanced the joy of both of his parents and the subjects.

Sunandā in her turn, gave birth to a lump of flesh which in time produced nine sons. They too, grew up, and when they were young, king Sarvārtha-siddhi called them together to advise on matters of state. After discussion and consultation with Maurya and minister Rākṣasa, it was settled that on the death of the king, the sovereignty would be vested in the nine princes reigning conjointly. But, only one of them should rule every year and the first ruler was to be selected by casting lot. Rākṣasa was made prime minister and Maurya was appointed commander-in-chief.

In course of a few years, Maurya became the father of one hundred chivalrous sons, all virtuous and skilled in politics. The people were attached to them ; and this made the Nandas jealous of them. On the pretext of being invited to a secret consultation, they were imprisoned in a dark underground dungeon, where all of them except Candra-gupta died. Three months later, this latter was taken out by the Nandas to see whether he could solve a riddle presented to them by the king of Laṅkā. (Baṅka or Baṅga ?) That king had sent the figure of a ferocious lion put in the midst of an iron cage.

They were to remove the image without opening the cage. Candra-gupta was of very keen intellect who easily concluded that the figure of the lion was of wax.

To remove it, he caused the wax to be melted by holding a bar of red hot iron near it. This success made him an object of hatred, and he on his part resolved to avenge the injuries caused by the Nandas. Soon an opportunity presented itself. The Śrāddha ceremony of the ancestors and relatives of the Nandas came and Candra-gupta was ordered to invite Brahmins. While on his way to the home of some Brahmins, he found Cāṇakya engaged in exterminating the roots of Muñja grass and eating the calx after burning it, since it had bruised his feet [and thereby postponed his matriage]. His determination, and also the skill in politics he displayed in conversation, made Candra-gupta sure of the help he could expect from such a man in his vengeance. He introduced himself as a Vṛṣala, and, relating to him the sad end of his father and brothers, asked him to come to the ceremony.

Cāṇakya was led to the Nanda court and placed himself on the seat of honour reserved for the most qnalified among the Brahmin guests. The haughty Nandas not knowing the facts and enraged at this intrusion, ordered his expulsion. Their servants caught him by the śikhā and expelled him from the hall. Thereupon the angry Brahmin swore that he would destroy the seed of the Nandas and place another—a son of a Śūdra on the throne He then departed and when he saw Candra-gupta, he promised to make him king on condition of his being made the Chief Minister.

Strict secrecy was maintained and when everything was ready, Cāṇakya devoted his whole attention to the destruction of the Nandas. He employed a Brahmin named Indraśarmā who had been his classfellow to watch over the conduct of Rākṣasa the minister. This man came to Pāṭaliputra in the garb of a Kṣapaṇaka by name Jīvasiddhi and proclaimed himself to be a master of astrology and spells. He won over Rākṣasa by curing one of the Nandas, and to ensure the freedom of Candra-gupta, he caused the latter to be banished from the city. Indraśarmā won the confidence of Rākṣasa and gathered all his secret Candra-gupta on his part won the confidence of the king of Śavaras and when everything was ready Cāṇakya incited the Mleccha king Parvataka to attack the Nandas, promising as his reward half of the Nanda Empire. His spies tampered with the loyalty of the enemy's troops and played on their superstition. This agreement concluded, the combined armies fell on the capital city and the Nandas were defeated and killed. The capital surrendered after a siege. Old Sarvārthasiddhi who had been made king was killed and at the same time, Parvataka was got rid of by a *poison-maid* (viṣa-kanyā). Candra-gupta became king with Cāṇakya as his prime minister. Rākṣasa whose life had been spared and on the advice of Cāṇakya allowed to remain one of the ministers, was left to be dealt with.

Rākṣasa, however, remained an enemy of the new state of affairs and plotted against Candra-gupta. He employed spies and assasins to kill the latter, but all such attempts were baffled owing to the vigilence and protective measures of Cāṇakya. Rākṣasa had secretly served the cause of Parvataka and tried to remove Candra-gupta by sending a poison girl of great beauty to him. Through Cāṇakya's activity, the plan had totally miscarried and Parvataka died coming in contact with the poison-maid, as stated already. The guilt of killing Parvataka was fastened on Rākṣasa.

Rākṣasa next fled from the city and joining Malayaketu (Parvataka's son), incited him to avenge the death of his father. But Cāṇakya sent his minister Bhāgurāyaṇa over to that prince and at the same time, employed such clever spies and stratagems that Malayaketu lost confidence in Rākṣasa, who had to fly for his life. Left alone, Malayaketu was easily defeated. Rākṣasa in despair, surrendered to his enemies, but Cāṇakya spared his life and made him Prime-minister to the Maurya, to whom he afterwards became devotedly attached. Having fulfilled his vow, Cāṇakya tied his tuft of hair and practically retired from active life, although he continued to advise the king in times of emergency.

The Mudrā-rākṣasa account opens at the point of Rākṣasa's alliance with Malayaketu, son of Parvataka, (killed by Cāṇakya through the *poison-maid*) and ends with the outwitting of Rākṣasa. The latter remained for a time the adviser of Malayaketu, but through Cāṇakya's intrigues, was discarded by Malayaketu who came to look upon him as a spy of Candra-gupta and Cāṇakya (act. V), and contemptuously dismissed him.* The rash prince not only dismissed Rākṣasa but ordered the cruel murder and imprisonment of the five kings in alliance with him *i.e.* Citravarmā of Kulūta, Siṃhanāda of Malaya, Puṣkarākṣa of Kaśmīra, the Sindhu king Suṣena and Meghanāda the Persian. This rather furthered the cause of Candra-gupta, and the hostile league was thus dissolved. Malayaketu was captured and imprisoned by the friendly princes and leaders Bhadrabhaṭa, Ḍiṅgarāta, Balagupta, Rājasena, Rohitākṣa and Vijayavarmā. (Act. VI, prelude.)

---

* मलयकेतु :—राक्षस, राक्षस, नाहं विश्रम्भघाती राक्षसः । मलयकेतुः मलयकेतुरहम् । तद्गच्छ समाश्रीयतां सर्वात्मना चन्द्रगुप्तः । पश्य—

विष्णुगुप्तञ्च मौर्यं च सममप्यागतौ त्वया ।
उन्मूलयितुमीशोऽहं त्रिवर्गमिव दुर्नयः ॥ Act. V. close.

Rākṣasa was also very cleverly outwitted. The most confided of his friends* turned to be the spies of Cāṇakya. He realised it too late. His seal-ring was stolen and his letters were forged by Śakaṭadāsa. Candanadāsa, in whose care he had kept his family, was imprisoned and taken to the execution-ground. Rākṣasa, informed (through a stratagem) of his danger and given up by all, came forward to save him.† Cāṇakya too appeared there in disguise, covered in a heavy mantle. The two rival politicians met at length. After recounting his own superhuman acheivements, ‡ Cāṇakya complimented Rākṣasa§ who did the same in return.¶ Candragupta, also appeared there, and on the recommendation of Cāṇakya, Rākṣasa was made minister to the Maurya king.

---

* Speaking of Kṣapaṇaka Jīvasiddhi, who was none else than Indraśarmā, the classfellow of Cāṇakya, Rākṣasa exclaims rather in anguish at his faithlessness :—

राक्षसः—"कथं जीवसिद्धिरपि चाणक्यप्रणिधिः। हन्त, रिपुभिर्मे हृदयमपि स्वीकृतम्" ॥ (Vth Act)

† व्यापत्तिं ज्ञातमस्य स्वतनुमहमिमां निष्क्रयं कल्पयामि ॥ (end of VIth Act)

‡ केनोत्तुङ्गशिखाकलापकपिलो बद्धः पटान्ते शिखी।
पाशैः केन सदागतेरगतिता सद्यः समासादिता ॥
केनानेकपदानवासितसटः सिंहोऽर्पितः पञ्जरे।
भीमः केन च नैकनक्रमकरो दोर्भ्यां प्रतीर्णोऽर्णवः ॥

§ येन महात्मना—गुरुभिः कल्पनाक्लेशैर्दीर्घजागरहेतुभिः।
चिरमायासिता सेना वृषलस्य मतिश्च मे ॥

¶ अयं दुरात्मा अथवा महात्मा कौटिल्यः—
आकरः सर्वशास्त्राणां रत्नानामिव सागरः।
गुणैर्न परितुष्यामो यस्य मत्सरिणो वयम् ॥ Act VII.

II

THE ARTHASASTRA AND ITS DISCOVERY

Except the tradition connecting him with the elevation of Candragupta Maurya to the Imperial throne, nothing more was recorded of Kauṭilya. His great work, attested to by ancient authors like Kāmandaka, Daṇḍin or Bāṇa, and by more recent writers and commentators like Medhātithi or Kulluka, was believed to have been lost.

This remained so till the beginning of the present century, when the manuscript of a work (together with a commentary on a part of it) "ascribing itself in unmistakable terms to the famous Brahmin Kauṭilya, also named Viṣṇugupta" was handed over by a pundit of the Tanjore district to the Mysore Government Oriental Library. This manuscript proved to be the long lost Arthaśāstra by Kauṭilya, and Mr. Shamasastry, the Librarian, who devoted much of his time to its study gave a tentative translation of it in the pages of the Indian Antiquary in 1905 and following years. Through the enlightened encouragement of the Mysore Durbar, the text was published in 1909, and the first English translation by the same learned scholar appeared in 1915. More recently, two other editions have been published. The first of these is by Prof. Jolly and has been published in the Punjab Oriental Series. The second has been edited with a commentary by the late Mahamahopadhyaya Pundit Gaṇapati Sastri of Trivandrum in the Sanskrit series published under the patronage of H. H. the Maharaja of Travancore.

The Kauṭilīya, as we have it now, comprises ten books (adhikaraṇas) and one hundred and fifty chapters (सपञ्चाशदध्यायशतम्) and is supposed to be complete in six thousand ślokas (षट् श्लोकसहस्राणि). In the first chapter of the first book, we find it distinctly mentioned that the work is based upon older Arthaśāstras* and that it was composed by Kauṭilya [after carefully consulting other authorities,†] bereft of undue enlargement, clearly explained and easy to understand.

In two other places we have statements which speak of Kauṭilya's authorship of the book. One of these occurs in the body of the book, at the end of the chapter on "royal writs" (Śāsanādhikāra).‡ Two more verses which occur at the end

* सुखग्रहणविज्ञेयं तत्त्वार्थपदनिश्चितम् ।
कौटिल्येन कृतं शास्त्रं विमुक्तग्रन्थविस्तरम् ॥

† पृथिव्या लाभे पालने च यावन्त्यर्थशास्त्राणि पूर्वाचार्यैः प्रस्थापितानि प्रायशस्तानि संहृत्यैकमिदमर्थशास्त्रं कृतम् (I. I. Page 1.)

सर्वशास्त्राण्यनुक्रम्य प्रयोगमुपलभ्य च ।
कौटिल्येन नरेन्द्रार्थे शासनस्य विधिः कृतः ॥ (II. 10).

‡ येन शास्त्रं च शस्त्रं च नन्दराजगता च भूः ।
अमर्षेणोद्धृतान्याशु तेन शास्त्रमिदं कृतम् ॥

of the book are more interesting, for they say that "this śāstra has been composed by one, who saved the sciences and the knowledge of weapons from decay, and rescued the world from the [misrule of the] Nandas."* and furthermore—"that Viṣṇu-gupta composed not only the sūtra, but also the bhāṣya, being mindful of the manifold errors and deficiencies of the commentators to the various śāstras."† The last statement is confirmed by the Arthaśāstra itself for the book comprises both sūtras and bhāṣya. This is apparent to all familiar with the Arthaśāstra text, but, unfortunately, it is difficult to separate the two and as yet no such attempt has been made in that direction.

Before we pass on to other topics, we must say something as to the character and contents of the Arthaśāstras. These books, if we are to believe in orthodox tradition embodied in the Purāṇas, formed part of the Artha-veda, which came to be regarded very early as an Upa-veda. This branch of study arose out of the necessity of enquiring into the means of gaining success in the material world. Agriculture, cattle-rearing, the attainment of prosperity in the world so far as the individual was concerned, the success of kings, and the progress of kingdoms,—

---

* दृष्ट्वा विप्रतिपत्तिं बहुधा शास्त्रेषु भाष्यकाराणाम् ।
स्वयमेव विष्णुगुप्तश्चकार सूत्रं च भाष्यं च ॥

† ततऋग्वेदस्यार्थशास्त्रमुपवेदः ।········वेदानामुपवेदाश्चत्वारः अथर्ववेदस्यार्थशास्त्रम् ।

were the topics dealt with by the authors of of these books. According to the evidence of the Caraṇavyūha of Śaunaka and others, Arthaśāstra was the Upa-veda of the Rig-veda or the Atharva-veda.* The importance of this branch of study has been clearly emphasised by later authorities.†

These books were thus the crude predecessors of our modern works on Political Economy or Philosophy. Writers on this subject were many and we find the names of such authors in the Epic (see Mahā. Śānti. ch. 56), in the Arthaśāstra itself and in later works like the Kāmandaka Nītisāra.

Kauṭilya was probably the last and the greatest exponent of the views of life that distinguished the Arthaśāstra writers. In his book, he constantly refers to older authors (pūrvācāryas) and metions the names of a large number of them. Some of these seem to have been closely connected with schools of Socio-ethical discipline, bearing the names of real or supposed

---

* For the tradition relating to the growth of the Uap-vedas, see Viṣṇu Purāṇa. III. ch. VI. 29.

See also my *Economic Life and Progress.* Vol. I. p. 13, 14.

† The author of the Sarva-siddhānta-saṅgraha clearly says—

अर्थवेदोऽन्नपानादिप्रदानसुखतत्परः ।
तत्पालनाच्चतुर्वर्गपुरुषार्थप्रसाधकः ॥ Ch. I. 13.

founders. Of these we may mention the following—

I. The Mānavāḥ
II. The Bārhaspaṭyāḥ
III. The Auśanasāḥ
IV. The Āmbhīyāḥ

Important single teachers, too, existed and of these may be mentioned the following :—

I. Viśālākṣa
II Parāśara
III. Piśuṇa
IV. Bāhudanti-putra
V. Kauṇapa-danta
VI. Vātavyādhi
VII. Kātyāyana
VIII. Kaṇiṅko Bhāradvāja
IX. Bhāradvāja
X. Dīrghaścārāyaṇa
XI. Ghoṭamukha
XII. Kiñjalka
XIII. Piśuṇa-putra.

Taking into consideration the evidence of the Epic and the names of some of these teachers, we find that several of them were closely associated with the worship of particular deities. Thus, Viśālāksa is evidently the name of Śiva. Bāhudanti-putra is clearly a follower of Airāvata, the elephant of Indra. According to the evidence of lexicons, Kauṇapa-danta was none else than Bhiṣma the great grandsire of the Kurus, who, when his life was drawing to its close, was regarded as the greatest repository of the wisdom of the ancients. Vātavyādhi or Pavaṇa-vyādhi is none else than Akrūra, the wise teacher of the Yādavas. Bhāradvāja was the same man as Droṇa, the Brahmin strategist in the Kurukṣetra war. Piśuṇa, according to some evidence, was none else than Nārada, who distinguished himself by his fine acquaintance with the Art of Government in the fifth chapter of Sabhā-parva. Kaṇiṅko Bhāradvāja may be identified with Kaṇika, the crafty politician who counselled old Dhṛtarāṣṭra in the Ādi-parva. Ghoṭamukha's identity is not known but probably his name occurs in the Kāmasūtra as a writer on a branch of that subject.* Dīrgha Cārāyana is rather a historical person well known to Pali tradition and he was the unscrupulous adviser of the reckless Virūḍhaka, who became king by deposing his old father Prasenajit. He is mentioned also in the Kāmasūtra.†

* घोटकमुखः कन्यासम्प्रयुक्तकम्। Vāt. kā. sū. I. I. 12.

† चारायणः साधारणं अधिकरणं प्रोवाच। Vāt kā. sū. I. I. 12.

III

THE ARTHASASTRAS AND THE CIRCUMSTANCES OF THEIR GROWTH.

It will be mere waste of time to attempt to identify these teachers with those of the Epic,* but, before we pass on to the study of the Kauṭiliyan ideas about government, we must emphasise the importance of the Arthaśāstras in the intellectual history of ancient India. In the days of Kauṭilya, the theorists of this school identified themselves with the realisation of sovereignty by means of political power or diplomacy on behalf of irresponsible princes, who scrupled not to use means, however dishonourable in the eyes of moralists* (पृथिव्या लाभपालनोपाय: शास्त्रमर्थशास्त्रम्). The period of their rise was also remarkable and in itself forms an interesting study. The Arthaśāstras carry us back to that remarkable age, in which was heralded a reaction against the teachings and ideals of the preceding ages. The Indian mind had for a considerable period been subjected to the influences of teach-

---

* In regard to this, I have gone rather into details elsewhere, and my views supported by evidences are to be found in part II of my 'Development of Hindu Polity and Political Theories.'

ings which harped on the darker side of existence. Life brought with it an association of sorrows, continually perpetuated by the cycles of rebirth and of Karma—of good and evil springing from the desires of man—and the passions engendered by them.

This, indeed, was the state of affairs since the close of the age of the Brāhmaṇas and Upaniṣads. The religion of the Brāhmaṇas had centred the attention of men upon sacrifice. Gradually, this old religion had died a natural death and a new one had come into existence. The essence of this lay in speculations about the impermanence of the world and the transient nature of its joys—its causes, and the ways enabling men to attain freedom from the influence of all evils. As a result of these, the outlook of life became gloomy and men thought constantly of the miseries of life, the evils of enjoyment and dread of rebirth. All sections of Indian philosophy were dominated by pessimism. The Buddhist harped on "Dukkha" and "Saṃvega." while the orthodox systems had their enumeration of the "Duḥkhas".

Such a mentality was favourable for the rise of philosophical sects—which all ignored the world of realities—scoffed at domestic happiness and harped on super-social ideals. Life with its joys and sorrows came to be dreaded—the more so because it was the cause of more miseries yet to come. Monachism came into vogue, the cares of life and their consequences were feared by all. Men entered the Saṅgha, women followed them ; the husband left the wife, the wife forsook the protection of her lord. The house-hold was shunned by all. Everybody made for the outside. In short, there dawned an age in which humanity forgot the real end of life, and yearned for death and the final dissolution.

How long this state of affairs lasted, we cannot say. But suffice it to say that ere long came a reaction. Rigorism had its consequences. This spirit of gloom and pessimism called into play the natural instincts of man. Schools of thought arose with extremely divergent views. Some became Sensualistic Hedonists, entirely opposed to any restraint or discipline, men who scoffed at spiritualism, men who regarded all religions as fraud, men who looked solely to carnal happiness as the real objective in life

But, while the hedonist denouncing religion or scoffing at laws and morals represented the extreme of a materialistic ideal, his views did not appeal to the Indian people as a whole. There were many who tried to resuscitate the old ideals regarding the duties of life. With them arose newer socio-ethical systems which attempted to justify a social existence by explanations of life and its duties, as well as schools of metaphysics, which tried to explain the origin, the meaning and the end of creation, along with the relation of man to this world and his ways of salvation.

In this respect, the age from the close of the period of the Upaniṣads to the fourth century B.C was one remarkable in the history of mankind, not only in India, but also in other parts of the globe, so far, as this intellectual activity was concerned. In the west, it saw the beginnings of philosophical speculation in Greece ; in Persia, the Zoroastrian revival took place ; in China, some of the great ethical teachers appeared. In India it saw the rise of Jainism, Buddhism, the Ājīvikas, or the schools founded by innumerable teachers, whose names or teachings have survived only in ridiculous epithets and nicknames, or have come down to us only in distorted versions which simply mark them out for contempt.

The influence of the older Metaphysical schools which arose in India about the sixth century B.C. and of those socio-ethical systems which followed them was immense, though in regard to these, our information is rather scanty. The teachings of the former contributed to a pessimistic mentality, but, gradually, a reaction was ushered in by their successors. They inculcated the necessity of joys in life. They protested against undue abstinence ; they pointed out the relative importance as well as the intimate connection of the Catur-varga *e.g.* Dharma, Artha, and Kāma in addition to Mokṣa. As a result of a compromise between extreme views. Mokṣa was regarded as the ultimate aim of life, but this, they taught, depended on the fruition of desires, desires ethically considered and aesthetically regulated. Man, according to them, owed duties to society and without these there would be a dissolution of social life and a consequent revival of anarchy. The individual, too, was meant not solely for gloomy pessimistic existence. In common with the animal world, he was meant for pleasures and enjoyment, without which life was no life at all.

Such were the views of the newer teachers who aimed at dispelling the pessimism and gloom of previous teachings. Among these, again, there remained important differences. Some extolled the position of Artha. Others dwelt upon the relative value of Kāma. Unfortunately for us, we have but received only a fraction of the literature bearing upon these subjects. In the case of the Kāmasūtra school, only one treatise, namely, that attributed to Vātsyāyana has reached us, but there is room for holding that we had a very ancient literature on Kāmasūtra, of which fragments are still preserved in some of the oldest parts of the Pali Canonical literature.

A detailed discussion of the above question is indeed out of place, but so far as the Arthaśāstra is concerned, the ideas of life as laid down in it are quite clear and show a harmonious compromise. Kauṭilya, as we shall see later on, presupposes the existence of certain fundamental institutions like marriage and private property, which are not only inevitable but ensure a regulation of lust and greed. Next, he goes on to emphasise the attainment of the Trivarga in human life and clearly expresses himself as follows :—

धर्मार्थाविरोधेन कामं सेवेत। न निस्सुखः स्यात्। समं वा त्रिवर्गमन्योन्यानुबन्धम्। एको ह्यत्यासेवितो धर्मार्थकामानामितरौ पीड़यति॥

From the above passage, Kauṭilya's views become clear. Clearly, he holds that the attainment of the Trivarga is the real objective of man. The three again are all closely related. Even Kāma has its proper place and a man should not live without happiness or pleasure. (**न निस्सुखः स्यात्**).

NOTE.—In the days of Kauṭilya, the Arthaśāstra formed part of Itihāsa and was an important branch of study. It held as high a position as the Purāṇas and Dharmaśāstras—[See Book I. Ch. 5.—पुराणमितिवृत्तमाख्यायिकोदाहरणं धर्मशास्त्रमर्थशास्त्रं चेतीतिहासः] Owing to various reasons however, the Dharmaśāstras came to be regarded as being of higher authority. Yājñavalkya expressly says—

स्मृत्योर्विरोधे न्यायस्तु बलवान् व्यवहारतः।
अर्थशास्त्रात्तु बलवद्धर्मशास्त्रमिति स्थितिः॥ II—21.

Gradually, the Dharmaśāstras became the repository of those measures which marked the later social reaction. The Purāṇas, as such, gained greater authority and they are so held by the champions of 'modern' orthodoxy, who attach great importance to minute rules relating to marriage, prohibition of sea-voyages, prohibition of food touched by men of lower castes etc.

Then, he proceeds to discuss the relative importance of these three, especially in a social existence. As a believer in the tenets of the Arthaśāstra, he lays stress on the supreme importance of Artha in this world. Contrary to many ancient thinkers who made Dharma the basis of all,* he extols the importance of Artha. "Artha" as he himself says, "[of these three] is of supreme importance, since Dharma and Kāma depend on it for their fruition. (अर्थ एव प्रधानः—अर्थमूलौ धर्मकामौ)" †

---

* Cf. the views embodied in S'āntiparvan. chap. 123. attributed to Bhīṣma (echoing the sayings of Kāmandaka)—

धर्ममूलः सदैवार्थः कामोऽर्थफलमुच्यते ।
संकल्पमूलास्ते सर्वे संकल्पो विषयात्मकः ॥
विषयाश्चैव कार्त्स्नेन सर्वं आहारसिद्धये ।
मूलमेतत् त्रिवर्गस्य निवृत्तिर्मोक्ष उच्यते ॥

123—(4—5)

† The same opinion is also held by the Pārāśarāḥ *e.g.*, —"अर्थदूषणादण्डपारुष्ययोरर्थदूषणं गरीयः" इति पाराशराः—"अर्थमूलौ धर्मकामौ । अर्थप्रतिबन्धश्च लोको वर्त्तते । तस्योपघातो गरीयान्" (Kau. Bk. VIII. ch. iii.)

IV

ON THE AIM OF LIFE

It will not be out of place here to point out the extreme views of some of the sensual hedonists and those of the Arthaśāstra writers. For, in that case, we shall be able to form an idea of the extremely materialistic doctrines which had once gained ground in India. in the age preceding the Arthaśāstras, or that which marked the composition of some of these treatises. The entire philosophy of the Lokāyatikas has perished. But, there are traditions recorded in verses collected by later writers like the authors of the Sarva-darśana-saṅgraha, the Sarva-siddhānta-saṅgraha, the Kāmasūtra of Vātsyāyana and the Ṣaḍdarśana-samuccaya, and from these we can form an idea of the basic principles of the Lokāyatic philosophy.

The Lokāyatikas represented a section of thinkers who in direct opposition to the pessimistic conception of the world, its unreality, and sorrow and the evils of Karma and rebirth, had evidently relapsed into the extreme of scepticism and doubt. They believed neither in creation nor in the Creator, nor even in life beyond death. They denounced sacrifices or rules of conduct in life, and regarded religion as the 'trick of the cleverer set devised to impose upon the unwary'* they believed only in this world† and in that alone which the senses could realise. They yearned after joys, since life was but fleeting.‡ "Take the cash and let the credit go" was their motto. It was the more so, since there was no knowing when life would dissolve.§ A man

---

* न स्वर्गो नापवर्गो वा नैवात्मा पारलौकिक:।
नैव वर्णाश्रमादीनां क्रियाश्च फलदायिका:॥
अग्निहोत्रं त्रयो वेदास्त्रिदण्डं भस्मगुण्ठनम्।
बुद्धिपौरुषहीनानां जीविका धातृनिर्मिता॥
... ...
त्रयो वेदस्य कर्त्तारो भण्डधूर्तनिशाचरा:।
जर्फरीतुर्फरीत्यादि पण्डितानां वच: स्मृतम्॥
(S. D. S. Ch. I)

† इहलोकात् परो नान्य: स्वर्गोऽस्ति नरको न च।
शिवलोकादयो मूढै: कल्प्यन्तेऽन्यै: प्रतारकै:॥
(S. S. Sangraha)

एतावानेष लोकोऽयं यावानिन्द्रियगोचर:।
भद्रे! वृकपदं पश्य यद्वदन्ति बहुश्रुता:॥
(S. D. Sanuccaya p. 72.)

‡ यावज्जीवेत् सुखं जीवेत् ऋणं कृत्वा घृतं पिबेत्।
भस्मीभूतस्य देहस्य पुनरागमनं कुत:॥
(S. D. Sangraha).

पिब खाद च जातशोभने! यदतीतं वरगात्रि तन्न ते।
नहि भीरु! गतं निवर्त्तते समुदयमात्रमिदं कलेवरम्॥
(S, D. Sanuccaya. p.73.)

§ Some of the following proverbs illustrate it.—*e.g.*

को ह्यबालिशो हस्तगतं परगतं कुर्यात्। वरमद्य कपोत: श्वो मयूरात्।

व सांशयिकान्निष्कादसांशयिक: कार्षापण:। इति लोकायतिका:—
Vāt. Kā. Sū. Ch. II. Sūtras 22 to 24.

must enjoy the more, since the future is shrouded in doubt and even if pleasant, that may not come at all.

Bṛhaspati was the reputed founder of the Lokāyatikas. A Bṛhaspati figures in the Artha-śāstra, as the founder of the school known as the Bārhaspatya. According to the Kauṭiliya, the followers of this school, rejected the Trayī as a source of knowledge since it was but the pretext for cleverer men of the world [for imposing upon the simple minded] and this view substantially tallies with what we find in the Sarva-darśaṇa-saṅgraha.*

The spirit of Kauṭilya was, however, quite different. He was a believer in material joys and aspirations, yet he did not go to extremes. His ideal was a compromise or a moderate synthesis of the two extreme views of life and its aims.

His views we have given already, but as he is very brief, we cannot expect to get his arguments in support of his own, or in rejecting the views of the other party. The Kāmasūtra, which contains materials belonging to the same or to some nearly proximate period, gives us arguments in support of the necessity of having a reasonable

---

* वार्त्ता दण्डनीतिश्चेति बार्हस्पत्याः—संवरणमात्रं हि त्रयी लोकयात्राविदः ।

Compare this with

कृषिगोरक्षवाणिज्यं दण्डनीत्यादिभिर्बुधः ।
दृष्टैरेव सदोपायैर्भोगाननुभवेत् भुवि ॥

ideal of life between the two extremes, *e.g.* rigorism and sensualism. In this respect, Vātsyāyana does for the Kāmasūtra school what Kauṭilya does for raising or improving the end and aim of the Arthaśāstra. Like Kauṭilya, he advises men to enjoy, and strive for the attainment of the prospects of life or Artha, (**विद्याभूमिहिरण्यपशुधान्यभाण्डोपस्करमित्रादीनामर्जनं अर्जितस्य विवर्धनमर्थः**) without detriment to the other two of the Trivarga. His views are clearer and are summarised in the beginning and the end of the second chapter of his book. (Trivarga-pratipatti). As he says—

शतायुर्वै पुरुषो विभज्य कालमन्योन्यानुबन्धं परस्परस्यानुपघातकं त्रिवर्गं सेवेत ॥ Ch II. S. I.

भवन्ति चात्र श्लोकाः—

एवमर्थञ्च कामञ्च धर्मं चोपाचरन्नरः ।
इहामुत्र च निःशल्यमत्यन्तं सुखमश्नुते ॥
किं स्यात् परत्रेत्याशङ्का कार्ये यस्मिन्न जायते ।
न चार्थघ्नं सुखञ्चेति शिष्टास्तत्र व्यवस्थिताः ॥
त्रिवर्गसाधकं यत् स्याद्द्वयोरेकस्य वा पुनः ।
कार्यं तदपि कुर्वीत न त्वेकार्थं द्विबाधकम् ॥

BOOK II

IDEAS ABOUT SOCIETY, STATE AND KINGSHIP.

I

THE ETHICAL CONCEPTS OF KAUTILYA.

Kauṭilya, as we have said, was a believer in the materialistic aspirations of man. His Arthaśāstra marked a reaction against the past tendencies. Yet, his position was not that of a hedonist believing only in pleasure and rejecting the future. His position requires definition. He was no extremist but stood between two extremes. He believed in pleasure in human life, but that was not its sole end or aim. He had no scepticism for the future. His "was not a life with a horizon shrunk within the narrow compass of the momentary present". He believed in a life after death. Hence, to sacrifice the present for the future or the future for the present joys was not a part of his creed. Both had a place and both had their respective importance. Without the present we cannot have a future and without a past the present cannot come into existence. Consequently, his was no creed of pessimism nor of shadowy unrealities, but a faith in life, with the prospect of a brilliant future for good done in the present.

In this respect he followed the old Indian or Brāhmaṇic precepts and ideals. The actions of men, he believed, are controlled (as individuals as also in the social life) both by themselves and by unseen agencies (दैवं मानुषं च कर्मलोक-मवति). Yet, according to him, man had freedom to act. He could mould his own life ; he could modify by his efforts the adversities in his path. (दैवादग्निरूदकं व्याधिः प्रमारो विद्रवो दुर्भिक्षमासुरी सृष्टिरित्यापदः । तासां दैवतब्राह्मणप्रणिपाततः सिद्धिः ॥ pp. 360—61).

The chief objects of life, were, according to him, a realisation of the Trivarga (अर्थो धर्मः-काम इत्यर्थत्रिवर्गः) and a discrimination between the Artha-trivarga and the Anartha-trivarga. Herein an analysis based on rationalism comes to find a place. The triad of evil, according to him, consists of Anartha, Adharma and Śoka अनर्थोऽधर्मःशोक इत्यनर्थत्रिवर्गः). Anartha is anything which of itself or from any other cause gives rise to fear (स्वतः परतो वा भयोत्पत्तिरनर्थः). Adharma is that which leads not only to nonfulfilment, but gives rise to despair therefrom, and, finally, Śoka is sorrow. In discriminating these, man is assailed by doubts. The question comes to his mind whether Artha is Anartha, Adharma is Dharma, and Kāma is not Śoka.

The discrimination of these is of vital importance and in doing so man is not to be guided merely by his will, since, will, unaccompanied by reason, leads to mischief. This seems to be the view of Kauṭilya from his definition of Sāhasa, which he describes as अन्वयवत् प्रसभकर्म. This definition of Sāhasa is, indeed, of interest to us, for, it shows how the great author of the Arthaśāstra assigns to reason its proper place and how he seems to think that mere will ought not to be our guide.

Again, not solely reason is to be the guiding principle to man. Man must look to his own happiness and in order to do that, so regulate his conduct as others may not come to grief. He must live for his happiness in society and in order that he may be happy, his happiness must be something which will not stand in the way of others. To attain such a state of existence, individuals must have recourse to a moral standard of life. This moral standard consists in showing due respect to the happiness and prosperity of others, and refraining from injury or perfidy to others or the adoption of such lines of action which may give rise to Anarthas to others *e.g.*

एवं वश्येन्द्रियः परस्त्रीद्रव्यहिंसाश्च वर्जयेत्। स्वप्नलौल्यमनृतमुद्धतवेषत्वमनर्थसंयोगं च अधर्मसंयुक्तमनर्थसंयुक्तं च व्यवहारम् ।

To attain such a state of moral excellence, man must undergo discipline. The object of discipline is to control sensuality and to attain a stage when knowledge and study will lead to intellectual and moral perfection. The necessity of *vinaya* or discipline has been more than emphasized by Kauṭilya who shows clearly how this depends on obedience to the precepts of elders and the carrying out of these into action. Thus, he says—

कृतकः स्वाभाविकश्च विनयः। क्रिया हि द्रव्यं विनयति नाद्रव्यम्। शुश्रूषाश्रवणग्रहणधारणविज्ञानोहापोहतत्वाभिनिविष्टवुद्धिं विद्या विनयति नेतरम्।

True discipline is attained by individuals when they have faith and obedience to their teachers, and this would lead to the control of the senses *e.g.* the mastery of the six senses and of those passions given birth to by them.

Kauṭilya again speaks in the same strain in the chapter on Indriya-jaya, *e.g.*

विद्याविनयहेतुरिन्द्रियजयः कामक्रोधलोभमानमदहर्षत्यागात्कार्यः। कर्णत्वगक्षिजिह्वाघ्राणेन्द्रियाणां शब्दस्पर्शरूपरसगन्धेषु अविप्रतिपत्तिरिन्द्रियजयः शास्त्रार्थानुष्टानं वा। कृत्स्नं हि शास्त्रमिन्द्रियजयः॥

Kauṭilya thus lays a great stress on the control of the senses, *i.e.* a mastery of the six organs of sense (*e. g.* of hearing, touch, taste, smell, sight etc.) which give rise to the six passions. Without discipline, everying will come to nought but when this is attained everything is realised

The sole end and aim according to him of the śāstras is to enable man attain a control over the senses.

After a control of the senses comes study which gives knowledge. Knowledge brings in concentration and from concentration comes perfection and the best understanding, *e.g.*

श्रुताद्धि प्रज्ञोपजायते, प्रज्ञया योगो, योगादात्मवत्तेति विद्यासामर्थ्यम् ।

These are the chief points which illuminate us on the ethical views of the great author of the Arthaśāstra and thus help us in defining his place in the history of Indian thought and culture.

An analysis of these above shows that in his views on ethics, Kauṭilya followed the old Brāhmaṇical teachers, some of whose views are embodied in the Āraṇayakas and Upaniṣads. It is difficult to designate this ethical system under any specific name, following the western thinkers on ethics and social morality. There is in it a predominance of elements of hedoeism and a belief in pleasure, Next to it, there is not only an element of rationalism in it, but an altruistic tendency is also present there. Hence, in Kauṭilya we find a fine synthesis of all these. The system which we find in his book is no innovation of his but something which is evolved out of the teachings and ideals of old.

Herein the importance of the Arthaśâstra can hardly be minimised and we must bear in mind the two facts that the Kauṭilyian system was reconstructed out of materials of old and marked a reaction against the pessimism and gloom of the preceding age.

II

THE SOCIAL CONCEPT

We proceed next with a consideration of the social ideals of Kauṭilya. It is difficult to find in his work, a detailed discussion about the origin of society, in as much as his treatise is mainly concerned with the attainment of Artha on the part of kings, and the details of a good administration. Furthermore, Kauṭilya with the characteristic brevity of the ancients devotes his attention mainly to practical topics and speaks little about theories. It is only incidentally that we find a glimpse of his ideas about the origin or the nature of society.

From what we get, we may come to the conclusion that Kauṭilya regarded society as the aggregation of communities and of individuals. Of the pre-social state, he gives us no description but he seems to believe that in those days men existed with rights undefined. Everything depended on might. Men were liable to be influenced by anger, greed, lust, and other passions, and consequently everything was topsy-turvy. To end this state of things in which the strong tyrannised over the weak, like big fish devouring smaller ones, a social arrangement was conceived with a code of generally-accepted conventions and a common superior was installed in whom resided the sole coercive authority and the right of awarding chastisement for wrong.

This seems to have been Kauṭilya's theory about the origin of social order. He alludes to Mātsya-nyāya in two places. Thus, in page nine he simply mentions this Mātsya-nyāya in which the strong devour the weak. (अप्रणीतो हि मात्स्यन्यायमुद्भावयति बलीयान् अबलं हि ग्रसते दण्डधराभावे—तेन गुप्तः प्रभवतीति pp. 9). In another place, he refers to the election of Manu as king by the people who were tormented by the evils of Mātsya-nyāya. (see pp. 23.—मात्स्यन्यायाभिभूताः प्रजा मनुं राजानं चक्रिरे)

From these, we may come to the view, that Kauṭilya believed along with some of his predecessors (whose views are summarised in the Śānti-parvan.—Rāja-dharma ch. 67) that the state of affairs preceding the establishment of social order was one of war. According to his view, furthermore, this social order was preceded by the establishment of covenants which respected marriage and private property. The observance of these two was vital to the well-being of the social order.

To facilitate this social well-being, men must learn according to Kauṭilya, to control the senses. The unbridled play of these lead only to the conflict of each other's interest and thus brings in a state detrimental to social life. This would appear from his primary injunction that never should a man covet other's wife or property. *e.g.* (एवं वश्येन्द्रिय: परस्त्रीद्रव्यहिंसां च वर्जयेत् ॥)

With proper respect for the conjugal rights and the property of others, men could carry on their social existence, and pursue the aims of life. These naturally are referable to four main objectives *e.g.* the attainment of what is not already in possession, the preservation of those already in hand, the increase of what is acquired, and lastly, proper distribution or enjoyment of the acquisitions. (*e.g.* अलब्धलाभार्था, लब्धपरिरक्षणी, रक्षितविवर्द्धनी, वृद्धस्य तीर्थेषु प्रतिपादनी च)

But this is not all. The attainment of the above objects of individual effort, as also the four general objectives of life *e.g.* Dharma Artha, Kāma and Mokṣa all depend not soley upon, the individual's own self-enlightenment, but also on the maintenance of a social standard through the exercise of a coercive authority. *i.e.* the chastisement of wrong and the reward of good.

The superior efficacy of coercion was recognised by all and almost everywhere in the globe. In India, too, the more ancient thinkers had recognized this. Kauṭilya following in their footsteps, could not remain blind to it and brief as he is, he enters into a consideration of how this coercive authority be regulated and exercised.

First of all, he dwells upon the importance of coercion and cites the opinion that there is nothing so efficacious as coercion (तस्माल्लोकयात्रार्थी नित्यमुद्यतदण्डः स्यात्—नह्येवंविधं वशोपनयनमस्ति यथा दण्डः इत्याचार्याः) Next, he goes on to explain that unlimited or unregulated chastisement leads to social wrong. If the punishment is too great, then men are afflicted, if mild, that is not cared for at all. Only when it is regulated and is properly inflicted that men benefit by it and are made to follow the right path of realising Dharma, Artha and Kāma. If it is unregulated or improperly exercised, then it affiicts all—even men like Vāṇaprasthas and the wanderers, who are not in society—not to speak of house-holders. Unregulated it leads again to Mātsya-nyāya *i.e.* to the very ills which it was applied for putting down. *e.g.*

तीक्ष्णदण्डो हि भूतानामुद्वेजनीयः। मृदुदण्डः परिभूयते। यथार्हदण्डः पूज्यः। सुविज्ञातप्रणीतो हि दण्डः प्रजा धर्मार्थकामैर्योजयति। दुष्प्रणीतो हि कामक्रोधाभ्यामज्ञानाद्वाणप्रस्थपरिव्राजकानपि कोपयति किमङ्ग पुनर्गृहस्थान्। अप्रणीतो हि मात्स्यन्यायमुद्भावयति।

Regulation is thus primarily necessary, and next to it, an authority in whom will reside this coercive power—a sole repository of coercive power. Of this coercive authority—the king, we shall speak in the next chapter. But, before we pass on to that, we shall try to give some details as to Kauṭilya's idea as to the nature and character of this Daṇḍaniti or coercive authority and discuss his views as to how to regulate coercion, how to demarcate between right and wrong, how to differentiate between policy or impolicy, how to measure pros and cons in an argument, what should be the standard of good, and how should success be measured.

Kauṭilya recognizes that an absolute standard, there could be none, nor could life go on without any. He therefore bases his ideal on the past and accepts the guiding canon of the scriptures. In the section on Vidyā-samuddeśa, he lays down the sources of knowledge and discusses the importance of the śāstras. He cites the opinions of his predecessors and rejecting some of their views, lays down his own. He enumerates four principal Vidyās *e.g.* Ānvīkṣakī, Trayī, Vārttā and Daṇḍaniti and then discusses their relative importance. According to him, right and wrong are to be discriminated according to the precepts of the Vedas, laws of social or economic welfare are to be found from Vārttā, policy or impolicy should be distinguished according to the standard laid down in the science of chastisment, and finally reason or speculative philosophy should be our guide in devising means for the attainment of good, in following the right line of conduct in distress as in prosperity,and in selecting a wise and right line of action.* Thus, of all ancient writers on polity, he is pre-eminently the one who assigns to reason or speculation its proper place.

It is as he says :—

प्रदीपस्सर्वविद्यानामुपायः सर्वकर्मणाम् ।
आश्रयः सर्वधर्माणाम् शश्वदान्विक्षकी मता ॥

From the above, we see that Kauṭilya gives to all the sciences their proper place in human life. His system moreover was not wholly an innovation, nor was he a believer in abstract principles. He wished no revolutionary changes, since life could not be entirely divorced from the predominating social ideals. Furthermore, orthodox as he was, he could not reject the authority of the Vedas or brush away the existing social order. He believed in the institutions and social ideas of his countrymen. He recognized the importance of Varṇa and Āśrama. As he himself says—

व्यवस्थितार्यमर्यादः कृतवर्णाश्रमस्थितिः ।
त्रय्या हि रक्षितो लोकःप्रसीदति न सीदति ॥

Absolute faith in the past, however did not sum up Kauṭilya's social ideal. For, Brahmin as he was, and a believer in the privileges of order, he was not blind to the interests of the other sections of the people. His ideas of the traditional social

---

* धर्माधर्मौ त्रय्याम् । अर्थानर्थौ वार्त्तायाम् । नयानयौ दण्डनीत्याम् बलाबले चैतासां हेतुभिरन्वीक्षमाना लोकस्योपकरोति व्यसनेऽभ्युदये च बुद्धिमवस्थापयति प्रज्ञावाक्यक्रियावैशारद्यं च करोति ।

order, his faith in the scriptures or in kingly rule, did not preclude a deep sympathy for the masses. It was not his idea that the commonality should live for others. They too had a right to existence, equally with the members of the three higher castes. Socially and economically they formed the basis of the life of the community.

His social outlook was indeed wider and more liberal for his age. The Śūdra he regarded as a member of the Aryan Community. He tried moreover as we shall see, to abolish that inhuman custom which made man the property of his fellow-man. While, in the west, his great contemporary Aristotle was justifying, nay vindicating the institution of slavery, he was the earliest to pronounce emphatically the noble doctrine "that an Ārya can never be a slave" and held that infamous custom as one which might exist only among the Barbarian Mlecchas (म्लेच्छानामदोषः प्रजामाधातुम् विक्रेतुं वा, नत्वेवार्यस्य दासभावः)

His social ideal was thus very high. Indeed it was higher for the age in which he lived. Yet, inspite of this, his enemies accuse him for his inhuman methods in politics. But as we shall see, Kauṭilya strove for a higher tone in social and political life. The inhuman methods of waging war or for attaining supremacy in politics are indeed to be found in his book, but, they are the usages of the world in which he lived and were not his own inventions.

III

POLITICAL CONSIDERATIONS

Such being the requirements of mankind, men lay the foundation of society, submit to laws and conventions, and have a superior wielding the rod of authority. Thus, the political organisation comes into being.

Next, we come to enquire as to what were the constituent elements and functions of this political organisation or the "state" as designated by the thinkers of the west. Here again, we find that Kauṭilya has not defined it—nor has he devoted his speculations towards its consideration. The omission is unfortunate but he cannot be accused for it, since, it was not his business and he does not pretend to be a theorist.

Yet inspite of this silence, we are not without means to have a clue to his ideas. They find expression in connection with his details about public administration. Passages which give us such hints, occur in more than one place. From one such passage, it appears that Kauṭilya regarded the Rājya, or kingdom—as primarily constituted of the people (*e.g.* पुरुषवद्धि राज्यं अपुरुषा गौर्वन्ध्येव किं दुह्वीत). In another place, we find an echo of the same idea—(न ह्यजनो जनपदो राज्यं जनपदमं वा भवतीति कौटिल्यः) ।

Another characteristic of the state, was that it occupied a definite territory. This idea of a definite territory is to be gathered from Kauṭilya's dissertations, where he speaks of the physical requisites of a state. As to the other elements *i.e.* a ruler and a code of laws—they are apparent from other passages, which have been referred to in the previous chapter on society. Thus, the chief requisites of the political organisation according to Kauṭilya, were a body of men, a definite territory, a king and a code of laws.

But this was was not all The object of the Kauṭilyan state was no mere police. The duty of the political organisation did not end with the protection of life and property. It had, as we shall presently see, a higher purpose namely, to help the individal in his self-realisation and as such it was founded on a strong economic basis. As in the case of the social order, Kauṭilya presupposes the necessity of primary institutions like marriage or private property, so, in the case of the political organisation, he presupposes the existence of a strong physical basis for the state. Without this foundation, there could be no question of a strong body politic in his eyes.

Consequently, we find him devoting one whole section (in the chapter on the requisites of a state) in which he discusses the qualities of the Janapada. The following according to him are the true requisites of a prosperous Janapada—*e.g.*

स्थानवानात्मधारण: परधारणश्चापदि स्वारक्षस्स्वाजीव: शत्रुद्वेषी शक्यसामन्त: पङ्कपाषाणोषरविषमकण्टकश्रेणीव्याल-मृगाटवीहीन: कान्त:सीताखनिद्रव्यहस्तिवनवान् गव्य: पौरुषेयो गुप्तगोचर: पशुमान् अदेवमातृको वारिस्थलपथाभ्यामुपेत: सारचित्रवहुपण्यो दण्डकरसह: कर्मशीलकर्षको वालिशस्वाम्यवरवर्णप्रायो भक्तशुचिमनुष्य इति जनपदसम्पत् ॥
(Kau. p. 256.)

We may not give a literal translation of the whole, but some of the requisites require our attention *e.g.* that the territory of the state should be capable of accommodating and supporting the people, capable of defending it against enemies and finding occupation for the people, peopled by men imbued with a patriotic spirit and hating the enemies, having manageable neighbours, free from the depredations of wild animals or of men banded in a league, provided with pastures, arable land, mines, or forests, not entirely dependent upon the mercy of gods, having good internal communications *i.e.* rivers and roads, having an outlet to the sea(?), capable of producing varieties of merchandise, and containing an energitic and industrious population of all castes including men of the higher orders.

The above enquiry into these requisites may not seem to be of any importance to many, yet in connection with Kauṭilya's socio-political ideals they are of supreme importance. In thus conceiving the duties and functions of the state, Kauṭilya simply followed the older line of Indian tradition of which the first indications are to be found in the Vedic literature. As I have tried to show elsewhere, the Hindu idea as to the duties of the state made it incumbent on the head of the state to help the people in the fruition of their aims in life. Consequently, it was part of the duties of the king, and hence of that organisation of which he was the sole-ruler, to look to the economic prosperity of the country, to look to agriculture, or to the other industries which all go to the well-being of the community as a whole.

The state, thus, according to Kauṭilya, must be based on sound economic foundations, so as to enable men to realise the aims of life, to lessen, as much as possible, the struggles of existence at home, to lessen the dependence of the community on the outside world, to be in a position to help other sections of humanity in distress, and thereby to ensure an existence conducing to the happiness of man in this life and paving the way to a brighter one beyond.*

* Students of modern history will readily admit how the crafty Brahmin anticipates the problems of modern states. An outlet to the sea has often been the cause of great wars in modern times. Want of room for an increasing population has goaded many nations to war. The history of the causes of the late war amply illustrates these points.

The importance of these economic foundations of life have been formally recognised in the political thought of modern Europe. Since the close of the 18th century and the beginning of the last one, the older political idealism has been supplanted by an understanding of the social good based on proper opportunities in life. History has received its proper economic interpretation and economic factors hitherto neglected by the historian have been recognized. Man has come more and more to be looked upon as a being of wants and desires and not solely of higher aims or objectives. Governments, too, have changed in their ideals. Today, we hear less of squables about political equality or the so-called equalisation of orders. The chief objective today with governments is to give each man a chance in life, to help him in fulfilling his own aims and thereby to help others in fulfilling theirs. A new era has dawned. The age of political reform has passed into one of social redress and re-adjustment.

The ancients though they talked less and though their outlook was rather narrow, recognised all these factors and this we find in the history of many ancient communities. Thus, in most ancient civilizations, social regulation of production and distribution had a place. The Jewish king had to look to the wants of his people. He had to regulate distribution of the necessaries of life, regulate profits, check usury, and thus he was saddled more with social duties, than what we now call political. In China, too, we find the same thing ; so also, in the records of Hammurabi, in the history of Rome, in the Taikwa reforms in almost prehistoric Japan, in Peru and in many other places.

In India, too, the Governmental system was not an exception to this general rule. From the earliest times, it was part of the king's duties to further social progress, to look to industrial and agricultural prosperity, to regulate profit, to check usury, to maintain the indigent poor and to utilise the resources of the community for the common good.*

In the hands of the author of the Arthaśāstra, the germs of the past developed into a system. Active social service came to occupy the highest place in it. His state was in its ends and functions, an economic state—a repository of resources for the common good, to be distributed to the subject with fatherly care. The Kauṭilyian state was thus more than political or merely social. It was as we shall see presently, a paternal one.

---

* This would appear from the Coronation Hymn in the Rājasūya—cf.

इयं ते राट्। यन्तासि यमनो ध्रुवोऽसि धरुणः।
कृष्यै त्वा क्षेमाय त्वा रय्यै त्वा पोषाय त्वा॥

IV

THE CONSTITUENT ELEMENTS OF THE STATE

After discussing the nature and functions of the state, we proceed with an enumeration of the elements, the totality of which went to constitute the state or the Rājya in the eyes of Hindu political thinkers. We use the word "element" to render into English an idea which has been variously expressed by the words Prakṛti, Aṅga or Ātmā. The older authorities of the Śānti-parva who had probably differences of opinion among them, recognized seven or eight such elements. Cf. the Śāntiparva verses :—

राज्ञा सप्तैव रक्ष्याणि तानि चैव निबोध ह ।
आत्मामात्यश्च कोषश्च दण्डो मित्राणि चैव हि ॥
तथा जनपदाश्चैव पुरञ्च कुरुनन्दन ।
एतत् सप्तात्मकं राज्यं परिपाल्यं प्रयत्नतः ।

Again, in CXXI. 47.

सप्तप्रकृति चाष्टाङ्गं शरीरमिह यद्विदुः ।
राज्यस्य दण्डमेवाङ्गं दण्डप्रभव एव च ॥

Kauṭilya does not enter into a discussion as to the number of such elements called prakṛtis. In his own way, he recognizes only seven which are laid down in the first chapter of his sixth book known as Maṇḍala-yoniḥ. (*e.g.* स्वाम्यमात्यजनपददुर्गकोशदण्डमित्राणि प्रकृतयः ।)

These seven were—the king or the ruler exercising sovereign authority, his ministers counselling him as to what should be done, his subjects settled in the kingdom, the fortifications, the defensive and offensive forces, and the treasury, which all went to constitute the well-organised body politic. Last of all, came the Mitras or allies who contributed to the safety of the kingdom, by helping to put down foreign enemies and preserving the political equilibrium which ensured the life and continuence of the state.

In our own days, such an enumeration may be regarded as un-scientific. Present day theorists may object to the recognition of the Mitra or ally as a constituent element of any state. So also, they may not accept the enumeration of the Treasury and the Army as separate units in the formation of the state. But, in regard to this, we must bear in mind that in an age when the theory of separation of functions on modern lines, was not known, when the state meant nothing but the sole embodiment of the highest executive authority (subject to the supremacy of the laws), this was essentially a practical concept. The King stood for the embodiment of the supreme executive, the ministers constituted a regulative agency, the fortifications and defences ensured the safety of the people and the

Janapada or territory was the chief physical basis of existence. It was pre-eminently a practical concept and took into consideration all the agencies which contributed to the moral and political existence of a community. Next, as regards Mitra or the ally, it determined the position of the community in the political world. Though not having a recognized place in the modern theories, the importance of the ally can hardly be minimised. In our own days, when a more stable political equilibrium has been established, and the right of existence even of minor states recognized, no state can do without an ally. A state in order to have a safe and prosperous existence, must have an ally and even in these days, political isolation means death. (Compare France before and after 1871 and note also the down-fall of Germany and her supporters owing to their complete isolatlon).

In ancient times the political world hardly knew anything like an equilibrium and necessarily, the need of an ally was even greater. Consequently, the enumeration of an ally as a vital factor points only to the recognition of a fact and nothing more.

Though enumerated separately, all these elements had no separate and independent existence. They stood in the closest possible relation to one another ; their harmony was essential to their own existence and of the whole which they constituted together. Their interdependence has been very beautifully expressed in the following verse.

अरिवर्जाः प्रकृतयः सप्तैताः सगुणोदयाः ।
उक्ताः प्रत्यङ्गभूतास्ताः प्रकृता राजसम्पदः ॥

Kau. pp. 257.

The relative importance of these elements has also been discussed in detail in the Artha-śāstra. Unlike most of his predecessors, Kauṭilya assigns the first place to the King. Next in precedence come the ministers and next to them the Janapada. After these, he reckons the army and next to it, the treasury. The importance of all these will be discussed in detail in their proper places.

V

IMPORTANCE OF REGAL AUTHORITY

As we have shown already, the state according to Kauṭilya required a head. This individual in whose person centred all executive authority, derived his power by virtue of the coercive authority vested in him. Without him, Mātsya-nyāya assailed the earth but with his properly wielding the rod of authority, the world was saved. cf.

वलीयानवलं हि ग्रसते दण्डधराभावे । तेन गुप्तः प्रभवतीति ।
चतुर्वर्णाश्रमो लोको राज्ञा दण्डेन पालितः ।
स्वधर्मकर्माभिरतो वर्तते स्वेषु वर्त्मसु ॥ Kau. p. 9.

Owing to his supreme importance, Kauṭilya assigns to him the highest place in the body-politic. He seems moreover to regard the authority of the king as the sole foundation of all the activities of the community. Laconically brief as he is, he gives expression to his sentiments in the chapter on Prakṛti-vyasana-varga, in which we have incidentally a discussion as to the gravity of dangers arising out of catastrophes befalling the various elements. Here, Kauṭilya controverts the opinion of Bhāradvāja the champion of ministerial autocracy and expresses the opinion that in the body politic everything depends upon the king. It is he "who looks to the interests of the people and averts dangers awating or befalling them. It is he who rewards virtue and punishes wrong. His prosperity leads to the prosperity of the kingdom. He imparts his quality to the elements of the state. Progress and downfall depend on him. Hence, he is the head and the consummation of all the other elements." *e.g.*

न इति कौटिल्य:—मन्त्रिपुरोहितादिभृत्यवर्गमध्यक्षप्रचारं पुरुषद्रव्यप्रकृतिव्यसनप्रतीकारमेधनं च राजैव करोति व्यसनिषु वाऽमात्येष्वन्यानव्यसनिन: करोति। पूज्यपूजने दूष्यावग्रहे च नित्ययुक्तस्तिष्ठति। स्वामी च सम्पन्न: स्वसम्पद्भि: प्रकृतीस्सम्पादयति। स्वयं यच्छील: तच्छीला: प्रकृतयो भवन्ति। उत्थाने प्रमादे तदायत्तत्वात्। तत्कूटस्थानीयो हि स्वामीति॥

Kau. pp. 320.

Such according to Kauṭilya, was the position of the ruler in the state. He was the moral and legal embodiment of sovereign authority. He was the chief executive head. He commanded the army. The administration of the country depended entirely on his discretion. The administration of Justice was in his hands. His person embraced everything. As such, it knew no limitations excepting that of the laws, and the social institutions which existed spontaneously and had orginated before the creation of regal authority itself.

Regal authority, however, underwent some limitations according to Kauṭilya. The fundamental Laws and institutions sacred to mankind existed apart from him. And, in regard to these great social institutions, Kauṭilya denied the king any authority to intermeddle with them. These he regarded as self evident and self-existent which were revealed to men by the great sages who composed the hymus of the Trayī. This view marks the real position of Kauṭilya in the Political thought of India. For, though a champion of royal power, he was not blind to the evils of extending regal authority over these, and so, pronounced his anathema upon any encroachment on these. Brief as he is, he puts it in his own characterstic and terse way. Such encroachments, in his eyes lead only to social dissolution and ultimately bring ruin on men. cf.

स्वधर्मः स्वर्गायानन्त्याय च । तस्यातिक्रमे लोकः सङ्करादुच्छिद्येत ।

तस्मात् स्वधर्मं हि भूतानां राजा न व्यभिचारयेत् ।
स्वधर्मं सन्दधानो हि प्रेत्य चेह च नन्दति ॥
व्यवस्थितार्यमर्यादः कृतवर्णाश्रमस्थितिः ।
त्रय्या हि रक्षितो लोकः प्रसीदति न सीदति ॥

Kau. p. 8.

He thus emphasises the necessity of ruling the world by maintaining Varṇa and Āśrama and preserving the svadharma of mankind, *i.e.* the traditional rules of conduct and morality. After enunciating this principle in the beginning of his book, he repeats it towards its close where he speaks of consolidation of authority subsequent to world conquest. (*e.g.* जित्वा च पृथिवीं विभक्तवर्णाश्रमां स्वधर्मेण भुञ्जीत ।)

BOOK III

THE KING, HIS DUTIES AND RELATION TO THE STATE.

I

KINGLY IDEAL IN THE ARTHASASTRA.

We have discussed the place of Royalty in the body politic, together with its functions, and the limitations on the irresponsible exercise of its authority. We shall, in this chapter, discuss the legal and personal relations in which the king stood to his subjects, the theoritical origin of his power and his duties to those who acknowledged his authority.

Kauṭilya as we have seen, was a firm believer in kingship. He regarded Royalty as being of vital importance to the body-politic. To sum up his views, it was the main-spring of all national exertions for the common good. It was further-more the embodiment of the unity of the interests of the various sections of the community. It was moreover the guiding authority which regulated all personal or political relations and thereby smoothened the life of the individual, and gave each a chance. In this respect the importance of kingship, could hardly be minimised. Next, we proceed to discuss Kauṭilya's views as to how the king should act and the relations which should subsist between him and his subjects.

In regard to his relations with his subjects, the

king according to Kauṭilya, was to act as a father to his children. This paternal ideal was not new in India. It had already found expression in the writing of the past. It is found in many places of the Rajādharma-parvādhyāya. Even, we find this idea among the Brāhmaṇical writers. In the borderland of Videha it had got a strong-hold in the remote past on the minds both of the people and of rulers. A long line of Videha kings had taken the significant title of Janaka or the father of their people.

This paternal ideal had a great significance in the history of Indian political development. It marked the growth of a distinctly higher stage of idealism in politics, though accompanied by a corresponding decay of popular sovereignty over the body politic. In truth, kings had become irresponsible, but in lieu of this irresponsibility they regarded themselves bound to protect the people like the father of children.

Like many of his predicessors, Kauṭilya was a believer in royal paternalism. The idea finds expression in numerous places. Thus, in the chapter on Jana-pada-nivesa, the king is instructed to protect the newly settled as if they were his children (तान् पितेव अनुगृह्णीयात्). A similar idea and an almost similar expression occurs in the chapter on superhuman calamities befalling a kingdom (*e.g.* उपनिपातप्रतीकारः) where we are told that during famines, the king must protect his subjects as if they were his children (पितेव अनुग्टह्णीयात्).

Beyond this, the paternal ideal is not more developed in the Arthaśāstra. For its further development and its boldest enunciation, India had to wait for two more generations, when it found in the person of the Emperor Aśoka its noblest and most veracious exponent. The latter pronounced in his edicts the noble ideal that all men were his children and he owed to them duties, similar to those to his own progeny. (सवे मुनिसे पजा ममा··· अथ पजाये इछामि हकं किंति सवेन हिदसुखेन हिद-लोकिक-पाललोकिकाये युजेवूति। मुनिसेपि इछामि हकं।

To Kautilya the type of the father represented the functions of the benevolent despot—irresponsible, accountable to none, like the father in the management of children, but guided by his affections and the duties which affection implanted in the paternal heart. Aśoka went a step further. Strung with remorse for the sins of an iniquitous and bloody youth, he devoted his efforts to make the paternal ideal a reality and thereby paved the way to the attainment of immortality.

Kauṭilya's idealism found further expression in identifying the king's own interest with those of his subjects. They were to have everything through him as the sole custodian of their interests; at the same time, it was his duty to identify himself with his people. His was a life of duty and not of enjoyment. Its aim and purpose was but to live for others—to make himself happy by ensuring his subjects' happiness. Verily says he :—

प्रजासुखे सुखं राज्ञः प्रजानाञ्च हिते हितम् ।
नात्मप्रियं सुखं राज्ञः प्रजानाञ्च सुखे सुखम् ॥

(Kau. p. 39.)

This noble idealism characterised all throughout its existence, the Hindu idea of royalty and the concept of regal duty. Centuries later, it found its noblest exponent in India's greatest poet, when he attempted to describe the king, through the idealistic vision of two youthful recluses addressing the king as follows :—

स्वसुखनिरभिलासः खिद्यसे लोकहेतोः
प्रतिदिनमथवा ते वृत्तिरेवंविधैव ।
अनुभवति हि मूर्ध्ना पादपस्तीव्रमुष्णम्
शमयति परितापं छायया संश्रितानाम् ॥

औत्सुक्यमात्रमवसाययति प्रतिष्ठा
क्लिश्नाति लब्धपरिपालनवृत्तिरेव ।
नातिश्रमापनयनाय यथा श्रमाय
राज्यं स्वहस्तधृतदण्डमिवातपत्रम् ॥

नियमयसि विमार्गप्रस्थितानात्तदण्डः
प्रशमयसि विवादं कल्पसे रक्षणाय ।
अतनुषु विभवेषु ज्ञातयः सन्तु नाम
त्वयि तु परिसमाप्तं बन्धुकृत्यं प्रजानाम् ॥

II

ROYAL AUTHORITY ; LAW AND THE ADMINISTRATIVE MACHINERY.

The king, according to Kauṭilya, was the embodiment of all authority. This authority he derived from "Law"—law which was the embodiment of all order, law which was the essence of the regulative maxims of the cosmical order, law, the eternal and the universal. The Hindu idea of Law was also peculiar. It was neither the will of the multitude nor merely the expression of social will. Itself regulating everything, it was above the reach of all human regulative agencies. With no parallels elsewhere in the world, it approached perhaps the Greek idea.

Law and law then was the final ruler of this universe. A counter-part of this was the law guiding the relations of men. The king, the master of all men was equally subject to it along with his subjects. and so Kauṭilya assigned to it the highest place. The king's business was neither to make, nor to alter the law, but to carry out its maxims. That was his principal duty and thence he derived his sole authority.

Dharma, self-existent and self-emanent, was the soul of being. If the wheel of Dharma stopped moving, the Varṇas and Āśramas were sure to perish. It was the king who, by ensuring the continuance of Dharma, contributed to the safety of the world. Cf.

चतुर्वर्णाश्रमस्यायं लोकस्याचाररक्षणात् ।
नश्यतां सर्वधर्माणां राजा धर्मप्रवर्तकः ॥
(Kau. p. 150.)

Though practically silent on the abstract conception of law, Kauṭilya was a believer in the older sacerdotal theory of Dharma and its excellence over the body-politic. According to him, as the god Varuṇa was the moral Judge *par excellence*, even so was the king on earth. He was, according to the sacerdotal theory, the counter-part of Varuṇa, and Kauṭilya enjoins on kings the duty of impartially administering law. This royal duty of adjudicating points of dispute between individuals, was not merely political but a higher and moral one. Kauṭilya points out that by virtue of his being the custodian of law, the king was to confer punishment and reward on the guilty or the worthy and thereby absolve himself from his moral liability. In cases of failure to punish wrong-doers, the king was liable to a fine thirty-six times the amount to be paid by the guilty. Says Kauṭilya—

अदण्डदण्डने राज्ञो दण्डस्त्रिंशद्गुणोऽम्भसि ।
वरुणाय प्रदातव्यो ब्राह्मणेभ्यस्ततः परम् ॥ (Kau. p. 234.

Similarly, in cases where a culprit robbing others could not be detected, the king was also to make good the loss from his own coffers.

Justice, then, was the first duty of the king, and in doing justice he was not to be guided by his own likes and dislikes. Impartiality was the first criterion of justice, and this opened to the king the way not only to the mastery of the world but also of the realm of Heaven. *e.g.*

राज्ञः स्वधर्मस्स्वर्गाय प्रजा धर्मेण रक्षितुः ।
अरक्षितुर्वा क्षेप्तुर्वा मिथ्यादण्डमतोऽन्यथा ॥
दण्डो हि केवलो लोकं परं चेमं च रक्षति ।
राज्ञा पुत्रे च शत्रौ च यथादोषं समं धृतः ॥
अनुशासद्धि धर्मेण व्यवहारेण संस्थया ।
न्यायेन च चतुर्थेन चतुरन्तां महीं जयेत् ॥

(Kau. p. 150.)

Next to impartiality, reason was the chief factor in judicial administration. Without reason, law could not be properly administered, since law, according to Kauṭilya, revealed itself to men through human reason. Thus reason itself must be the guide in points of difficulty or doubt. Kauṭilya, thus assigns the highest place to Nyāya or reason. As he himself says—

संस्थाया धर्मशास्त्रेण शास्त्रं वा व्यावहारिकम् ।
यस्मिन्नर्थे विरुध्येत धर्मेणार्थं विनिश्चयेत् ॥
शास्त्रं विप्रतिपद्येत धर्मन्यायेन केनचित् ।
न्यायस्तत्र प्रमाणं स्यात् तत्र पाठो हि नश्यति ॥ (p. 150.

We pass on, next, to the king's control over Law. All disputes, according to Kauṭilya, could be settled in four ways, *e.g.* through

(1) Dharma— or truthful acknowledgment of the disputed claim by the other party.

(2) Vyavahāra—or through the agency of witnesses to the transaction.

(3) Caritra—or by following the time-honoured customs.

(4) Rājaśāsana—or by royal adjudication. Cf.

धर्मश्च व्यवहारश्च चरित्रं राजशासनम् ।
विवादार्थश्चतुष्पादः पश्चिमः पूर्वबाधकः ॥
अत्र सत्यस्थितो धर्मो व्यवहारस्तु साक्षिषु ।
चरित्रं संग्रहे पुंसां राज्ञामाज्ञा तु शासनम् ॥

(Kau. p. 150.)

Of all these various ways of settling disputes, royal adjudication had the highest place.

Theoretically, the king had no legislative authority, since Law seemed to have a rigid character. Yet, in practice, it was hardly so. The king indirectly exercised considerable influence over the laws. For, though no new law could be made or altered, the king had ample opportunities of modifying it, *e.g.*

(1) Firstly, he could repeal, modify or introduce customary laws.

(2) Secondly, so far as the administration was concerned, he could, by edict, issue regulations and ordinances, which had the force of laws and which were stringently enforced by royal officials. The old Dharma-code was silent on many points and defective in many respects. There was no provision for the punishment of certain crimes at all. This was remedied by the regulations issued by the king

Character of the Arthasastra laws :—The character of the Arthaśāstra laws calls for consideration. As it is, the Arthaśāstra was the first attempt at codification of laws in India. Prior to that, the king or the judges were mainly guided by customs We have no history of the evolution of law in ancient India, and our knowledge does not go beyond the Dharma-sūtras. These contain for the most part customary laws and seem to be hopelessly deficient in most branches. In these, the law of crimes does not exist at all. Murder or other offences are regarded more or less as torts and could be expiated by fines, which had the same nature as the weregilds in the early Saxon or Teuton laws. Fines were levied on persons accused of theft, though a house-breaking thief was punished with death. Adultery and unchastity was similarly punished.

Originally, civil and criminal jurisdiction was exercised by the king in person, when he was no more than a mere clan-head or a tribal chief. Later on, officers with judicial functions came to be appointed. The evidence of the Jātakas shows two or three classes of such officials, *e.g.*

(1) the royal Amātyas

(2) the Codakas

(3) the Viniścaya-mahāmātyas.

They tried all sorts of cases and awarded sentence according to castomary laws, which included fines, and various forms of capital punishment, *e.g.* by impaling, burning or by mutilations. In matters of disputes relating to succession or inheritance, the old law was administered by the Elders or Judges.

As the Imperial administrative system came into existence and kingly prerogative was strengthened, the royal edicts and ordinances multiplied. The sources of taxation multiplied, new offences were created by royal order and a considerable body of such edicts hardened into a code which we find in the Kaṇṭaka-śodhana chapter of the Arthaśāstra.

The chief objects for promulgating these laws were

(1) the preservation of the king's person. (In this connection the law of Treason requires our attention.)

(2) and of the king's rights *i.e.* to preserve the regal incomes from various departments and to check theft or defalcation.

(3) to ensure the benefits of good government to the people by checking the economic tyranny of classes, *e.g.* by regulating prices, wages, profits, and by the checking of criminals and wrong-doers.

(4) to punish crimes not included in the old law.

Now, when we come to summarise our view, we find the following characteristics of these laws.

e.g. (1) their stringency.—This would appear from the nature of punishments meted out to the culprits. All sorts of horrible punishments appear in the Kauṭilyan statute book *e.g.*, simple death ; death by burning ; by impaling ; by throwing to dogs and wild animals ; by burning off the limbs ; by drowning.

The severity of the code was, however, modified by the practice of levying heavy fines in lieu of mutilation.

(2) their comprehensive and all embracing character. No part of the body politic was free from their jurisdiction.

Not only was the punishment heavy, but the law gave little chance of escape. Thus, in cases of sale of children as slaves, not only were the seller and buyer punished, but even those who happened to hear of the transaction or witnessed it.

Furthermore, the stringent law did not in all cases respect traditional privileges. Thus, the Brahmin's immunity from capital punishment vanished when he was accused of treason. The only privilege he got was that he was drowned instead of being burnt alive.

Lastly, so far as their interpretation was concerned, these laws recognised no higher authority above the king. We find, indeed, a mention of the old Dharmasūtra theory of all laws emanating from the Śruti, but there is hardly any room for the interpretation of these laws by the Dharmajñas or the Śiṣṭas. The law knew no higher authority than the King and no interpretation except that of the Royal Judges.

As we pass on from the Jātakas to the Arthaśāstra, we find in that book a code of laws which falls under two great divisions :

(1) The Dharma Laws—occuring in the IIIrd book, based mainly on the old customary laws.

(2) The Regal or Kaṇṭaka-śodhana laws in the IVth book of the Arthaśāstra.

The chief divisions of the Dharmasthīya laws are :

(1) Vyavahāra—or agreements in general.

(2) (*a*) Vivāha and Strīdhana—marriage and the laws relating to maintenance and woman's property.
(*b*) Laws regulating the relation between husband and wife ; divorce or separation.
(*c*) Enforcement of marital privileges ; absence or desertion of the husband.

(3) (*a*) Inheritance and succession (दायविभागे दायक्रमः).
(*b*) Division of heritable property—(अंशविभागः and पुत्रविभागः).

(4) Laws relating to house-hold property —(गृहवास्तुकम्) and sale of house-property (वास्तुविक्रयः).

(5) Non-performance of Agreements (समयस्थानपाकर्म).

(6) Law of Debt (ऋणादानम्).

(7) Law of pledges and deposits (औपनिधिकम्).

(8) Law of slaves and servants (दासकल्पः).

(9) Laws relating to agreements for service (कर्मकरकल्पः).

(10) Laws of co-operative undertakings (सम्भूयसमुत्थानम्).

(11) Recission of sales (विक्रीतानुशयः).

(12) Sale without ownership (अस्वामिविक्रयः).

(13) Laws regarding Sāhasa or heinous and violent crimes (साहसम्).

(14) Laws regarding defamation and slander (वाक्पारुष्यम्).

(15) Laws regarding bodily injury, battery and assault (दण्डपारुष्यम्).

(16) Law of Adultery (स्त्रीसङ्ग्रहणम्).

(17) Miscellaneous (प्रकीर्णकम्).

(18) Law of Gambling (द्यूतः).

These laws were administered by the Dharmasthas, whose status we shall discuss later on, assisted by three Amātyas. It is apparent that out of these divisions arose the eighteen titles of law in the later Smṛtis. This law was mainly the old customaty law, and seems to have been inviolable, except by a process of legal fiction or through the agency of the commentators. Many legal schools existed, and Kauṭilya expressly mentions two of them *viz.*, the Auśanasāḥ and the Mānavāḥ.

The other division of law was administered by the Kaṇṭaka-śodhana Commissioners. The growth of this law is interesting from the social and constitutional point of view, though, unfortunately, we are not in a position to trace its development, owing to the lack of earlier material. Probably, this law arose out of royal ordinances, which as in medieval England had the force of law, until and unless they were declared illegal. For the administration of these laws, which regulated many social and economic problems, there were royal ministers and Commissioners. (अमात्य and प्रदेष्टा:). The business of these men were manifold, *viz.*,

(1) To regulate the guilds, their work and wages (कारुरक्षणम्).

(2) Protection of merchants, price-regulation and regulation of profits (वैदेहकरक्षणम्).

(3) Protection and preservation of the rights of the state (सर्वाधिकरणरक्षणम्), *e.g.*, prevention of theft from royal stores, mines, or other government departments, detection of forgery of royal

writs, punishment of Judges for misdemeanours, of dishonest clerks, or those who break prisons or lock-ups, and punishment for the cruelty of prison officials.

(4) Suppression of theft of all descriptions (not contemplated in old law), dishonesty in dice-playing; violation of game laws, insult to superiors; impersonation as a Brāhmaṇa or injuring them; false use of royal writs, sale of adulterated meat or of human flesh; various descriptions of murder (*e.g.* in quarrel), carrying out the administration of the laws of Treason, punishment for breaking of dams and embankments, punishment of poisoners, incendiaries, slanderers of the king, of those who steal weapons and armours, or those who destroy the virility of men;

(5) Suppression of rapes and outrages on women of various descriptions, (कन्याप्रकर्म) *e.g.* punishment of adulterous women, or those forming liaison with low-class people, general regulation of relations of men or women.

(6) Suppression of offences known as अतिचार which comprised forcing a Brahmin to eat unclean food, house-breaking, violation of his moral liabilities on the part of a responsible officer, destruction of houses, rash-driving and causing death thereby, theft or slaughter of sacred animals, witchcraft, incest or incestuous adultery, intercourse with low class women, violation of nuns, forcible

intercourse with prostitutes, homo-sexual vice, intercourse with lowclass women, and many other heinous crimes.

All these comprised offences not all included or contemplated in the old codes of Dharma law. As time went on, as society became complex, as the royal authority increased, and as the administrative body extended its jurisdiction, the necessity of new laws became evident. As there was no legislative agency, the right of issuing ordinances or of making laws, devolved on the king and his ministers, who worked with the object of protecting the people—by "eradicating and destroying the thorns which imperilled the life of the people". We shall discuss merely the importance of some of these laws and do nothing more, since it would be out of place here to go into details about their nature or character.

The Kaṇṭaka-śodhana Commissioners, moreover, exercised the authority and jurisdiction of Police Officials and Criminal Investigators. They acted with the object of preventing crimes, and also of saving the country from epidemics, famines or pests injurious to the community. In addition to their duties mentioned above, they had the authority—

(1) to employ spies for the detection of crimes and criminal tendecies in men ; for examining the conduct of government officials suspected of bribery or perverse intention, for detecting the

making of counterfeit coins, poisoners, and abettors of thieves, robbers, and adulterors ;

(2) to apprehend criminals in the very act of committing wrongs, *i.e.* while engaged in enticing women, house-breaking, or committing theft etc. ;

(3) to enquire into the cause of the sudden death of subjects and to hold postmortem examinations ;

(4) to apply judicial torture to make suspects confess their guilt.

Their jurisdiction thus appears to be very comprehensive. In their functions and summary jurisdiction, the commissioners nearly approached the officers of the Star Chamber, the High Commission Court or the Eccleciastical courts of medieval England.

III

LEGAL THEORY OF THE ROYAL PERSON.

If such were the extensive powers of the king, a growing legal theory had stepped in to make the regal powers more and more comprehensive. As the result of the influence of this theory the idea of the royal person became finer everyday, and it was freed from all obstacles or encumbrances. The king was in theory bound by no shackles or legal disabilities.

This legal theory clothed the royal person with a number of privileges, which had their germs in the sacerdotal theories and ideals of the Brāhmaṇic period.[1] Some of these we find mentioned in the Brāhmaṇas, while others find expression in the Dharma-sūtras. Prominent among the privileges of the king were the following—

(1) He was adaṇḍya or immume from the jurisdiction of any one else in the kingdom.

(2) He was free from ferry-dues and all other taxes.

(3) His property did not lapse with adverse possession. cf.

आधिः सीमा बालधनं निक्षेपोपनिधिः स्त्रियः।
राजस्व श्रोत्रियस्वः च न भोगेन प्रणश्यति॥
ज्ञातयो न हरेयुः उपनिधिमाधिं सीमानं राज-
श्रोत्रियद्रव्याणि Cf. the D. S of Vaśiṣṭha.

(4) He had the escheat to all property without any heir (cf. Vaśiṣṭha, तयोरलाभे राजा हरेत्। नतु ब्राह्मणस्वं ch. XVIII 62 ; also Kauṭilya III. V. अदायादकं राजा हरेत्।).

(5) All treasure-troves went to him (अदायादकं राजा हरेत्। "शतसहस्रादूर्ध्वं राजगामी निधिः।—Kauṭilya IV. Ch. I.

(6) All lost articles without owner went to him (नाष्टिकं च—...तच्च द्रव्यं राजधर्मंं स्यात् तच्च द्रव्यं त्रिपक्षादूर्ध्वंराजा हरेत्)—Kauṭilya Bk. III ch. XVI.

(7) He could not be cited as witness in a law-court. (Cf. राजश्रोत्रियग्रामभृतक etc. न साक्षीनृपतिः कार्यो न कारुकुशीलवौ। Kauṭilya III. ch. IV and Vaśiṣṭha.

(8) He had privileges of social eminence and was regarded as the first gentleman of the realm. Everyone including even Brāhmaṇas and Śrotriyas were to honour him when he came as a guest.

These were the traditional privileges of the king in ancient India, which grew out gradually. We find the growth of similar ideas in the history of other nations. Some of these added to the social position of the king, some freed him from obligations otherwise imposed on common subjects, while others added to his source of revenue. The law of freedom from prescription even now holds good in England, where, in the eighteenth century, the crown lawyers invented the theory of "Nullum tempus", in the crown duchies. The other privileges still attach to the royal person, and are recognized by the English legal system. No one can sue the Crown, but instead, the minister in charge is sued. The present law of England also recógnizes the king as the ultimate heir to all properties without owner.

If these traditional privileges of the king added but to his security or to the safety of the exercise of his royal authority, there were other causes and circumstances which further consolidated the regal position itself and contributed ultimately to its irresponsible exercise.

For the safety of the Royal person, we see in the Arthaśāstra the promulgation of a Law of Treason which bears a curious similarity and a close resemblance to that English law which arose in the reign of the Plantagenets. It is interesting to compare the details and provisions of the Law of Treason in England with that we find in the

Arthaśāstra. The English Law may be summarised in the following offences which constituted, treason, and for which it inflicted the highest punishment (25 Edward III. St. 5). *e.g.*

(1) Waging war against the King in his realm or adhering to his foes.

(2) Compassing the death of the King, queen or their eldest son.

(3) Violating the Queen, the King's eldest unmarried daughter, or his eldest son's wife.

(4) Counterfeiting the King's seal or money or importing false money.

(5) Slaying the Chancellor, Treasurer or Judges in the discharge of their duty.

These are the chief offences which the law of Edward made punishable with death. When we turn to India, we find in the Arthaśāstra almost all these offences made capital, and heavy sentences imposed on the culprit which were executed with rigour. The section of the Arthaśāstra law bearing on treason runs thus : *e.g.*

"राज्यकामुकमन्तःपुरप्रधर्षकमटव्यमित्रोत्साहकं दुर्गराष्ट्र-दण्डकोपकं वा शिरोहस्तप्रादीपिकं घातयेत् ।
ब्राह्मणं तमपः प्रवेशयेत् ॥

Thus according to Kautilya, the following offences were primarily regarded treasonable *e.g.*

(1) Coveting the royal domains (राजत्रकामुक)

(2) Inciting enemies or forest tribes, joining or inviting foreign enemies.

(3) Inciting revolt or tampering with the defensive forces, or exciting revolt among subjects, or in the Army.

(4) Violating the sanctity of the harem *e.g.* outraging the chastity of the queen or the female members of the royal house-hold.

Curiously enough, these sections are almost parallel and bear the closest possible resemblence to the English law.

In addition to these, the forging of royal seals and edicts is, in the Arthaśāstra punished with death, though not attended with so great cruelty. For, in the chapter on the protection of departments we find the following section:

कुटुम्बाध्यक्षमुख्यस्वामिनां कूटशासनमुद्राकर्मसु पूर्वमध्यमोत्तमवधा दण्डाः। यथापराधं वा॥ P. 222.

Next to these, we have in the Arthaśāstra a section on slander on the king, which was punished with the loss of the tongue. The chief offences under this head were—

(1) slander on the king;

(2) divulging his secrets.

Cf. **राजाक्रोशकमन्त्रभेदकयोरनिष्टप्रवृत्तिकस्य ....जिह्वामुत्पाटयेत्॥** Kau. p. 228.

The operation of the law of treason did not end here. It did over-ride even the Brāhmaṇa's privilege of immunity from capital punishment

(सर्वापराधेष्वदण्डनीयो ब्राह्मणः) and made him liable to be drowned (ब्राह्मणं तमपः प्रवेशयेत्). This law even suspended or abrogated civil rights arising out of the old traditional laws (p. 154). Thus, through the operation of the law of treason, a wife could renounce her husband if he proved a traitor to the king. Cf.

नीचत्वं परदेशं वा प्रस्थितो राजकिल्विषी ।
प्राणाभिहन्ता पतितस्त्याज्यः क्लीबोऽपि वा पतिः ॥

Women also lost all rights to their Strīdhana if they incurred the royal displeasure. Cf.

राजद्विष्टातिचाराभ्यामात्मातिक्रमणेन च ।
स्त्रीधनानीतशुल्कानामस्वाम्यं जायते स्त्रियः ॥

(Kau. p. 157).

IV

OTHER CIRCUMSTANCES AND CAUSES CONTRIBUTING TO THE DEVELOPMENT OF ROYAL POWER.

The development of royal prerogatives and the subsequent growth of irresponsibility was not the work of a single day or of a single individual. It was a long continuous process which had begun centuries ago and was fostered by favourable circumstances. As is evident to all students of Indian history, popular participation in politics almost came to an end with the close of the period which saw the decay of the tribal states. Buddhism arose, and with it the cause of absolutism and of Imperialism indirectly got a strong impetus. The idea of an universal religion loosened the cohesion of the clan. Humanity in some respects, was freed from old world dogma, but the cause of democracy suffered, inasmuch as the religious upheaval diverted the attention of men from politics to religion. Far from religion influencing politics, the influence was just the reverse. Those who stood in opposition to tyranny became weakened and the feared loss of privilege made the priest an ally of despotic power

In the trail of these, came the rise of the

Arthaśāstra school. Its expounders advocated the extension of royal authority. Politics became unmoral. Neither force nor fraud were condemned. Force became the sole criterion of success in politics ; fraud was rather welcomed as a surer means of success, since it smoothed all other obstacles. Militarism became the order of the day ; standing armies came into being ; conquest expanded the realm of the king, and with conquests the king's coffers became filled and the conqueror became irresponsible. New territories, more numerous subjects, vast acquisition of wealth all made princes no longer depend on the will of the people, as in the past.

Such was the history of India from the sixth century to the fourth. Graduaily, the whole of Northern India came under the sway of the Nandas and, later on, of the Mauryas. All the other monarchies—Kośala, Avanti and Kausāmbī, became parts of the great Empire. Not only were these the only acquisitions but all the intervening forest area fell into the hands of the conqueror. Hitherto these were but "no man's land",—no one's property. Under the Mauryas, these became practically the imperial domains of the sovereign. If we compare the state of affairs described in the Arthaśāstra with that in the Dharmasūtras, we are in a position to note the great changes which had taken place.

The Dharmasūtras recognize these areas as

belonging to nobody. In the words of the Roman jurists they were "Res communes" and everybody had the right to enjoy them. The pictures in the Jātakas confirm the above idea, and one of the authors of the Dharmasūtras, Vaśiṣṭha, expressly says that "those deriving income from these are to be free from taxation" (नदीकक्षवनशैलोपभोगानिस्करा: सुग्र: ?) ।

The picture in the Arthaśāstra, on the contrary shows quite a different state of affairs. The forests are king's property. They are under the jurisdiction of the royal forest officers—not only the trees, shrubs, and plants, but also the animals —elephants, ferocious beasts, and the deer. These latter, again, are protected by the most stringent of game-laws ever promulgated in the East. They bear a close resemblance to those introduced in medieval England under the Normans and Plantagenets, who shrank not from inflicting capital punishment accompanied by the most brutal tortures on those who violated the king's rights in the forest.

Next to the forests, the waste lands and, as we shall see later on, the mines were claimed in the name of the king. The waste came under the jurisdiction of the Śūṇyapāla, while the mines were worked or let on hire under the supervision of the Ākarādhyakṣa.

The forest. the mine, or the waste land, thus became new sources of income to the king, over which the people had no right to claim any control. They could cite no authority, no custom, no law, to restrict the king's ownership over these.

From these, flowed to the king's coffers a regular supply of silver and gold and other accoutrements of war *e.g* materials for the bow and arrow, the lance or the javelin or the greater implements of war. The horse and the elephant strengthened the army.

Once financial independence was ensured and a regular money-supply guaranteed, the king was irresponsible and could rule by the sword.

V

THE KING'S DAILY LIFE

The king was the centre of political life and the pivot of the whole constitution. All power remained concentrated in him and from him emanated authority which was delegated to the agents of administration. Everything therefore depended on his exertions and he had to work hard for the discharge of the onerous duties which were imposed on him. As such, he was no mere figure-head.

The king's life, consequently, was not one of enjoyment or pleasure. It was one hard routine of work. Desire for supremacy, hankering after the safety of the vast fabric, mistrust of officials, who might turn the royal confidence reposed in them to their own advantage and to the detriment of their sovereign master the king, all made the king remain constantly on the alert. Consequently, the king's life as described in the Arthaśāstra was one of hard labour and constant worries. Under similar circumstances, the burden on the king naturally becomes heavy. The Maurya king had his counterparts in the ancient world and also in later times. Not to speak of ancient kings, Phillip II and Aurungzeb were also hard workers.

Kauṭilya constantly inculates the necessity of exertion. Since, with it, the king imparted his energy to his servants and made them work for the common good. Otherwise, they shirked their duty and neglected the affairs of state. As Kauṭilya says :—

राजानमुत्तिष्ठमानमुत्तिष्ठन्ते भृत्याः ।
प्रमाद्यन्तमनुप्रमाद्यन्ति । कर्माणि चास्य भक्षयन्ति ।
द्विषद्भिश्चातिसन्धीयते ।

After pointing out the evils of lethergy, he further observes :—

तस्मान्नित्योत्थितो राजा कुर्यादर्थानुशासनम् ।
अर्थस्य मूलमुत्थानमनर्थस्य विपर्ययः ॥
अनुत्थाने ध्रुवो नाशः प्राप्तस्यानागतस्य च ।
प्राप्यते फलमुत्थानाल्लभते चार्थसम्पदम् ॥

Exertion on the part of the king was thus the first consideration. With it, the king attained all his desires, without it everything was reversed. With active supervision, he could make new acquisitions, preserve both the old and the new, and then distribute his favours among the worthy.

In the chapter on Prakṛti-sampat, where the virtues of a good monarch are enumerated, energy and absence of indolence are therefore mentioned by Kauṭilya as the foremost qualities of the king. (महोत्साहोऽदीर्घसूत्रः)

Daily routine.

To enable the king to carry on the work of administration and supervision, Kauṭilya calls upon him to follow a hard routine of working hours, for the proper performance of the multi-ferious work concentrated in his hands. The king was to divide the day and the night into sixteen equal parts (either with the help of hour glasses or by marking the hours of the day by noting the daily shadow variations. (नालिकाभिरह्वरष्टधा रात्रिं च विभजेत्)

1. The first Yāmārdha was to be devoted to the consideration of measures for defence and of income and expenditure. (रक्षाविधानमायव्ययौ)

2. The second was to be spent in judging the complaints of the Paura-jānapadas. (पौरजानपदानां कार्यानि पश्येत्)

3. The third and the fourth were to be spent in ablution, eating and in rest or with study.

4. During the fifth, he was to receive money from the officers and consult the Superintendents. (अध्यक्षांश्च)

5. During the fourth, he was to exchange letters with the members of the Council and to consider the information supplied by spies.

6. The sixth was to be spent in consultation or in rest (स्वैरविहारं मन्त्रं वा सेवेत)

7—8. The seventh and the eighth parts of the day were to be reserved for the inspection of the various branches of the army or in discussing affairs relating to it, along with the commander-in-chief.

After performing his prayers at the end of the day, the king was to receive his spies again, during the earliest part of the night. Then, after performing his ablutions and taking his dinner he was to retire to rest. After spending three hours, he was to rise from bed and to spend the sixth part of the night in meditating on the duties of the coming day. During the next period, he was again to deliberate with his ministers and to send and direct his spies.

During the closing hours of the night, he was to receive the benediction of the priests, sacrificers and the royal chaplains, and having consulted the Physician, the Master of the kitchen, and the Sooth-sayer, he was to enter the Public Hall, after passing round a cow with its calf and bull.

The most important of the daily duties of the king was his consultation with ministers and the holding of a daily Durbar to hear the complaints of his subjects. This last practice held its ground under the Pathan Sultans of Delhi and the Mogul Emperors. Kauṭilya dwells upon its importance in the strongest possible terms. The king according to him must come in contact with his subjects and earn their gratitude by dealing out even-handed justice to all. Any monarch who failed to do this, and any king who was out of the reach of his subjects, made himself liable to their anger and was thus sure to bring ruin on himself. As Kauṭilya himself says :—

उपस्थानगतः कार्यार्थिनामद्वारासङ्गं कारयेत्। दुर्दर्शो हि राजा कार्याकार्यविपर्यासमासन्नैः कार्यते। तेन प्रकृतिकोपमरिवशं वा गच्छेत्॥

In discharging this duty of redressing the grievances of his people, the king was bound to give preference and precedence to the business of gods, hermits, sectaries, Śrotriyas and members of religious orders. Similarly, the cases of weak-lings, children, the sick, or women without protection, received the prior attention of the monarch. To state in brief, urgent attention was paid to the those business which pleaded emergency. (कार्यगौरवादात्ययिकवशेन वा)

As everything depended on the safety of the king, his personal protection engages the attention of the author of the Arthaśāstra. With all his characteristic wisdom of men and matters, he details all those safe-guards, which were calculated to ensure the personal safety of the king. The dangers in those days, in India as in all countries and in all ages, which beset the life of despotic kings, arose from the following *e.g.*

(1) secret assasins ready to poison the king or to encompass his death, in alliance with his concubines and mistresses, or by setting the palace on fire.

(2) the rebellious hands of the king's own relatives, queens and sons, both legitimate or illegitimate, acting

on their own initiative or in league with powerful subjects.

The details of precautions against these are to be found in the four following chapters of the book *e.g.*

(*a*) निशान्तप्रणिधिः
(*b*) आत्मरक्षितकम्
(*c*) राजपुत्ररक्षणम्
(*d*) अवरुद्धवृत्तमवरुद्धे च वृत्तिः ।

The chapter on royal harem begins with the description of the requisites of a properly constructed palace and details its concealed underground chambers (गूढ़भित्तिसञ्चारं मोहनगृहं तन्मध्ये वा वासगृहं भूमिगृहं वा), its numerous doors and subterranean passages (द्वारमनेकसुरुङ्गासञ्चारम्), its pillars containing concealed ways of escape, and numerous such other contrivances. Next, we have mention of the precautions against fire or lightening or snakes. For exterminating snakes mongoose and other animals were directed to be kept. While, for the two other dangers, the construction of the palace was to be modified. As precaution against poison, certain kind of birds and animals, as well as experts in healing the effects of snake-bite or poisoning by other means, (जाङ्गलीविदः) were to be kept.

Within the harem itself, separate quarters were allotted to the Princes and Princesses, while harem-guards were stationed at different places under the Antarvaṃśika.

The queens and royal concubines were not to be regarded as objects of trust. Spies in various guises were to watch their quarters. Eunuchs were to exercise supervision. Maids in the harem were liable to examination and courtesans were to watch their doings. Their own relations, too, were not to be allowed to enter their quarters. Men over 80 years or women over 50 were to be employed to watch them. Everything coming for them or despatched out by them was to be examined, and nothing was to be allowed to go unexamined or without pass-ports.

This was not all. The king was not to visit any of the women until and unless their purity was vouch-safed for by the elderly ladies or men who acted as the guardians of the harem. This might appear rather too huminating to the women or too mean of the king, but, trust or faith in one, especially in women, was no part of the political life of those days. Kings were not to be guided by love, affection or sentiment. They were to be guided by the example of the past and Kauṭilya here cites a list of those kings who had been murdered in the harem, with a view to remind them of the consequences of good faith or carelessness in dealing with women. The list he gives, occurs in the works of many subsequent writers and became a sort of stock-list always to be remembered with horror. It contains the names of princes who met death even in the asylum of love, either through the hand of the queen professing loyalty to her lord or of the son or brother in league with such rebellious women. We find thus, the names of Bhadrasena murdered by his brother-in-law concealed in the queen's room, of the Karuṣa king murdered by his son concealed in the bed of his mother, of the king of Kāsi murdered by his queen who mixed poison in his food, of Vairanty, the king of Sauvīra, of king Jaludha or of king Vidūratha— all murdered by their queens with weapons concealed under their garments, in the braid of their hair, or with poison in their ornaments. *e.g.*

देवीगृहे लीनो हि भ्राता भद्रसेनं जघान ।
मातुः शय्यान्तर्गतो हि पुत्रः कारुशम् ॥
लाजान्मधुनेति विषेण पर्यस्य देवी काशिराजम् ।
विषदिग्धेन नूपुरेण वैरन्त्यं मेखलामणिभिः सौवीरम्,
जालूथमादर्शेन वेण्यागूढं शस्त्रं
कृत्वा देवी विदूरथं जघान ॥

For further precautions, the king was to protect his person by surrounding himself with armed females, men armed and covered with mail, or with foreign mercinaries like the Kirāta guards. All these were selected after the most careful examination of their temperament and a thorough test of their loyalty. More often, these men were the descendants of the most trusted hereditary servants of the royal family (पितृपैतामहं महासम्बन्धानुबन्धं शिक्षितमनुरक्तं जनमासन्नं कुर्वीत ॥)

Food for the royal table was also directed to be cooked by the most trusted culinary experts, and before being offered to the king, was to be carefully tested. Part of it was to be thrown in to the fire and its purity was tested by noting any chemical effect on the plates, or by being given first of all, to chickens or other birds and animals. In every action precautions were to be taken. The King was not to take medicine, unless it was tasted by others ; he was not to take a walk in the garden until and unless the same was cleared of enemies or was declared free from snakes. He was not to dip in water unless it was declared free from dangerous aquatic animals. In his excursions, in his hunting expeditions, in his river trips, he was to be protected by spies accompanied by trusted guards. If he was out on walk, or went on elephant, guards were to line the route of his journey. If he were to be present in festivities, or witnessed any theatrical representations, or appeared in assemblies, the "Ten Kinds" of spies and guards were to protect him. (**यात्रासमाजोत्सवप्रवहणानि दशवर्गिकाधिष्ठितानि गच्छेत्**) The same measures were to be taken, even if the king went to visit a hermitage or any holy men* (**आश्रमस्त्वग्राह्याधिष्ठितः सिद्धतापसं पश्येत् ।**)

*The Buddhist literature gives us many more instances of royal assassination or deposition. For such, see Jātakas nos. 150, 461, 338, 373, 465. The deposition and death of

ROYAL CHILDREN.

In all despotic systems, these who stand nearest to the throne, often prove the most dangerous enemies to royalty. What is true everywhere, was true also in India. Even as early as the Vedic period, the King always prayed for safety from the enmity of his kinsmen. Inspite of the development of hereditary kingship and of royal authority, that danger continued to subsist. Kings found their greatest enemies in their own sons, who impatient of waiting, always aspired to the throne to the detriment of their royal father. To royalty, progeny was thus more a source of danger than of relief. The popularity of a son often caused vexation in the mind of the father while his debasement, depravity or cruelty was also a cause of anxiety for his future. In the Jātakas, we have more than one instance of a royal father exiling or imprisoning a prince, if he happened to be popular with the people or proved tyrannical. (Cf. Jātakas nos. 181, 193, 234, 320, etc.)

In that age of mistrust and suspision, princes came to be regarded as the natural enemies of their fathers. "They are like the brood of the

---

Bimbisāra by Ajātaśatru points to the disloyalty of sons, while the story of Pasendi's expulsion from the capital while on a visit to Buddha shows the necessity of protection even while the king visited holy men.

crab" says one politician "who devour their own parent". (कर्कटकसधर्माणो जनकभक्षाः राजपुत्रा एव ।)

All the predecessors of Kauṭilya had recognized this danger and consequently most of them like Bhāradvāja, Viśālākṣa, Parāśara, Piśuna, Kauṇapadanta and Vātavyādhi, regarded princes as a necessary evil to their parents. In trying to devise means for getting rid of them they advocated their chastisement or suppression. Some suggested their death as soon as they were born, some suggested banishment to the frontier, while some advocated exile to a foreign land. Others went so far as to advise the king to tempt his sons in the company of young women or to bring in their moral and intellectual depravity, by making them drunk or addicted to women, gambling or the chase.

Kauṭilya herein differs and shows his own excellence. Unlike his predecessors and contemporaries, he recognises the folly of such measures. He point out that the dynasty and with it the state was to suffer thereby. Consequently, he calls upon kings to perform religious ceremonies to impart noble qualities when the princes were in the womb, and to give them the right training in childhood. They are to be reared virtuous, honest and educated in all sciences. (काष्ठमिव हि घुणजग्धं राजकुलमविनीतपुत्रमभियुक्तमात्रं भज्येत । तस्मादृतुमत्यां महिष्यां ऋत्विजश्चरुमैन्द्राबार्हस्पत्यं निर्वपेयुः etc., and…तस्माद्धर्ममर्थं चास्योपदिशेन्नाधर्मं अनर्थं च)।

Far from allowing them to indulge in wine, women, gambling or the chase, Kauṭilya calls upon kings to rectify their manners and character and suggests methods of right training for them. In case of many sons fighting with each other, he advises kings to banish them to the frontier posts,—not all of them but the unruly. As for the well-disposed, steady and loyal son, he was to be associated with the father in the government. He could be made a Yuvarāja or Heir-apparent or made the Commander-in chief. (आत्मसम्पन्नं सैन्यापत्ये यौवराज्ये वा स्थापयेत् ।)

An wicked prince on the other hand, even if he were the only son, was to be exiled, and the king was to ensure the safety of his line, either by adopting his daughter's son as heir, or even by raising a son on the wife* by a virtuous relative. In no case the throne was to be allowed to be occupied by a worthless prince. (न चैकपुत्रं अविनीतं राजेऽ स्थापयेत्)

Kauṭilya's observations as to the king's duties towards the princes are indeed important from more than one point of view. First of all, they show, the originality of his views and point out boldly the fact that far from slavishly following the teachings of his predecessors, he was a real re-

*The Jātakas seem to refer to such adoptions, and even to the practice of raising issue by *niyoga* (see Kuśa Jātaka No. 53.) For banishment of princes, see Jātakas No. 181, 193, 234, 320.

former. They prove moreover that he was a firm believer in royalty—royalty as an institution beneficial to the subject and not a mere despotic *regime*. The traditions of a hereditary monarchy descending in the heirs male, subsisting on popular loyalty and continuing the highly organised administrative system—was his goal. In his eyes, as in the eyes of prosterity, hereditary monarchy backed by a system, had undoubtedly an advantage over short-lived usurpations. His views on the comparative merits of hereditary monarchy and usurpations backed by force, are to be found in the chapter on the 'Calamities befalling the King and the Kingdom' (राजराज्ययोर्व्यसनचिन्ता). In that chapter, he discusses the relative merits of a diseased or sick king with a hereditary title and a new one with no hereditary title but who is a strong usurper. In course of a discussion in which he cites the views of his predecessors, he shows his reasons first of all for preferring a blind but wise king to one not guided by the Śāstras. Then, he discusses the merits of a discarded prince and a new-comer and cites older authors who preferred a new king, since, being a new comer he was sure to please his people by confering privileges and immunities (नवस्तु राजा स्वधर्मानुग्रहपरिहारदानमानकर्मभिः प्रकृतिरञ्जनोपकारैश्चरति इत्याचार्याः)।

To these, Kauṭilya raises objections which are worthy of note as showing us his mind. He points out that a new king is sure to regard monarchy as solely acquired by his strength and thereby work without restraint. This may give rise to a combination which may easily remove him. (*e.g.* **नवस्तु राजा बलावर्जितं "ममेदं राज्यम्" इति यथेष्टमनवग्रहश्चरति** etc. Kau. VIII. ch. 2)

Next, in regard to the comparative merits of a weak hereditary monarch and a new usurper, Kauṭilya points out that though the former may be weak, the "elements" easily bow down to a hereditary ruler and as loyalty is the basis of permanence, the hereditary rule of a weak king is to be preferred. (**नेति: कौटिल्य:—दुर्बलमभिजातं प्रकृतय: स्वयमुपनमन्ति । जात्यमैश्वर्यप्रकृतिरनुवर्तत इति । बलवतश्चानभिजातस्योपजापं विसंवादयन्ति । अनुयोगे साद्गुण्यम् ॥**)

This faith in hereditary royalty leads Kauṭilya to devote one more section of his great work to the consideration of measures to be employed in case the king died all on a sudden, or in a foreign land leaving no competent heir.* The crafty and unscruplous politicians of that unscruplous age regarded it as merely affording a fine opportunity for the minister to usurp the throne. Indeed, one of them—the crafty Bhāradvāja, not only advocated it but justified such a usurpation as an act (illustrating the rule of might in nature) frequently happening in nature.

*Hyder Ali's death was also not made public by his minister Punniar who waited for Tippu's return.

e.g. प्रम्रियमाणे च राजनि अमात्यः कूल्यकुमारमुख्यान् परस्परं मुख्येषु वा विक्रामयेत्। विक्रान्तं प्रकृतिकोपेन घातयेत्। कुल्यकुमारमुख्यानुपांशुदण्डेन वा साधयित्वा स्वयं राज्यं गृह्णीयात्। राज्यकारणाद्धि पिता पुत्रान् पुत्राश्च पितरमभिद्रुह्यन्ति। ete. (Kau. V. ch. 6)

Kauṭilya's views on the contrary are just the reverse. Far from approving this usurpation, he points out the iniquity of such an act which would surely bring the revolt of subjects. In his own terse way he points it out that—it was "प्रकृतिकोपकमधर्मिष्ठमनैकान्तिकं चैतत्।

According to him, to prevent anarchy and discontent among subjects, it was the sacred duty of the minister to set up the real heir on the throne, or in his absence any other prince or princess or even the queen if she were pregnant, and to conduct the affairs himself. At the same time, he should try his best to gain the good will of the Magnates by constantly harping on the topic that the prince on the throne was but a symbol and a phantom and they—the great dignitaries were the real sovereigns. (ध्वजमात्रोऽयं भवन्त एव स्वामिनः) With these declarations, the usurpers are to be cajoled and thereby the minister should defer violence on their part. Biding his time, he should do his best to give the prince a sound education or in the case of the princess find a suitable bridegroom, who will present her with a son. When favourable opportunity occured, the regency was to be terminated and the prince placed secure on the throne.

These were but measures to be taken in cases arising out of emergency. On the other hand, the question of succession when there were many claimants to the throne proved often a more difficult problem which presented itself to the legislator. The more so, since, as regards state-succession, it is doubtful as to whether as yet there was any fixed rule about primogeniture. The evidence of the Mahābhārata shows that primogeniture was hardly an accepted principle and Princes often made it a point to deviate from the normal line of succession if the eldest proved incompetent, perverse or devoid of manly qualities. As in the case of Yajāti, who chose the youngest, and in the case of Pratīpa who was prevented from choosing the eldest suffering from leprosy, Princes often selected younger sons in preference to the eldest. Custom had given such deviations a moral sanction. Kauṭilya recognised the validity of primogeniture, but with reservations. As he himself says :—

बह्वनामेकसंरोधः पिता पुत्रह्तितो भवेत् ।
अन्यत्रापद ऐश्वर्यं जेयष्ठभागो तु पूजयते ॥

i.e. Except in cases of incompetency, the eldest is to be preferred. Other alternatives have already been mentioned. *e.g.*, procreation of children on the Queen or adoption of an heir. When all these become impracticable, Kauṭilya recommends even the custom of vesting regal authority in the whole royal family as was the case in the time of the Nandas, who according to tradition ruled conjointly. Cf.—

कुलस्य वा भवेद्राज्यं कुलसङ्घो हि दुर्जयः ।
अराजव्यसनाबाधः शश्वदावसति क्षितिम् ॥

*The absence of a hereditary title stood in the way of a superlatively great man like Napoleon, while the Bourbons returned simply because they "represented the principle of legitimacy". The Spaniards also experimented in the XIXth century with an elected prince to the exclusion of the Bourbons, but they failed. Hereditary limited monarchy holds its own against revolutions or chronic disorders as is proved by the case of England.

VI

CONCEPT OF REGAL DUTIES AND GOVERNMENTAL FUNCTIONS.

Great as the concentration of powers was in royal hands, it was compensated and balanced by a loftier conception of royal duties. In India, Government never signified mere police work. As I have shown elsewhere, (Government Ideals in Ancient India. Calcutta Review, 1922) the Hindu conceived of the government's functions as comprising in its entirety the whole of protective and disciplinary measures, in addition to active duties necessary for ensuring the subject a proper realisation of his material ideals in human existence. According to the views expressed in the Arthaśāstra, the king's duties may be summarised as follows :—

(1) To protect life and property, by putting down violence and thus enable the subject to pursue freely his independent efforts in life.

(2) To deal out justice with impartiality and to administer the laws with a view to redress wrongs whenever there was any cause of trouble.

(3) To promote agriculture and industry by active help. These will be described in detail later on.

(4) To promote the prosperity of all industrial and productive classes.

(5) To protect hermits, Śrotriyas and students and to help them and to encourage education.

(6) To protect the people from the tyranny of capitalists and to regulate the means of livelihood in the case labourers and artisans.

(7) To maintain the widow, the orphan, the sick, and the indigent and to save people in times of emergency.

[(8) The king as a rule has no right to interfere in social and religious matters or to change the law ; but even there the prerogative was stretched by the lawyers, as we shall see very soon.]

The conception of these duties vested in the king was the result of a natural process of which we have parrallels in the histroy of other countries. Thus, we see that in England, the king who was the feudal overlord of the country, became by virtue of feudal custom the natural guardian of widows and orphans. The law of the church entrusted him with poor-relief. He became the highest Judge in his realm and gradually his prerogative was exercised to grant reliefs, even when the law was silent, and this led to the growth of the body of rules known as Equity adminstered in the Chancery court by the Chancellor of the kingdom who came to be regarded as the keeper of the Royal Conscience.

BOOK IV

ADMINSTRATION

I

THE ADMINSTRATIVE MACHINERY

In the administrative system the king was the central figure. All authority issued from him and everything was conducted in his name. But, as the empire was of vast extent, a wholly personal administration was impossible. Consequently, a highly organised administrative machinery, manned and regulated by a well-trained bureaucracy, came into existence. The beginning of this is shrouded in mystery. It was not the work of a single day or of a single genius, but the outcome of a natural process which had begun with the movement for administrative centralisation and of Imperialistic government. The germs of the system, which later on came to require a numerous body of trained officials and confidants of the king, are to be found even in the Vedic period. The earliest references to the existence of such important state fuuctionaries is found in the Brāhmaṇas in connection with the Rājasūya ceremony. Thus, all the Brāhmaṇas give us lists of the Ratnins or the "Jewels" at whose house the king had to offer oblations. The more prominent among these were the Bhāgadhuk, the Akṣavāpa, the Senānī, the Saṇgrāhitṛ, the Grāmaṇī and several others. It is not the place to mention their names or functions in detail, or to note the differences in the various lists, but this fact at least shows that towards the close of the Vedic period, the king had succeeded in gathering round him competent advisers and personal friends. Various chapters of the Mahābhārata, both old and new, give us the names of many such officials. In the Jātakas, too, we find mention of the Amātyas, Daṇḍanāyakas, Purohitas, the Viniścaya-mahāmātyas and other officials of higher and lower grade. The Jātakas represent a simpler stage marked by the existence of small kingdoms. But, as time went on, these states were conquered by the king of Magadha and were welded together into an Empire embracing the whole of Northern India.

The process of conquest brought in great political and constitutional changes. In place of so many small and democratic states, there came one central government, which had not only to look after the administration of the region directly under its control but of that of the Provinces. Consequently, the old system had to be modified and supplanted by one in which a more complicated and elaborate machinery was devised to suit the requirements of changed circumstances. Gradually, the system described in the Arthaśāstra, or that under Aśoka, was evolved into existence.

The Arthaśāstra does not give a detailed

historical description of the system, but seems to make suggestions about a growing Empire. As we shall see later on, the object of the author was not to describe a system in its entirety, but to suggest the lines on which a system coping with the increasing requirements might be built up. The object of writing the treatise is not yet clearly understood. Different scholars have arrived at different conclusions, but as we shall see later on, those who believe the Artha-śāstra to have been intended for a small kingdom, have come to a wrong conclusion and have lost sight of some of the chief points of interest in the aim and scope of the book.

To study the administrative machinery of the period, we must discuss in detail the following heads, and deal separately with each of them :

(1) The Central Executive Machinery.
(2) The Consultative Body.
(3) The various Departments of Central Government.
(4) Provincial and City administration.
(5) Local government in the villages.
(6) The Bureaucracy.
(7) The relation between the Central body and the Provincial bodies.

II

THE CENTRAL EXECUTIVE

At the head of the central executive, stood the King, his most trusted advisers and the departmental heads having office or head-quarters in the capital. The chief officials included—

One or more Mantrins, the Purohita, the Senāpati or Commander-in-chief, the Yuvarāja or Heir-apparent, the Dvauvārika, the Antarvaṃśika, the Praśāstā, the Samāhartā, the Sambidhātā, the Pradeṣṭā, the Nāyaka, the Paura, the Vyavahārika, the Kārmāntika, the Mantri-Pariṣadadhyakṣa, the various Adhyakṣas, the Daṇḍapālas, the Antapālas, and the Āṭavikas. In regard to the higher official body, Kauṭilya seems to designate them by the word *Eighteen-tirtha*, but, nowhere does he emunerate them. We have only scattered references to the higher officials in connection with the employment of spies (Ch. on Gūḍha-

The Aṣṭādaśa-Tīrthas are mentioned in the Mahābhārata, and, according to Nīlakaṇṭha, included many of the above officials.

The word "Tīrtha" is obscure in its meaning. Probably, they were so called on account of their constant association with the king (Peers ?) ; or, it may be that they were the men through whom the king received information or the people received redress or justice. The word occurs in the Rājataraṅginī and several other books.

puruṣha-praṇidhiḥ) and in the chapter on the Payment of royal servants. The word Eighteen Tīrthas, though occuring elsewhere and explained otherwise, here seems to be merely suggestive. In practice, the number was multiplied to suit the needs, and though Kauṭilya is silent on this point, his direction as to the number of Councillors (*e.g.* यथा सामर्थ्यम्) is really suggestive of the fact that even in the case of these, the number should be allowed to be larger, though the old name was to be retained.

Mantrin—It is not clear whether there was only one Mantrin or more. Some passages contemplate the existence of more than one Mantrī (*e.g.* सर्वोपधाशुद्धान् मन्त्रिणः कुर्वीत). Whatever might have been the case, the Mantrins occupied the highest place among officials. They seem to have been the most trusted advisers, and as such, they it were who were called upon to advise the Sovereign in times of emergency. In the absence of any detail, we may regard them as exercising general superintendence over the work of other officials.

The chief qualifications of the Mantrin, according to Kauṭilya were that he must be a native of the country, learned, above all temptations, and a favourite of the people.

Purohita—This office was one of the earliest to come into existence. In the Vedic period, this office had a great importance attached to it. The Purohita was once the *alter ego* of the King and was regarded as the mediator between the king and the gods, and the king and his people. According to Dr. Haug, he often accompanied the king in battle. He derived further importance from his administering the oath to the king. In the days of the Dharmasūtras, he advised the king on points of law and in cases of miscarriage of justice imposed fines and penance on himself. In the Epic, the Purohita occupied a similar position. In the days of the Arthaśāstra, this officer held a high and important position, though he had to yield his precedence to the Mantrin. Kauṭilya advises the king to regard the Purohita as a preceptor and to venerate him as a son does his father. He was no mere priest or Chaplain, and Kauṭilya asks the king to select a man (Brāhmaṇa) of noble family, learned in the Vedas, the six aṅgas and in the art of government, and competent to avert distress by means of divine knowledge and excellence in the Atharva-Vedic lore. (पुरोहितमुदितोदितकुलशीलं षडङ्गे वेदे दैवे निमित्ते दण्डनीत्यां च अभिविनीतमापदां दैवमानुषीणां अथर्वभिरुपायैश्चप्रतिकर्तारं कुर्वीत। तमाचार्यं शिष्यः, पितरं पुत्रो, भृत्यः स्वामिनमिव चानुवर्तेत।) In cases of dishonesty or disloyalty, he could be dismissed, as the evidence of some passages suggests, but in no case he was to be put to death

(महापराधेऽपि पुरोहिते संरोधनमपस्रावणं वा सिद्धिः ।). In serious offences he could only be dismissed or imprisoned.

Senapati (*or the Minister of War*)—It is doubtful whether this man was the Commander of the army in battle. This office arose early, probably to relieve the king from the duties of leading troops in battle when urgent state business necessitated his stay at home. In the Brāhmaṇas, we find an officer, the Senānī, included in the list of the Ratnin. He was an influential officer and probably performed the duties now entrusted to a Minister-of-war and exercised administrative control in times of peace over the leaders of Foot, Chariot, Elephant and Horse.

In the Arthaśāstra, we find the practice of making the Yuvarāja or a prince of the blood the Senāpati. As this office carried great influence with it, the king had to be watchful lest the Senāpati raised a revolt.

Yuvaraja—The Yuvarāja, or the Heir-apparent, was often associated with the government. When and how that practice arose is doubtful, but, this is quite clear that the association of the Heir-apparent in the government gave that prince a chance of learning the art of government and, at the same time, removed much of the probability of a war of succession. The practice of crowning a Yuvarāja is found in the Rāmāyaṇa and the Epic, and the Jātakas confirm this practice.

Dauvarika (*lit. keeper of the Royal-gate*)—It is doubtful as to what were his original duties. Probably, not only he was the Keeper of the Gate, but through him, all applications and claims for redress reached the king. It may be pertinent here to note that the office of Deoḍhi existed in the Punjab under Maharaja Ranjit Sing and the holder of this office was an influencial minister.

Antarvamsika (*Lit. leader of the Harem and Harem-guards*)—His ministerial position was due to the fact that under the old system the officer who protected the royal person was entitled to a high positlon. In the Middle Ages, such officers protecting the royal person, or doing personal service, attained a high position in Europe and vestiges of it still remain.

Prasastri (Superintendent and regulator)—His exact functions are not known ; but the chapter on the Sāṅgrāmika shows that he had important military functions. He administered punishments, preserved peace in the royal camp, and the auxiliary forces of the army were under his control.

Samaharta—or the Collector-general of Revenue. He was one of the "Eighteen Tīrthas" and combined the duties of revenue-collection and preservation of peace (the two being combined as in the case of our modern Indian magistrates and collectors). The Gopas, police officers and spies, were under his control. But, his principal duty was, as his name suggests, the assessment of the various royal dues and their exaction. The detailed description of his duties is given in the chapter on Samāhartr-pracāra.

Sannidhata—Receiver-general or Chamberlain. His business was to receive all dues and keep accounts, not only of cash payments but of payments of commodities. He was also to build store-houses, granaries, prison-houses and armouries.

Pradesta—Superintending official, whose business was multifarious. Probably, in the days of the Arthaśāstra, many Pradeṣṭāraḥ existed. They were probably travelling officials, who superintended the work of the Gopas, and collected the *Vali*. (गोपस्थानिकस्थानेषु प्रदेष्टारः कार्यकरणं वलिप्रग्रहणं कुर्युः). They also had criminal jurisdiction and inflicted punishment and assessed them. The evidence of one passage shows that they probably it was, who exacted fines in lieu of mutilation. In the chapter on "Fines in lieu of Mutilation", we are told that the Pradeṣṭa was to assess punishment after considering the offence. Cf.

उत्तमापरमध्यत्वं प्रदेष्टा दण्डकर्मणि ।
राज्ञश्च प्रकृतीनां च कल्पयेदन्तरान्वितः ॥

Nayaka (*Lit. Leader of Forces*)—Was a military official, who had to lead the vanguard of the Army. The chapter on Sāṅgrāmika gives us some idea of his duties. Thus, in the chapter describing the movement of the camp, (स्कन्धावारप्रयाणम्) we are told that the Nāyaka was to occupy the frontal position (पुरस्तान्नायकः. मध्ये कलत्रं स्वामी च etc., Kau. p. 362.)

Paura (Leader of the city)—Probably, he was the Superintendent of the Capital City. The capital occupied a higher position than that of other cities. Hence, its superintendent or the Prefect of the capital occupied a ministerial position. We can compare his position with that of the Prefect of the city of Paris in the French administration.

Vyavaharika (City judge or Recorder)—We have hardly any details, nor can we suggest anything.

It is doubtful whether this officer was a judge or an official who preserved the records of agreement. The word Vyavahāra means, in Kauṭilya, among other things an agreement or contract. In later literature, it meant a law-suit. Hence, it is difficult to define his duties. Judges are mentioned elsewhere as Dharmasthas or Amātyas.

Karmantika—Superintendent [or superintendents] of Manufactories. They are to be described later on. Probably, there were many such Superintendents.

Mantri-parisadadhyaksa—It is difficult to find out exactly what Kauṭilya means. The two words in the compound may be taken separately meaning.

(1) The Mantri-pariṣat.

(2) Adhyakṣas.

The Council of Advisers, had a separate existence. We shall discuss its constitution and functions later on.

The **Adhyaksas** were many. They were heads of departments and performed various duties to be described in detail.

Dandapala—(*Lit.* in charge of the rod or chastisement)—army officials. Probably, the Daṇḍapālas were both in charge of the Police and the military or were merely Police officials.

Durgapala—Governor of Forts. Probably, there were many such chiefs of fortresses, with one commanding above them.

Antapala—Governor of frontier. Probably, many such officials existed on the various frontiers.

Atavikas—*e. g.*, ruler of forests. Probably, they were royal officials mainly recruited from the aboriginal forest chiefs.

III

THE MANTRI-PARISAT.

Generally speaking, the executive authority vested in the king was exercised by him through the officers mentioned above. They formed, as it were, an executive Council or a Ministry, which looked to the best ways of carrying on the administration of the country. They advised the sovereign in matters of state business, and after proper deliberation looked to the carrying out of the regal instructions. Their exact relation in this respect to their sovereign master, as also the amount of latitude granted to them, is unknown. Some of them, indeed, claimed expert knowledge, and superintended the business and work of under-officials ; others exercised an executive function and simply carried out the Royal orders.

Among these officials and high dignitaries, there were some whose advise the king constantly sought. These men were the ministers of the highest grade or Mantrins—the most trusted advisers of the Crown. In addition to these, there was a Council in which the business of the state was formally discussed. The existence of these two bodies seems rather to be anomalous in our own days, but it was justified by the desire for secrecy and for maintaining the personal interests of the king.

Kauṭilya advises the king to undertake nothing without consultation or deliberation. "Every act and venture", he says, "ought to be preceded by proper deliberations" (मन्त्रपूर्वाः सर्वारम्भाः). But, in doing this, the king must be careful to guard the secrecy of his deliberations and the final decisions arrived at. According to Kauṭilya, not only should he guard his secrets from men, but even from talking birds or animals (तदुद्देशः संवृतः कथानामनिस्रावी पक्षिभिरप्यनालोक्यः स्यात्………श्रूयते हि शुकशारिकाभिः मन्त्रो भिन्नः। श्वभिरन्यैश्च तिर्यग्योनिभिश्च।) The man who may give out secrets must be carefully removed and care should be taken that the secrets do not go out of the circle of trusted advisers (उच्छिद्येत मन्त्रभेदी).

This desire for secrecy characterised all higher deliberations. As is known to students of History, this led the Turkish Sultans to take inhuman measures for their safe-guard. In medieval England, it led to the creation of the Privy Councillors acting under oath, and very recently during the great war, the same led to the creation of the Inner Council of the Cabinet—the War-council, consisting of the Premier, the War-minister and one or two others.

In ancient times the desire for secrecy was even greater than it is now. So much so, that one of the predecessors of Kauṭilya, Bhāradvāja, advised the king to deliberate alone since ministers were sure to divulge to others and thus all secrecy was sure to be lost. So, to preserve secrecy, he says that the king must deliberate alone and in secret. Ministers were sure to have their own confidants and these latter had some more in their turn. Thus, deliberation was sure to be divulged to others and all secrecy lost. (गुह्यमेको मन्त्रयेत—इति भारद्वाजः—मन्त्रिणामपि मन्त्रिणो भवन्ति। तेषामप्यन्ये। सैषा मन्त्रपरंपरा मन्त्रं भिनत्ति।)

Against this view, stood the opinion of Viśālākṣa who went to the other extreme and advocated consultation and disputation with all the learned men available (नैकस्य मन्त्रसिद्धिर्भवति।… तस्माद्बुद्धिवृद्धैः सार्धमासीत मन्त्रम्।) But, in opposition to this view, Parāśara gave his opinion that in order to have proper advice the king must approach those men, who are more or less inclined to the same views as those of the king. This was sure, in his opinion, to ensure good advice along with the preservation of secrecy.

Against all these views, Kauṭilya advances his own opinion. He lays down the principle that the king should as a rule consult with three or four ministers (मन्त्रिभिश्चतुर्भिः सह वा मन्त्रयेत). This was his opinion, since, consultation with one does not enable a man to come to a satisfactory conclusion, inasmuch as he may proceed wilfully and without care (एकस्य मन्त्रो यथेष्टमनवग्रहश्चरति). Similarly, if the consultation is carried on with two, they might unite and overpower the king's judgment, or, differing they might divulge or counter act each other (द्वाभ्यां मन्त्रयमानो द्वाभ्यां संहताभ्यामवगृह्यते । विगृहीताभ्यां विनाश्यते) ।

After all these discussions Kauṭilya, defines the nature and object of deliberations. In his opinion, the chief elements of a consultation are the following five ; (1) How to begin, (2) How best to utilise men and money, (3) How best to select time and place, (4) How to avert evil, (5) How best to attain success. (कर्मणामारम्भोपायः, पुरुषद्रव्यसम्पत्, देशकालविभागः विनिपातप्रतीकारः कार्यसिद्धिरिति पञ्चाङ्गो मन्त्रः ।)

Finally, Kauṭilya lays down the general principle that the king must act according to circumstances, time, place, the object in view being taken into consideration. He might consult or ask the opinion of his ministers individually or may consult them as a united body, but, he must always bear in mind that the proper opportunity must not be allowed to pass in vain (अवाप्तार्थः कालं नातिक्रामयेत्) ।

Apart from individual ministers, there existed

a Council of Advisers. It was probably descended from the Sabhā which gathered round the king even in the Vedic age and which gradually became a Council of ministers of the king. It became the real consultative body in the state, with the gradual extinction of the Samiti or the democratic gathering of armed freemen of the tribe. During the Brāhmaṇic or Upaniṣadic period, this body came to be known as the Pariṣat, on account of its being essentially a body of royal friends, sitting round him (lit. *pari*—round and *sad*—to sit.)

In the days of Kauṭilya, this body existed, though, composed of the King's servants it no longer reflected free or independent opinion of the people. Its constitution varied in number. According to the Mānavas, it consisted of 12 advisers. According to the Bārhaspatyas, 16 amātyas constituted a Pariṣat, while the Auśanasas raised the number to 20 such men. (**मन्त्रिपरिषदं द्वादशामात्यान् कुर्वीत इति मानवाः** etc.) Kauṭilya lays down no hard and fast rule as to number, but simply enjoins the necessity of having as many as the needs of the state required. (**यथासामर्थ्यमिति कौटिल्यः**) This was perhaps due to the needs of a growing empire, of which he cherished the hope, and for which he laboured. Personally, he was for a large Assembly of advisers and according to him, a king with a big Council (**अक्षुद्रपरिषत्कः**) was sure to win success, while another with a small one was sure to go to ruin (क्षुद्रपरिषत्कः). He supports his contention for a big Council by citing the case of the god Indra, whose 1000 counsellors gave him the designation of Sahasrākṣa, though really he had but two eyes. (इन्द्रस्य हि मन्त्रिपरिषद्दषीणां सहस्रम् । तस्मादिमं द्व्यक्षं सहस्राक्षमाहुः ।)

Kauṭilya lays down the rule that in all urgent business, the king should not only consult his most trusted advisers, but also summon the Council of Ministers. (आत्ययिके कार्ये मन्त्रिणः मन्त्रिपरिषदं चाहूय ब्रूयात्) He was to consult at least all of those who were present, the opinion of the absentees being taken by sending letters to them inviting their views. (आसन्नैः सह कार्याणि पश्येत् -अनासन्नैः सह पत्रसम्प्रेषणेन मन्त्रयेत—P. 29 also ch. on, राजप्रणिधि— पञ्चमे मन्त्रिपरिषदा पत्रप्रेषणेन मन्त्रयेत ।)

In case of differences of opinion among the councillors, generally the opinion of the majority was followed. But, this does not seem to have been obligatory, nor was the king legally bound by it. He seems to have had his own free judgment and was unfettered in its exercise. (तत्र यद्भूयिष्ठा ब्रूयुः, कार्यसिद्धिकरं वा तत्कुर्यात् ।)

The discussion as to whether the opinion of the majority was absolutely binding on the King, is important. It is easy to recognize that the acceptance of this rule of the majority raises the question of the king's liability to act according to the opinion expressed by the Council. Many indologists have inclined to the view that it was absolutely binding and have thereby tried to prove that as such, the government was a limited monarchy in which the Legislature or the Consultative Body checked the irresponsible exercise of sovereign power by the King. The acceptance of this view may be palatable to the majority of Indians, proving as it does undoubtedly, the existence of a constitutional government in the past.

A careful consideration of the system described in the Arthaśāstra shows, however, something to the contrary. For, the passage itself as it stands, does not prove any legal obligation on the part of the king to obey the mandate of the majority. The force of the words यद्भूयिष्टा: ब्रूयु: is taken away by the other expression कार्यसिद्धिकरं and proves that, though morally liable to follow the opinion of the majority, it was left to the king to select the course which was best calculated to bring success.

Next to this, we must bear in mind that the king was at liberty to consult any number of his councillors and there was no limitation in that respect. Any number of them might be taken into confidence and there was no obligation to call a meeting of all the councillors. This power of selection together with the fact that no principle of ministerial responsibility or of concert of action was recognized, stand in the way of accepting the above view.

Furthermore, these ministers were all royal servants, selected and appointed by the king and holding office during "royal pleasure". They depended solely on the favour of the monarch for their advancement and had no other alternative but to follow the king unreservedly. The chapters on समयाचारिकम् and अनुजीविवृत्तम् show, that they were more of courtiers seeking royal favour, than the custodians of public right, maintained by the support of the people.

Such was the state of the Council of Advisers, which was nothing more than an advisory body Under Aśoka it existed, as is proved by the references to the "Parisā" in the Edicts. It subsisted during the time of the Suṅgas and Kāṇvas and if we are to believe in the tradition recorded in the Mālavikāgnimitraṃ, it was regularly called and was allowed to express its opinion on all important affairs of the state.

IV
BUREAUCRACY AND DEPARTMENTS.

Before we pass on to the departments which carried out the various administrative business, we must say something about that powerful and highly-trained bureaucracy, which contributed to the successful working of the system and the permanence of the government.

The members of this higher bureaucracy were designated by the name Amātya. The office of these Amātyas seems to have come into existence at a very early period, and the Jātakas repeatedly refer to them. In the days of Kauṭilya, the Amātyas were numerous, performed onerous duties and wielded responsibility and power. Their qualifications are discussed in the chapter on the "Creation of Amātyas," and from this, we know that young men of respectable family, wisdom, purity, and loyalty, were recruited into the government service. Their abilities were then tested by putting them in work and tempting them by means of allurements. And then, those who proved their worth, were selected to fill responsible offices. Perhaps, the lowest rank were taken to fill offices in connection with mines, forests, or manufactories. Those who proved themselves to be brave and courageous, were put near the king's person. Those who were above the temptations of lust, were made officers of the royal palace or the harem. Those who did not care for money or bribes, were placed in charge of collecting departments. Those who proved themselves to have been endowed with a high moral ideal, were placed in judicial offices or in charge of the Destruction of Thorns, while, those who were endowed with the highest virtues and were above all sorts of allurements, were made highest ministers or Mantrins.

The evidence of this section thus shows that there were several grades of Amātyas; the highest of them were the Mantriṇaḥ. Kauṭilya uses these two words rather loosely in many places. Thus, in the chapter on "Mantri-Purohitot-pattiḥ", he speaks of the qualities of Amātyas and this shows that broadly-speaking, the Mantri-naḥ were included among the Amātyas. But, in more than two places he draws a fine line of demarcation. Thus, in the same chapter of Amātyotpattiḥ, he says that capable men should be made Amātyas but not Mantrins. (अमात्यास्सर्व एवैते कार्याः शुद्धाः न तु मन्त्रिणः) This showes that the latter occupied a higher position. Further, elsewhere, he says that the Mantrinaḥ are to be selected from men above all allurements (सर्वोपधाशुद्धान् मन्त्रिणः कुर्वीत ।)

To these Amātyas (together with officers of similar grade like the Pradeṣṭāraḥ) was entrusted the work of various departments. The departments again were multiferious and each was concerned with the business of a particular branch of administration. Most of these are described in thc chapter on Adhyakṣa-pracāra. Of these, thc following are the most important :—

(1) Department of Revenue-collection. The whole department was under the Samāhartā or the Collector-general.

(2) Department of receipts into the Treasury and the management and up-keep of the receipts. These were under the Sannidhātā or Receiver-general.

(3) Department of Audit of receipts and expenses. This was under the chief officer of the Akṣapaṭala.

(4) Department for the issue of Royal writs. It was under the Superintendent of Writs.

(5) Department for the keeping of the roval treasure. It was under the Treasury-superintendent or Koṣādhyakṣa.

(6) Department of Mining under the Akarādhyakṣa, who had his subordinates for thc manufacture of metal goods—*e.g.*

(*a*) The Lohādhyakṣa—in charge of base metals.

(b) The Khaṇyadhyakṣa exploiting ocean mines.

(c) The Lavaṇādhyakṣa or the salt-Superintendent.

(d) The Rūpadarśaka or manufacturer and examiner of coins.

(7) Department regulating and controlling the work of jewellery-manufacture for the citizens and subjects. This department was presided over by the Sauvarṇika

(8) Department of gold-mining and manufacture. This was under the Suvarṇādhyakṣa.

(9) Department for the receipt and upkeep of agricultural and forest produce and also for keeping grain-reserves for emergency—under the Koṣṭhāgārādhyakṣa.

(10) Department for the control of supply of commodities under the Paṇyādhyakṣa.

(11) Department for receiving raw vegetable and forests-produce, under the Kūpyādhyakṣa.

(12) Department for the preservation and up-keep of weapons and implements of war, under the Āyudhāgārādhyakṣa.

(13) Department for regulating weights and measures, under the Pautavādhyakṣa.

(14) Department for the regulation and measurement of time under the Mānādhyakṣa.

(15) Department for toll-collection under the Śulkādhyakṣa.

(16) Department for the Superintendence of weaving under the Sūtrādhyakṣa.

(17) Department for Agriculture and royal farms, under the Sītādhyakṣa.

(18) Department for the regulation of wine-shops and liquor-manufacture, under the Surādhyakṣa.

(19) Department for regulating slaughter-houses, under the Sūnādhyakṣa.

(20) Department for regulating the trade of courtesans under the Gaṇikādhyakṣa.

(21) Department for regulating the royal ferries, guarding of rivers and for the navy, under the Nāvadhyakṣa.

(22) Department for the royal cows and for protecting cattle, under the Go'dhy-akṣa.

(23) Department of royal stables under the Aśvādhyakṣa.

(24) Department for royal elephants under the Hastyadhyakṣa.

(25) Department of royal charriots for peace and war under the Rathādhykṣa.

(26) Department for superintending the infantry under Pattyādhyakṣa.

(27) Department of passports under the Mudrādhyakṣa.

(28) Department of pastures and uninhabited meadows under the Vivītādhyakṣa.

(29) Department of waste-lands under the Śūnyādhyakṣa.

(30) Department for regulating guilds, under the Kaṇṭaka-śodhana Commissioners.

(31) Department for regulating shops and prices under the Saṃsthādhyakṣa.

It will be needless for our purpose to follow the arrangement of the Arthaśāstra and to describe the detailed duties of each of the officials or his department. For our own convenience and to make the subject morc easily understandible to a modern reader, we shall describe the duties of all these departments in connection with the following :—

(1) Revenue-collection and Fiscal policy *e.g.*

(*a*) Collection of land tax, ferry-dues, taxes from artisans, loans, interests, road-cess, etc.

(*b*) Indirect taxation—*e.g.* tax on sales, tax on goods, and animals carrying load, etc.

(*c*) Collection from royal farms, royal studs etc.

(*d*) From mines and forests and other sources.

(2) Audit and account. Income and Expenditure.

(3) Police Adminstration.

(4) Army, Navy and Commissariat arrangements.

(5) Protection and regulation of Commerce and Industry ; sale and supply of commodities ; labour and guilds.

(6) Prevention of adulteration of food, and destruction of social evils, regulation of drinking, or gambling etc.

(7) Destruction of evils and thorns.

(8) Provincial and Local Government in villages and towns.

V

REVENUE COLLECTION

Revenue collection was entrusted to the Samāhartā and his officials, who were also in charge of the ordinary police and [directed the activity of] the espionage emissaries. They were directly employed in collecting land-tax from village-areas and townships, while the revenue derived from the royal ferries, toll on commodities, fines, collections from towns, from the coinage, or passport, taxes paid by courtesans, keepers of gambling-houses and of wine-houses, and various other dues passed to the Samāhartā through officials in charge of them respectively. We shall discuss all these taxes in detail, in connection with the Fiscal policy.

The chief officials under the Samāhartā were the [four] Sthānikas and under them were the Gopas, each of whom was in charge of five or ten villages. These Gopas were the busiest agents of the Central government in the local areas and not only made collections but kept detailed registers of the income and expenditure of all men under their jurisdiction. They maintained complete and detailed records, as regards the varieties of land and their produce, areas under cultivation, areas not cultivated, dry land, land for houses, forest-areas, houses of gods, Caityas, irrigational dams, cremation grounds, transfers or sales of land or houses, so as to enable them to understand the income of local areas *e.g.*

तत्प्रदिष्टः पञ्चग्रामीं दशग्रामीं वा गोपश्चिन्तयेत्। सीमावरोधेन ग्रामाग्रं कृष्टाकृष्टस्थलकेदारारामषण्डवाटवनवास्तु-चैत्यदेवगृहसेतुबन्धश्मशानसत्रप्रपापुण्यस्थानविवीतपथिसंख्यानेन-क्षेत्राग्रं ; तेन सीम्नां क्षेत्राणां च मर्यादारण्यपथिप्रमाणसम्प्रदान विक्रयानुग्रहपरिहारनिबन्धान् कारयेत्। गृहाणां च करदाकरदसंख्यानेन। (Kau. P. 142.)

They also noted the privileges and immunities enjoyed by individuals or localities, local tradition, and also, the status of house-holders, *i.e.*, whether they were taxpayers or non-taxpayers. They also recorded the number of houses, the caste of house-holders, number of inmates in houses, their sex and occupation *i.e.*, whether they were peasants, or cowherds, or traders or artisans, or slaves, the number of cattle, the hoarded wealth of people, taxes or tolls payable by the inhabitants or forced labour, if it was due. Thus, there was a most detailed census which no other country in antiquity except Egypt ever kept. The Greeks also mention such Indian census records. (तेषु चैतावच्चातुर्वर्ण्यमेतावन्तः कर्षकगोरक्षकवैदेहककारुकर्म करदासाश्चैतावच्च द्विपदचतुष्पदमिदं चैष हिरण्यविष्टिशुल्कदण्डः समुत्तिष्ठतीति। कुलानां च स्त्रीपुरुषाणां बालवृद्धकर्मचरित्राजीवव्ययपरिमाणं च विद्यात्। Kau. P. 142.)

Under the Gopas, were the village officials themselves. We shall describe their duties and functions in their proper place. The work of the Gopas was probably supervised by the travelling Pradeṣṭāraḥ who also collected the Bali. (गोपस्थानिकस्थानेषु प्रदेष्टारः कार्यकरणं बलिप्रग्रहं च कुर्युः ।)

Sources of Taxation. – We proceed now to the various sources of revenue. As is well known to all, from time immemorial, certain customary revenues were vested in the king. The primary sources of revenue comprised in the Vedic period—(1) the Bali and the (2) booty of war. To these, were added gradually

(1) a share of the produce of land
(2) tax on gold [earnings or hoard ?]
(3) tax on animals

The amount of these varied. Thus, according to the Mahābhāratā (Śān. ch. 67), the king by contract with his people was entitled to

(1) 1/50 of gold and animals
(2) 1/10 of grains and other produce.

Again, this land-tax, seems to have been 1/16 in the days of the Atharva-veda. Later on, in the days of Bodhāyana and Vaśiṣṭha, it was 1/6, (षड्भागभृतो राजा प्रजां रक्षेत्, Bod ; राजा तु धर्मेणानुशासन् षष्ठमंशं धनस्य लभेत, Vaś.) while, according to Gautama, who records an older tradition, it varied from 1/10 to 1/6. As to the tax on gold, we are at a loss to understand whether it was on the hoard or capital or on the annual income.

In addition to these, the king came to have in course of time, other sources of revenue, *e.g.*

(1) Tax on artisans.

(2) Offerings in lieu of forced labour.

(3) Toll on commercial commodities.

The other traditional sources were

(4) Fines paid by criminals.

(5) Property of those dying without heir.

(6) Lost articles without owner and treasure-troves.

With the growth of the Empire in north India, other sources were added. Land-tax was increased and additional imposts on various pretexts were levied. Monopolies were created and in the Arthaśāstra we find the king regarded not only as the sole owner of mines and forests, but also enjoying monopolies in salt and some other articles.

There was a time, as would appear from the evidence of the Mahābhārata, when the king could neither levy new taxes nor increase those already imposed. A chapter of the Mahābhārata, Śānti-parva, (ch. 87) expressly states that in case the king intended to levy new taxes, he was to notify by proclamation his royal intention, and state the causes which created this necessity. If the people agreed, then and then only could the king levy a new tax ; otherwise it was not valid.

Kauṭilya is careful lest fiscal tyranny would lead to popular discontent. As he himself says "a king suffering from want, eats up his people". (अल्पकोषो हि राजा पौरजानपदानेव ग्रसते. Kau. P. 47.) Elsewhere, he again describes the consequences of the people becoming angry from fiscal and other tyrannies He points out that such people revolt and thus the king's authority is overthrown by their revolt or through their alliance with the enemy. Consequently, in cases of distress he asks the king to "beg of his subjects" by going through the old formality of a proclamation, which however was more of form than anything real. As he himself says :—

क्षीणाः प्रकृतयो लोभं, लुब्धा यान्ति विरागताम् ।
विरक्ता यान्त्यमित्रं वा भर्तारं घ्नन्ति वा स्वयम् ॥
तस्मात् प्रकृतीनां क्षयलोभविरागकारणानि नोत्पादयेत् ।

(Kau. P. 275.)

Yet inspite of this carefulness, the author of the Arthaśāstra leaves nothing unturned to ensure an ample revenue to the king. "Money" [Artha] in his opinion "was the most important requisite to man in this world, since Dharma and Kāma depended on it" (अर्थ एव प्रधानः अर्थमूलौ धर्मकामौ) For kings, this was the more so, in as much as to ensure sovereignty through the loyalty of the Army and the officials, money was of vital necessity to the king (कोशाभावे ध्रुवं दण्डविनाशः).

The sources of revenue according to the Arthaśāstra, were many. They included the following :—*e.g.*

(1) Various forms of land-tax ; produce of crown lands (सीता); share of produce payable to the king (भागः) ; tax on houses in cities (वास्तुकः) ; Vali, Kara, Senābhakta and occasional taxes.

(2) Duty levied on the sale of commodities in market ; tax on imports and exports together with miscellaneous dues.

(3) Road-cess (वर्तनी), canal-dues (जलभागः), ferry-dues (तरदेयः), conveyance-cess, tax on loads, tax on markets (पट्टनं), various other taxes levied on roads, or toll-houses, fee from passports.

(4) Taxes received from artisans, levied on and probably paid through their guilds (कारुशिल्पिगणः) ; those paid by fishermen etc.

(5) taxes levied on prostitutes (वेश्या), gambling-houses (द्यूतम्), wine-houses (सुरा) or slaughter-houses etc.

(6) Income from properties and monopolies belonging to the king, these comprising—

(*a*) the forests including forest produce and games.

(*b*) mines and manufactories attached thereto, together with the income from the manufacture of golden ornaments for the people, or that from the coinage.

(*c*) monopoly-income from salt and other commodities.

(7) Forced labour.

(8) Fines from law-courts.

(9) Accidental incomes—*e.g.* from property passing to the king owing to the death or disappearance of the owner ; lost articles ; treasure-troves etc.

(10) Occasional taxes like the Utsaṅga.

(11) Interest on loans advanced to the people.

(12) Miscellaneous taxes like those imposed for prevention of theft etc.

VI

LAND POLICY AND LAND REVENUE

Before we pass on to the detailed treatment of all these sources, we must say something on the Land-policy of the Government. Land was and is even now the chief source of revenue to the Indian Government. In the days of Kauṭilya, the Government did much to ensure an ample revenue from land and with a view to this, it tried its best to ensure the retention of control over land in the hands of the Government. A large area of land was directly under the ownership of the king and this was probably due to the conquest of hostile territory or the plantation of new villages on waste-lands at the instance of the king.

We have nothing to prove that the Government of the Arthaśāstra was regarded as the sole owner of land. On the other hand, there are evidences pointing to the existence of land in the absolute ownership of individuals. These lands were the Brahmadeya land, belonging to Brāhmaṇas. Next to these, were the lands in the hands of the A-karada tenants, who seem to have paid only a tax in lieu of protection. Both these two classes had rights of alienation by sale and gift. But, the Government insisted on restricting these rights only to among themselves. Thus, a Brahmadeya-owner could sell his land only to a Brahmadeya-holder and an owner of A-karada land to an A-karada-holder Evidently, the object of this was that the privileges and immunities attaching thereto should remain confined to the classes for whom they were intended.

The Brahmadeya and A-karada tenants probably enjoyed their rights from time immemorial, and the Government did not dare to disturb their rights. But, with the settlement of new areas, new classes of tenants arose. They were known as the Karadas who comprised—

(1) either village-officials, physicians, or village-craftsmen, enjoying land for life (without right of alienation) in lieu of service to the public.

(2) or the cultivators planted in waste-land and helped by loans of money and corn by the Government, holding under similar conditions.

In regard to these, the Government had direct relations with them. Evidently, it did not favour the creation of a class, not directly tilling the ground but enjoying easy and unearned profits, and to ensure it further, all such holders enjoyed merely life-tenancy without the right of perpetual alienation. (करदेभ्यः कृतक्षेत्राण्यैकपुरुषिकाणि दद्यात् विक्रयाधानवर्जम्)

Next to these three classes of land, there were the crown lands directly held by the king. These were either worked by royal officers by means of slaves, criminals, or hired labourers, or plots were let out to tenants who worked on the basis of a getting share of the produce.

In addition to these, there were those lands subject to and held under certain [feudal ?] obligations. In the Arthaśāstra, we find mention of villages supplying soldiers, labourers, or various kinds of raw material. The villages supplying soldiers may be described as feudal holdings, while those furnishing labour (विष्टि) as holdings under servile tenure.

VII

TAXES AND TOLLS

As to the taxes levied on land, they were first of all assessed after observing the average of produce for a number of years. Villages were classified according to the productive capacity of the land and this was determined by noting the amount of labour spent in raising crops. Thus, those lands which depended entirely on rain, paid least, those on the side of rivers something less, while land in those places where the labourer had to work hard in finding water for his fields, the royal share was the least. This system which has been described by Kauṭilya in the chapter on "Filling the Depleted Treasury" survived all throughout the Hindu and Mussalman period. Under the Guptas, the Dhruvādhi-karaṇika assessed the royal share after due observation, and in the revenue system of Sher Shah and Akbar, the royal assessment followed such an ascertainment of the average produce. Payment was both in cash or in kind. Payment in kind was the rule during the age of the Jātakas, when the Droṇamāpaka appeared in the fields during the harvest, and after measuring the grains took the royal share, leaving the rest to the cultivator.

As to the various taxes, Kauṭilya mentions the Piṇḍakara or tax paid in lump when it was paid by the whole village. The meaning however is not clear. The Ṣaḍbhāga (see p. 93 ch. on Koṣṭhāgārādhyakṣa) was the traditional 1/6, though in reality it was more and often approached 1/3 or 1/4th.

Vali was the old Vedic tax, (R. V. X. 173) paid by the subject to the king. It was not a religious tax as supposed by Dr. Shamasastry on the authority of the commentator. Its existence as a separate tax is proved beyond doubt by an inscription of Aśoka (at Lumbini garden) which makes the village of Lumbini free from Vali and confirms on it the favour of paying 1/8 instead of 1/6 on account of the village visited by the king being the birth-place of the Buddha (उबलिके अट्ठभागिये कटे)

As to Kara, mentioned again in the chapter on Koṣṭhāgārādhyakṣa, no meaning can be assigned. Probably, it was that paidby the Karada tenants. According to Dr. Shamasastry, it was paid by tributory princes, but, this is rather doubtful. As to canal dues, (जलभाग) it was levied on those who took water from royal canals and reservoirs. In the Punjab, the government derives even now a large income from such water-taxes. Loans of corn, also brought in income in the shape of interest. Such royal loans to agriculturists existed from an earlier period.

In addition to these above, there were occasional imposts levied on particular occasions. Their mention is important, in as much as they show the rising demands of an absolute Government and also because they show us a parallelism, between Indian and European fiscal policy. These taxes mentioned in the Kauṭilīya are—

(1) Senābhaktaṃ—or contributions levied for the maintenance of troops. It is not clear whether they were levied on all places and throughout the country, nor can we determine as to whether they were punitive imposts. According to the commentator, they were, but contributions in kind to support a marching army.

(2) Utsaṅga—a tax paid on the occasion of the birth of a royal prince. [Cf. Khīramūla of the Jātakas.]

(3) Pārśva—the true meaning is not clear.

(4) Pārihīnaka—compensation of crops for damages by cattle (?)

(5) Aupāyanika— presentations to the king [on his visit ?]

These show the beginnings of the levy of the various "extras" which continue to our own days. Some taxes remind us of the feudal aids.

Utsaṅga reminds us of the European feudal impost on tenants, for the marriage of a lord's daughter or to make his son a knight. In present day Bengal, Zeminders get Nazarana not only on their visit but also on account of their daughters' marriage or the srādh ceremony of their parents.

So much for ordinary land tax. In times of distress, the normal rates were enhanced. (अकोशः जनपदं महान्तमल्पप्रमाणं वा देवमातृकं प्रभूतधान्यं धान्यस्यांशं तृतीयं चतुर्थं वा याचेत यथासारम् । Kau. P. 240.) But, with these we are not concerned at present. They will be described in connection with extraordinary taxation and emergency measures.

House-owners in cities were evidently freed from these taxes, in lieu of which they paid another tax. Probaly, this has been referred to by Kauṭilya as Vāstuka (वास्तुक)

(2) **Indirect taxation** and taxes levied on commerce.

Next to land tax, the chief source of income was the customs and and excise duties. The attitude of the Kauṭilya Government to traders was not so liberal as in our own days when *Laissez faire* principles have allowed them great latitude in fixing prices and profits. Traders were regarded as thieves though not in name (अचौरश्चोरः). Moreover, the Government looked with askance, on their prosperity gained at the cost of the consumer. There were various taxes imposed on commodities *e.g.*

(1) tax on the sale of all articles.

(2) tax levied on merchandise as duty.

(3) tax levied on goods during transit.

As regards the tax on the sale of goods, it was was very important and was noticed by the Greek travellers. No commodity could be sold at the place of its production and everything was taken to the market. Any contrary transaction was punished with fine. (जातिभूमिषु च पण्यानामविक्रय: खनिभ्यो धातुपण्यादानेषु षट्‌कृतमत्यय: etc. Chap. on śulka-vyavahāra (Kau. P. 112—113).

Consequently, all commodities were taken to the market and before being transported were visited by royal officers, who sealed them and stamped them. In the city, they passed under the jurisdiction of the Śulkādhyakṣa and the Paṇyādhyakṣa. All goods were examined, as regards their seals. The owners of those the seals of which were defective were punished. Articles, trading in which was forbidden, were confiscated. Afterwards, these were allowed to be put up for sale. Attention was paid to realise the "proper price". Then the Śulka was exacted together with the market-dues. As a rule, the government levied duty both on imports and on exports (निष्क्राम्यं प्रवेश्यं च शुल्कम्) The general rate exacted was 20% on imports, while on exports a similar duty [about 10% [?] was levied.

As to the scale of duty, the chapter on Śulka vyavahāra, gives us a table. It was as follows—

1/6th—on fruits, flowers, grains, meat, fish.

1/15 to 1/10 on linen goods, varieties of cotton fabric, on antimony, mercuric sulphide or cinnabar, metals, sandal-wood wines, varieties of cloth etc.

1/25 to 1/20—on cotton-fabric, animals, medicines, leather-work, grains, rice, oils, wine, cooked rice etc.

The toll levied at the entrace-gate was varied for the benefit of the people. In addition to these, other dues were exacted *e.g.*

1. Taxes levied by the frontier officials. (अन्तपाल: सपादपणिकां वर्तनीं गृह्णीयात्).

2. Tax at ferries which were managed by the the king.

3. A conveyance cess was levied.

4. Tax on loads or beasts of burden was also levied (पण्यवहनस्य पणिकामेकखुरस्य········अंसभारस्य-माषिकाम् etc.)

There were other minor imposts on sale transactions *e.g.* discounts, compensation for losses etc.

---

* There is very little information on the customs policy of the government. Kauṭilya distinguishes between Vāhya, Abhyantara and Atithya (on transit). The duty on imports is mentioned (प्रवेश्यानां मूल्यपञ्चभाग:) but not on exports which is taken from Bodhāyana.

(3) Artisans and craftsmen also paid taxes, and these were probably not paid individually, but by their gaṇas as a whole. In the chapter on Samāhartṛ-samudaya-sthāpanaṃ, Kauṭilya speaks of (कारुशिल्पिगण:) the artisan-guilds as a source of revenue. This seems to show that artisans or craftsmen had the privilege of paying through their guilds. Probably, there was some such arrangement as we had elsewhere. Similarly, fishermen, or members of the Servile Arts paid taxes.

(4) Taxes were levied on prostitutes, who seem to have remained under the direct jurisdiction of royal officials and were regarded as royal property as in some countries of the Middle Ages. They were under the Superintendent of Prostitutes, who fixed their rates and fees, settled their disputes and complaints, or decided cases relating to their succession.

(5) Gambling-houses were a source of income. Each gambling-house was watched by a royal official, and a part of the gambling profits went to the royal coffers.

(6) Wine-houses, liquor establishments as well as the manufacture of wine was similarly controlled. Kauṭilya gives us details about the preparation and the ingrediants of wine and its varieties. (*e.g.* सुरा मैरेय and अरिष्ट). The sale of wine was centralised, and nobody could manufacture or sell without a license. Wine-

drinking was very common in those days and thus fetched a large income. Occasionally however, the government granted permission to manufacture wine to householders, for home consumpation, and this was for a specified period during festivities or ceremonies.

Royal properties—We pass on to consider the royal income from Royal properties or monopolics vested in the king.

These proved very important sources and brought large incomes to the king. They comprised the revenue derived from crown-lands, forests, mines, and the royal monopolies like the manufacture and supply of salt.

Crown lands when cultivable were placed under the officer in charge of agriculture, (Sitādhyakṣa) who either cultivated these lands directly or let them out on hire to peasants agreeing to pay a share of the produce.

In case of direct cultivation, the government employed hired workmen slaves, or condemed criminals, or those working in lieu of nonpayment of fines.

In case of land being handed over to peasants working for a share, they paid from 1/5 to 1/3 to the government. The royal share varied inversely as the farmer had to work hard in carrying water to the fields.

Next to the crown lands, were the forests. These fetched in those days, as they even now do to our own government, a large income. Their appropriation by the king belonged to the Kauṭilyan or the immediate Pre-Kauṭilyan period. The forest-produce was collected by forest officials, who also preserved game and administered the stringent game-laws. Some portions of the forests were entirely set apart for wild animals which remained preserved games. In other parts were established factories for various purposes. (द्रव्यवनकर्मान्तानटवीश्च द्रव्यवनापाश्रयाः प्रत्यन्ते हस्ति वनमटव्या रक्षन् निवेशयेत्)

The preservation of elephants was under the charge of different officials (नागवनपालाः) who were under the Nāgavanādhyakṣa. They carried on khedda operations and tamed young elephants. Injury to elephants was visited with severe penalties (हस्तिघातिनं हनुः). Tusks, bones and other parts of dead elephants were collected. Kauṭilya attaches great importance to the possession of elephants, owing to the great part they played in the war-fare of those days. (हस्तिप्रधानो विजयो राज्ञाम्) In his opinion, the best elephants were those of the East *e.g.* Kaliṅga, Karūśa and of the extreme East. Those of Daśārṇa and Aparānta were of medium quality, while, those of Saurāṣṭra and Pañcajana were of inferior qnality.

Forests otherwise supplying various articles

were under the Dravya-vanādhyakṣa and sent supplies to the Kūpyādhyakṣa. (कुप्याध्यक्षो द्रव्य-वनपालैः कुप्यमानाययेत्). These forest-products included—(1) varieties of timber, (2) bamboo, (3) canes and creepers, *(d)* bark of plants, *(e)* materials for rope-making, *(f)* various flowers and leaves, (9) Various roots, medicinal herbs and plants, (10) poisonous plants and poisonous herbs, (11) various animals, their skins, bones, etc. (12) metals and metal-products including [crude] iron, copper, bronze, and other natural ores and alloys, (13) earthenware, (14) miscellaneous products including charcoal, wood, logs and leaves.

Royal manufactories for weaving and rope-making existed, as well as cattle-farms. All these were sources of great gain. These were stocked in royal godowns, and either sold to the people or were utilised in all possible ways. Consequently, these were a source of income and benefit to the state.

Mines—The royal ownership of mines and minerals extracted therefrom, was again a great source of income to the king. When and how the ownership of the mines was vested in the king, is not easy to find out but probably, it arose with the appropriation of the *res nullius* and waste belonging to nobody, and in course of time, these came under the direct ownership of the king. Kauṭilya more than emphasises the necessity of royal ownership of mines, since they produced gold, silver and precious metals. This contributed to a welfilled treasury, which in its turn, ensured a permanent military force, vital to the safety and permanence of a king's authority. As he himself says—

आकरप्रभवः कोशः कोशाद्दण्डः प्रजायते ।
पृथिवी कोशदण्डाभ्यां प्राप्यते कोशभूषणा ॥

Theoritically, all mines, whether of precious metals or of base metals belonged to the king and all profits went to him. But, in regard to their working, the government did not stand in the way of private effort or tried to kill it entirely. It did not discourage private enterprise, but, on the other hand, invited such enterprise and capital, and let out extensive mines requiring great outlays of capital to capitalists. These latter either paid a fixed rent or worked for a share of the profits. Smaller mines requiring less capital or less labour, the state reserved for its own working. Thus says Kauṭilya—भाण्डोपकारिणं च व्ययक्रियाभारिकमाकरं भागेन प्रक्रयेण वा दद्यात् । लाघविकमात्मना कारयेत् ।

In addition to these above, the government derived a substantial income from other sources one of the most prominent of which was the depreciation of the currency. As we know from the chapter on mines, the state in those days monopolised the manufacture of the metallic currency and employed two officials, the Lakṣaṇādhyakṣa and the Rūpadarśaka to superintend the work. From the directions given in connection with their duties, it is clear that the government did not scruple to make out something of a depreciation of the metal, out of which coins were made. In the Middle Ages, too, such practices were resorted to by European kings.

All mines worked by the governmeut, as well as those worked by private capitalists, were under the jurisdiction of the Ākarādhyakṣa, the highest officer in charge of mining. In all mines, workmen with expert knowledge, men well-up in the science of detecting valuable ores and in the art of extraction of metals, or those who belonged to guilds of experts, (शुल्बधातुशास्त्ररसपाकमणिरागज्ञस्तज्ज्ञसङ्घो वा)। or expert miners themselves were employed.

Kauṭilya gives us details of the crude metallurgical processes of those days, the ways of detecting various ores or the methods of their extraction. These are of no importance to us, but, their explanation is of importance in other connections. The superintendent's work consisted in putting down clandestine trade or theft of minerals. (आकरिकमपहरन्तमष्टगुणं दापयेत् ।

अन्यत्र रत्नेभ्यः । स्तेनमनिसृष्टोपजोविनं च बद्धं कर्म कारयेत्)
His next and more important work was to supervise the storing and collection of such minerals, their classification and superintendence of their manufacture for commercial purposes.

For these various purposes, there were different officials acting under him. The most important of them were the following—

(1) The Lohādhyakṣa—who was in charge of base-metal manufacture. (लोहाध्यक्षः ताम्रसीसत्रपुवैकृन्तकारकूटवृत्तकंसताललोध्रकर्मान्तान् कारयेत्। लोहभाण्डव्यवहारं च) He superintended the manufacture of various alloys in common use and articles made of these *e.g.* of bell metal, bronze, etc.

(2) The Lakṣaṇādhyakṣa—who manufactured coins and tokens of silver or copper, mixed with alloys (लक्षणाध्यक्षः चतुर्भागताम्रं रूप्यरूपं......कारयेत्) *e.g.* Rūpyas Paṇas, Ardha-paṇas etc.

(3) The Rūpadarśaka—who manufactured token coins and tested them (रूपदर्शकः पणयात्रां व्यवहारिकीं कोशप्रवेश्यां च स्थापयेत्)

(4) The Suvarṇādhyakṣa—who was in charge of the extraction of gold. This

officer was in charge of gold extraction, while, another superintended the manufacture of gold utensils and ornaments for the people, which industry also appears to have been solely in the hands of government officials. This official was named Sauvarṇika and had his office in a prominent part of the city (विशिखामध्ये सौवर्णिकं शिल्पवन्तमभिजातं प्रात्ययिकं च स्थापयेत्। सौवर्णिकः पौरजानपदानां रूप्यसुवर्णमावेशनिभिः कारयेत्।)

In addition to these, there were other officials associated with the Ākarādhyakṣa. *e.g.*

(5) The Khanyadhyakṣa—in charge of sea mines, and extracting corals, conch-shells, pearls, etc. (खन्यध्यक्षः शङ्खवज्रमणिमुक्ताप्रवालक्षारकर्मान्तान् कारयेत्) The extraction of alkali (क्षारः) and its supervision was also a part of his duties, while, the extraction of salt was entrusted to the next official.

(6) The Lavaṇādhyakṣa—who superintended the manufacture of salt (लवणाध्यक्षः पाकमुक्तं लवणभागं प्रक्रयं च यथाकालं सङ्गृह्णीयात्) and collected the excise income arising therefrom. He supplied the public demand and fixed the price.

Salt seems to have been a royal monopoly, and on imported salt a duty of 1·6 was levied (आगन्तुलवणं षड्भागं दद्यात्) Any infringement of this monopoly right or income was severly punished. Clandestine manufacture of salt [adulteration ?] was punished. (विलवणं उत्तमं दण्डं दद्यात्)

The rigor of the monopoly rules was mitigated in the case of the Vāṇaprasthas, Śrotriyas, hermits and royal labourers (अनिसृष्टोपजीवो च । अन्यत्र वाणप्रस्थेभ्यः । श्रोत्रियास्तपस्विनो विष्टयः भक्तलवणं हरेयुः), who were given salt for their own consumption.

Next to these monopolies, goods in which the king had a trading right, or those which were manufactured or produced in royal farms and manufactories, had a preference in the market over those of private manufacture or produce. This preference was probably in the shape of freedom from duties and preferential treatment, which enabled them to have a readier sale. In regard to these, we have no specification by name or detail, but there is reason for believing that such a preference existed, and that these were vested in favoured individuals who had sole agencies therein. (स्वभूमिजानां राजपण्यानामेकमुखं व्यवहारं स्थापयेत् etc. P. 98.)

(7) **Forced labour**—was again a source of benefit and income to the state.

(8) **Fines**—from law-courts brought considerable revenue. The Arthaśāstra laws hard and rigorous as they were, were profitable to the state, in as much as, the principle of levying fines in lieu of mutilation or imprisonment made a large number to pay.

(9) **Accidental Income**—In addition to these, there were accidental incomes from the following :—

(*a*) The king had his escheat on all properties without heir. (thus, in the chap on. Samāhartā, we find mention of डम्मरगतकस्वमपुत्रकम्.)

(*b*) Lost property without owner passed to the king. (नाष्टिकम्)

(*c*) Treasure-troves went to the king. (निधिस्वान्यजातः)

(10) **Occasional** and extraordinay taxes were levied in times of distress, war or other emergencies. These took the form of enhanced revenue exactions and Praṇayas, mentioned in the chapter on कोशाभिसंहरणम्. In addition, there were exactions like the forced loans and Benevolences which we find in Medieval England.

(11) **Interest**—on loans of money and corn advanced to cultivators brought something more to the treasury.

VIII

RECEIPT AND AUDIT

This vast income derived from all these heads mentioned above, was when collected, handed over to the Receiver-General or the Sannidhātā, who was entrusted with the duty of receiving these. His real functions are not clearly explained in the Arthaśāstra, where we find him not only in charge of receipts, but also in charge of constructing treasury-houses, trading houses and store-houses. But, the general evidence of the chapter shows that he was the highest receiving officer, and we have passages which speak of his receiving collections of all sorts. (तस्मादाप्तपुरुषाधिष्ठितः सन्निधाता निचयानानुतिष्ठेत्)

(1) *e.g.* gems and precious stones.

(2) precious metals and coins (रूपदर्शकविशुद्धं हिरण्यं प्रतिगृह्णीयात्)

(3) pure and fresh grains (शुद्धं पूर्णमभिनवं च धान्यं प्रतिगृह्णीयात्)

In regard to receipts in kind, probably, there were other officers who acted under him, both as collecting and receiving officials *e.g.*

(1) The Kūpyādhyakṣa,—who collected mainly forest-products which have already been enumerated.

(2) The Koṣṭhāgārādhyakṣa,—who collected all payments in kind. These were all stored, one half being especially kept in reserve for the people in case of famines or other emergencies. (ततोऽर्धं रक्षेत् आपदर्थं जानपदानाम्)

In regard to all kinds of receipts, there was a strict account department, with a number of officials who constantly audited the income. In all offices, government officials were required to know the various sources of income, the various local customs (धर्मव्यवहारचरित्राणि), the various forms of royal dues and gains, the [local] rates of exchange and barter, the obligations and dues of families and corporations, the immunities granted to men or castes, grants to courtiers, remissions of taxation and various other factors connected with collection.

There were offices and sub-offices under the treasury, and in each place, detailed registers were kept by the official in charge assisted by his scribes and accountants (कार्मिकाः). The work of each office was supervised by a superintendent (कारणिकः)

The account books were kept in detail. In all entries, the names of the treasurer (निधायकः), the prescriber (निबन्धकः), the receiver (प्रतिग्राहकः) the payer (दायकः) and the person who caused payment (दापकः), were clearly written down.

Generally, all accounts were submitted in the month ot Āṣāḍha, which marked the close of the financial year.[?] But, all the officers were bound to keep their accounts up to date, and the superintendents checked daily. All receipts were checked and verified, in reference to place and time, the form of collection, the person paying or the one receiving it. Tampering with accounts was severely punished, as well as attempts at falsifying the registers.

Foremost attention was paid to financial administration, since, it was upon the well-kept treasury that all undertakings depended. (कोशपूर्वाः सर्वारम्भाः). Dishonesty on the part of the collecting or receiving officials was severely checked. The use of royal articles, exchanging these for other such of similar though lower quality, carrying on trade with state money, or lending royal money on interest, defalcation, theft, or all such fradulent practices were severely punished. It is needless to enumerate the forty kinds of enbezzlement mentioned by Kauṭilya, since, they would be out of place here, though, surely instructive to those that study details of the various branches of administration. The attention paid shows the perfect and efficient system, which existed in those days.

In all offices, measures were taken to punish indifferent or dishonest officials. In the head-offices, the higher officials had to meet and present their accounts collectively, otherwise, they were punished. Similarly, clerks failing to keep or present daily accounts were punished, though occasionally, time was given. For fraudulent tampering with accounts or for thefts of various description, the punishment varied from fines of various sums to the penalty of death. Informers and spies (सूचकः) were kept, who constantly apprised the higher officials of the doings and malpractices of subordinate officers. If proved, they were heavily fined and the informants were rewarded.

IX

PUBLIC EXPENDITURE

Having given a detailed account of the revenue and its collection, we pass on to discuss the public expenditure of those days. Broadly speaking, the vast revenue was spent partly in maintaining the royal dignity, in defending and protecting the country, as well as in discharging the obligations which the government had taken upon itself.

The chief heads of expenditure were :—

(1) Maintenance of the Royal Household, the Harem, including the queens, the concubines, princes (and their education), the harem-guards, spies, the king's kitchen and the guards that protected the Royal person.

(2) Maintenance of the religious establishment with the priests, and the sacrificers.

(3) Payment of the salaries of higher officials, and their subordinates including the magistracy and the judiciary, the police, the espionage and the menial staff.

(4) Maintenance of the Army and the Navy *e.g.* payment of soldiers, and pensions, together with the cost of maintaining the fortifications and implements of war.

(5) Maintenence of factories, manufacturing establishments, mines, forests etc.

(6) Payment and maintenance of hired labourers, miners and the vast menial establishment etc.

(7) Grants and loans to cultivators, irrigation expenses, or grants in aid of co-operative irrigation, settlement of villages, aids to new settlers etc.

(8) Maintenance of widows and orphans and the infirm or the distressed.

(9) Grants to teaching establishments and pensions to learned men or teachers, both of the sacred lore as well as of the secular sciences.

(10) Pensions to the children and relatives of deceased officials, and the widows and orphans of soldiers killed in battle.

(11) Public works and the maintenance of roads, canals, embankments etc.

Royal Household—We have no means of ascertaining approximately the amount of money or the proportion of revenue spent on each of these various heads. But, undoubtedly, the Royal Household, as in the case of most European countries in the 17th and 18th centuries, (where all collections and expenses were made in the name of the king) absorbed a large part of the revenue. The personal requirements of the king, the safety of his person and the ministration to his pleasure cost a huge sum.

Kings of those days kept harems full of concubines in addition to their lawfully-wedded queens, and each of these ladies had a large number of attendants or servants. The harem itself required for its protection and the preservation of its health and sanctity, a number of higher officials, physicians, spies, courtisan-spies, old men, poiosn-detectors, and eunuchs. To these, must be added the cost of keeping different house-holds for princes and princesses and their education.

We have neither details nor any account of the expenses of the royal house-hold. Only in the chapter on the "Payments to Servants" there is a statement that the Chief Queen was paid 48,000 [gold?] pieces a year.

The Religious Establishment—It also entailed a great expenditure. The Purohita whom the king regarded almost as a father enjoyed the salary of the Mantrin (48000). Under him were the Ṛtvij, Ācārya, and minor sacrificing priests. The Ṛtvij and the Ācārya enjoyed the same remuneration as the Purohita, while Astrologers, Omen-readers, and the Purāṇa-reciters received 1000 paṇas a year.

In addition to these who formed a permanent establishment, grants were made to the Siddhas and Tāpasas, while, to the ordinary Śrotriyas or the priests of villages, were given Brahmadeya land and immunity from general taxation, in addition to certain grants of salt and other articles.

Payment of Officials—Next to the religious establishment, comes the important head of expenditure on the payment of officials. As in our own days, the India of the fourth country B. C. was governed by a powerful and highly-paid bureaucracy. The government took care to pay them handsome renumerations and salaries in cash, so that they might live comfortably and might not have recourse to fraudulent means of adding to their income. The details are given in the chapter on the "Payment of servants", but, only this may be mentioned that officials of the highest grade—the Mantrins got 48000 paṇas a year, while, those of the second grade, including the Dvauvārika, Antarvaṃśika, Praśāstā, Samāhartā and the Sannidhātā, got 24000 a year. Adhyakṣas, city-superintendents, judges, the President and members of the Mantripariṣat all got 12000 a year. Accountants, clerks, counters and scribes of the lowest grade got 500 a year. Physicians and surgeons got 2000 a year. The salary of spies varied from 500 a year to upwards. Village labourers got less or the same.

When we consider the vast number of officials, we are bound to conclude that the administration was costly and the government paid with both hands to make it efficient.

The Army and the Navy—As in the case of modern India, the defence of the Empire was a costly one. Huge sums were spent on the

Army and the Navy and the allied departments of Commissariat, Transport, Armoury, Espionage and various other sections. The Maurya army, if we are to believe in Greek accounts, approached a million in its personnel (*e.g.* 600000 foot, + 30000 horse, + 4 × 9000 elephant-riders, + 3 × 8000 charioteers.). The salary of men, even if we compute at the rate given by Kauṭilya was a huge sum. According to him, foot soldiers got 500 a year, servants, horse-attendants and menials attached to the departments got 60 paṇas a year, while higher officials like charriot-leaders, got 2000 paṇas a year. The next higher in grade were the commanders of bands of horse, elephant, foot and chariot, who got 4000 a year each. Higher grade commanders of the four sections got 8000 a year along with the Pradeṣṭaraḥ. The Nāyaka got 12000 a year, while the Praśāstā got 24000. The highest official, the Senāpati got 48,000 a year. The hugeness of the amount appears simply from a calculation of the pay of foot soldiers e.g. 600,000 × 500— 300,000,000 paṇas. This huge total was further swelled by the cost of maintaining the soldiers and the huge number of horse, elephant and cattle attached to the fighting and transport wings of the Army, and in giving food and clothing to the forced labourers impressed into the army service. The food supplied to men in those days was not scanty and in even in these days when Indians as a rule live on a low diet, the expense for maintaining a foot soldier would be considerable.

Factories and Mines—After the army and the navy, the various factories were a source of expenditure. The various farms, manufactories, cattle-farms, the royal agricultural establishments, too, cost a very huge sum, though they were productive of great benefits to the state.

Other important items of expenditure were the Mines and Forests. There, too, large numbers of men were employed and vast expenses were caused.

Agriculture and Arts--From these, we pass on to heads of expenditure of quite a different character. These were caused mainly with a view to further the happiness of the people actively, by grants to agriculture or the arts. In regard to the encouragement of agriculture, we find in the chapter on Janapada-niveśa, the direction that the king must give poor agriculturists privileges and exemptions without injuring his revenue. (cf. अनुग्रहपरिहारौ चेभ्य: कोशवृद्धिकरौ दद्यात्। कोशोपघातिकौ वर्जयेत्। अल्पकोशो हि राजा पौरजानपदानेव ग्रसते। निवेशसमकालं यथागतकं वा परिहारं दद्यात्। निवृत्तपरिहारान् पितेवानुगृह्णीयात्। p, 47.) Not to speak of this, loans were granted, and in times of famine and pestilence, special loans and advances were made. As I have shown elsewhere, we find these things in the Epic, and in the Sabhā parva. ch. V, this rate of interest is put down at 1% per annum.

Educational Pensions—Another item of importance was the royal grant to the cause of Education. This existed from time immemorial. Not to speak of gifts to sages in the Brāhmaṇic age, we have in the Buddhist literature, the Mahā-śāla (**महाशाल** and **महाश्रोत्रिय**) class enjoying royal grants of villages. In the days of the Arthaśāstra, the Ācāryas and Vidyāvantas who were teachers of the non-sacred branches, got pensions varying from 500 paṇas to 1000 paṇas (**आचार्या विद्यावन्तश्च पूजावेतनानि यथार्हं लभेरन्, पञ्चशतावरं सहस्रपरम्**) and probably, along with these, the Adhyakṣas, Vaktṛṇaḥ and Prayoktṛṇaḥ, who taught agriculture and the technical arts. Śrotriyas, too, were the receipients of their usual privileges and favours.

Pensions to Officials—The grant of pensions to retired officials was also another source of expenditure. Not only those who retired after meritorious service, but those dying in harness, had their wives and children provided for. (**कर्मसु मृतानां पुत्रदारा भक्तवेतनं लभेरन्। बालवृद्धव्याधिताश्चैषामनुग्राह्याः। प्रेतव्याधितसूतिकाकृत्येषु चैषामर्थमानकर्म कुर्यात्।** Kau. p. 246.)

Public Poor Relief—While these people enjoyed the special favours of the king, the relief of the poor was regarded as a royal duty in ancient India. The king was regarded by the jurists and thinkers of India as the natural guardian of the orphan and the widow *(parens patriae)*, the patron of the Śrotriya and the protector of the decrepit, the aged or the starving poor. Kauṭilya too, inculcates upon kings this royal duty though, with his own characteristic brevity he speakes less of theory or principle and simply entrusts to the king the above duty of maintaining the orphan or indigent. (*e.g.* **बालवृद्धव्याधितव्यसनानाथांश्च राजा विभृयात्। स्त्रियमप्रजाताम्। प्रजातायाश्च पुत्रान्**). Beyond this, we know nothing until we come to the Śukranīti. Poor relief was thus an important duty of the king and in this, there was no distinction of caste or creed.

Relief of Distress—The Royal government was not content with these provisions, but remained always prepared for greater emergencies. In times of famine, it took emergency measures as well as in times of pestilence or epidemics. It did something more. It kept in reserve ½ the produce of the royal farms or the taxes paid in kind, for relieving the distress of its subjects (**ततोऽर्धं रक्षेत् आपदर्थं जानपदानां**). We shall discuss these emergency measures elsewhere.

Public Works– The last though not the least important head of expenditure was that on public works. Even in those days, the government spent money in works of public utility. They constructed roads and built embankments and reservoirs of water for the good of the agriculturist. In some cases, the government helped co-operative irrigational works. The Greeks bear testimony to the existence of the Grand Trunk Road joining Pāṭaliputra with the western-most provinces of India, as also to the canals and reservoirs which were maintained and repaired by the king and supervised by royal officials. A late inscription of the time of Rudradāmana bears testimony to the creation of the Sudarśana lake under the direction of Candragupta's Yavana* viceroy Puṣyagupta. Kauṭilya gives us no details, nor mentions any contemporary undertakings, but, he expressly says that the king should—

शोधयेत्पशुसङ्घैश्च क्षीयमाणं वणिक्पथम् ।
एवं द्रव्यं द्विपवनं सेतुबन्धमथाकरान् ॥
रक्षेत् पूर्वकृतान् राजा नवांश्चाभिप्रवर्तयेत् ॥

(Kau. p. 49.)

* The reference here is to the Girnāra lake which was also reconstructed in the days of the Guptas. In that connection, a later history of the lake is given by the officer in charge. As to the public works of Aśoka, some vihāras, pillars, stūpas and monuments have still survived, and his inscriptions bear testimony to his roads with *serais*, his hospitals for men and animals and his religious buildings.

X

POLICE ADMINISTRATION

By the time of the Arthaśāstra, an efficient police system had grown up. The simple yet summary methods of dealing with the law-breaker which subsisted in the Vedic age, had been followed by the creation of special officers with criminal jurisdiction. The Jātakas give us a picture of the methods and measures of the times. There were first of all the village-headman and his officers, the Codakas, and then above them the Viniścaya-Mahāmātyas with their higher criminal jurisdiction. These did all for the preservation of peace. In the small tribal states, these measures were sufficient for the preservation of peace. But, the state of affairs changed when the Great Monarchy embracing the whole of Northern India came to be established and consequently a higher organisation came into existence.

Kauṭilya gives us a general description of the police measures to be adopted by the king. Of these, the following are important—

(I) First of all, the kingdom was to have its frontiers protected by officials appointed for that purpose. (जनपदद्वाराणि अन्तपालाधिष्ठितानि स्थापयेत्। अन्तेष्वन्तपालदुर्गाणि।)

The frontiers were moreover fortified and in important places, frontier-guards watched new-comers whose antecedents were enquired into. Then, they were disarmed and allowed to enter with pass-ports.

(2) Within the kingdom, there were police head-quarters established in all principal centres where there were also law-courts. Thus, in the midst of 800 villages there was a Sthānīya, a Droṇamukha in the midst of 400 villages, a Kharvaṭa or Khārvaṭika in the midst of 200 villagers, and a Saṅgrahaṇa in the midst of 10 villages.

All these places were probably garrisoned with troops commanded by officers of various grade. Whenever any emergency arose, these troops lent assistance to the officers in charge of villages or towns. Probably, there was in these days no fine distinction between the civil and the military as regards police. The duty of preserving peace was entrusted to the Samāhartā and the Sthānikas under him. They also instructed their subordinates in matters of police-duties and employed spies.

This was the general arrangement. In addition to these, there were local officers entrusted with the duty of keeping peace in their respective areas.

(1) In towns, the Nāgaraka was in charge of the city-police

(2) In villages, the Grāmika or Grāmādhyakṣa was in charge of the police. He possessed inferior criminal jurisdiction, watched new comers and could summarily expel from the village thieves or adulterers. In case of abuse of power, he was himself liable to pay a fine.

(3) In the intervening areas there was the Vivītādhyakṣa, who seems to have exercised criminal and police powers. He enquired into the whereabouts of passersby and did not allow anybody to pass except with passports. He protected travellers from thieves, dacoits or wild animals and made arrangments for supplying the regions with water and caused places of rest to be established. Under him, were hunters and guards accompanied by dogs who watched the approach of thieves or gangs of outlaws. If they apprehended danger, they sent men on horseback to inform villagers, or in case of risings of wild tribes, gave the alarm by sending out royal carrier-pigeons, or by means of a series of beacon-fires. (*e.g.* विवीताध्यक्षो मुद्रां पश्येत्।.........लुब्धकश्वगणिनः परिव्रजेयुररण्यानि। तस्करामित्राभ्यागमे शङ्खदुन्दुभिशब्दमग्राह्याः कुर्युः। शैलवृक्ष-विरूढा वा शीघ्रवाहना वा अमित्राटवीसञ्चारं च राज्ञो गृहकपो-तैर्मुद्रायुक्तैर्हारयेयुः धूमाग्निपरम्परया वा। Kau. p. 141.) Ordinarily, Candālas, Śavaras, and Pulindas, were

employed for police duties. (तेषामन्तराणि वागुरिकशबरपुलिन्दचण्डालारण्यचरा रक्षेयु: Kau. p. 46.) ।

To facilitate the work of these police officials, a strict watch was kept on all movements of people from one place to another. Men travelling from one part of the country to another had to show passports and answer querrics of police officials. For issuing passports, there were officers in charge of passports which were granted on the payment of one māṣaka. (समुद्रो जनपदं प्रवेष्टुं निष्क्रमितुं वा लभेत। मुद्राध्यक्षो मुद्रां :माषकेन दद्यात् Kau. p. 140). These were liable to be examined. Anyone who could not prove his *bona fidcs* by showing these was fined. (द्वादशपणं जानपदोऽमुद्रो दद्यात्). These were examined by the Vivītādhyakṣa, by the officers of the Nāvadhyakṣa at the ferries, or the officers at town-gates or during entrance into villages.

Next to these impediments on movements of people from one part to another, there were spies of various classes and under various garbs. We have an enumeration of these spies in the chapter on Gūḍha-puruṣotpattiḥ and the following one. The more important classes of spies were the Kāpaṭikas, the Udāsthitas, the Vaidehakas, the Gṛhapatikas, and the Tāpasa-vyañjakas, while in addition to these were the Satriṇaḥ, the Tīkṣṇas, and the Bhikṣukī. These were employed both by the Samāhartā and his subordinates or by the officers of the Kaṇṭaka-śodhana. These men not only gave information about thieves, adulterers, criminals, coiners, forgers, poisoners, assasins and themselves, tempted wicked criminals of various description, but, in the guise of holy men or pretending to be criminals themselves learned their secrets, and either caught them red-handed in the act of committing crimes, or detected young men with evil tendencies. It is not the place for describing in detail the methods they employed in detecting criminals, but the description of their duties and methods form an interesting and amusing study. Nobody can help admiring the author of the Arthaśāstra for his knowledge of men and methods.

Some more spies were employed by the civil administration and were stationed in disguise, at cross-roads, ruined temples, Caityas, ferries, in wine-shops, or brothels, and in all possible rendezvous of the wicked. (पुराणचोरव्यञ्जनाश्चान्तेवासिनश्चैत्यचतुष्पथेषु स्तेनामित्रप्रवीरपुरुषानां च प्रवेशनस्थानगमनप्रयोजनान्युपलभेरन् Kau. p. 143.) ।

To ensure the efficiency of these measures, the government imposed responsibility both on localities and on the officers in charge of them. Thus, in the chapter on Aticāra, we are told that merchants on entering a village had to inform the headman about their goods. If, during their stay, the merchants lost anything, the village-chief had to make good the loss. If the theft was committed during a journey from one village to another, the Vivitādhyakṣa had to make the loss good. (ग्रामेग्न्यत: सार्थिका ज्ञातसारा बसेयु: । मुषितं प्रवासितं चैषामनिर्गतं रात्रौ ग्रामस्वामी दद्यात् । ग्रामान्तरेषु वा मुषितं विवीताध्यक्षो दद्यात् । अविवीतानां चोररज्जुक: । Kau. p. 232.)

For detecting thieves, a special officer was employed named Cora-rajjuka and a special tax was levied on localities.

Further, to prevent crimes, not only men of evil tendencies or their movements were watched by officials, but, restrictions were put on the indiscriminate trading in arms or their carrying by subjects. Private citizens trading in arms had such goods confiscated by the customs officials or the Nāvadhyakṣa's men. (pp. 114 and 126) Merchants from abroad had to deposit their arms with the frontier-guards (a practice still enforced by the British at Khyber against the Kabulis and the border people) or were allowed to carry them on receiving permits to do so. (सार्थिकानां शस्त्रावरणमन्तपाला गृह्णीयु: समुद्रमवचारयेयुर्वा । Kau. p. 247). Carrying of weapons at night in towns was also forbidden. (चाररात्रिषु दण्डग्रस्त्रहस्ताश्च मनुष्या: दोषतो दण्ड्या: p. 146). Movements near the king's palace or climing on to city walls was also punishable. Visitors in cities to wine-shops, hotels of cooked food or meat, brothels or houses of ill-fame were registered (शौण्डिकपाक्वमांसिकौदनिकरूपाजीवा: परिज्ञातमावासयेयु: p. 144).

XII

THE ARMY AND THE NAVY

According to the theorists of the Arthaśāstra school, a strong army was one of the most important requisites of the state. Consequently, great attention was paid to the maintenance and organisation of the army.

According to the Greek travellers, the affairs of the army and the navy were managed by six boards which supervised the work of the following different sections :—

(1) The Infantry (2) The Supply and Commissariat (3) The Horse (4) The Elephant (5) The Chariot (6) The Navy.	(All these boards according to the Greeks, being constituted of six members each.)

The Arthaśāstra mentions no such boards, but it mentions a number of heads of departments. *e.g.*

(1) The Āyudhāgārādhyakṣa.
(2) The Pattyadhyakṣa.
(3) The Hastyadhyakṣa.
(4) The Rathādhyakṣa.
(5) The Nāvadhyakṣa.
(6) The Aśvādhyakṣa.

The Āyudhāgārādhyakṣa was in charge of the Armoury. He had to collect or manufacture the requisite weapons, keep them in proper order and make them up to date, *e. g.*, the arms and weapons of soldiers, the armours of men-at-arms, cavalry-men and chariot troops.

(*b*) He had to keep weapons and implements for defending forts or for assailing those of the enemy. (*e.g.* आयुधागाराध्यक्षः साङ्ग्रामिकं दौर्गकर्मिकं परपुराभिघातिकं चक्रयन्त्रमायुधमावरणं च तज्जातकारुशिल्पिभिः कारयेत्। Kau. p. 101.)

All these weapons are enumerated in the chapter on Āyudhāgārādhyakṣa, where full details are given. From these, it would seem that the ordinary weapon of the infantryman was a sword, a bow and arrows, a javelin, and in some cases lances, with a body-covering of tough bull-hide. Higher class officers had armours both of iron-netting or of sheet-steel with coverings for the head, arms, breast or the thighs.

Elephants, chariots and horses, too, had coverings and helmets. For resisting sieges, there were various devices, the exact nature of which is difficult to determine. These included iron or wooden beams to crush the enemy, revolving discs turning in the path of the enemy's way of advance, devices for throwing stones or setting fire, as well as those for throwing numerous arrows all at once.

It is needless to enumerate them. Weapons for investment or destruction of forts are interesting. They included implements like the catapult or the ballista for throwing stone-balls, devices for setting fire to the enemy's camp, (including balls fired along with an arrow), devices for breaking the walls and high moving towers to enable men to climb the walls of the fort. They are similar to the moving towers used in Babylonian and Persian warfare.

The Āyudhāgārādhyakṣa was in charge of all these. He had to make arrangements for their manufacture and up-keep in proper condition. All weapons were marked with the royal emblem and were issued to troops either on active duty or in parade. When the active duty or parade was over, the weapons were again returned to the armoury. (कृतनरेन्द्राङ्कं शस्त्रावरणमायुधागारं प्रवेशयेत् । अशस्त्राश्चरेयुरन्यत्र मुद्रानुज्ञानात् । p. 247).

II. Infantry:—The officer in charge of the infantry was entrusted with the training, discipline and organisation of foot soldiers. He superintended their regular drilling and training in various forms of warfare (p. 247). In the absence of all details, our knowledge is supplemented by an important passage in which Kauṭilya mentions the various forms of warfare *e.g.* fighting in low-lands, fighting in the open, fighting with missiles (आकाशयुद्ध), fighting with tunnelling or entrenchments, fighting at night and in day-time (**निम्नस्थलप्रकाशकूटखनकाकाशदिवारात्रियुद्धव्यायामं च विद्यात्**)

III. Cavalry :—The officer in charge of the cavalry had (with the assistance of his subordinates) to take charge of the horses, as well as cavalrymen. Horses were regularly trained for war and great pains were taken to make them servicable. Veterinary officers took care of their health, and efforts were made to keep them in good condition of training. The details of the chapter on the Cavalry superintendent are really interesting and supply valuable information even to the specialists of the present day.

IV. Chariots:—The section of chariot-fighters formed a separate department. Special care was taken for the construction and protection of chariots with armours. According to Kauṭilya, chariots were generally 10×12 puruṣa in measurement. Another form of chariot was smaller. No more details are given. They were of various type and construction. Some were used in drawing idols or men of positions, while, others were specially constructed for war fare or for assailing the fortifications of the enemy (**देवरथपुष्यरथसाङ्ग्रामिकपारियाणिकपरपुराभियानिकवैनयिकांश्च रथान् कारयेत्** p. 139) No more details are given in the Arthaśāstra, but, the Greek accounts show that in war they were drawn by two or more horses, and were very servicable on account of their swift movement. This enabled the chariot force to assail or turn the flank of the enemy or to pursue a flying coloum. The chariot troops were given special training, in fighting. The importance of the chariot is proved by its use by Porus in the war against Alexander. Fuller details are obtainable from Greek authors.

V. The Naval force—It was under the Nāvadhyakṣa. According to the evidence of Kauṭilya as well as that of the Greeks, the naval force was considerable and had to perform multifarious duties. The state maintained both big sails (**महानाव:**) controlled by captains, steersmen, and expert keepers of the sail and rigging, and small boats (**क्षुद्रका:**) The officials of the also Nāvadhyakṣa had not only to protect the coastal regions or rivers from enemys, or to put-down piracy (**हिंस्त्रिका निर्घातयेत्**), but, they were also in charge of administering the maritime and water-way regulations and those relating to markets and harbours. (**पत्तनाध्यक्षनिवन्धं पण्य पत्तनचारित्वं**). They were in charge of the following duties :—

(1) Collection of maritime customs.

(2) Protection of ports and shipping.

(3) Prevention of the smuggling of arms and weapons or prohibited articles of commerce.

(4) Guarding of the ferries and fords and the collections arising from the former.

(5) Apprehension of criminals, run-aways from justice, smugglers, men taking to orders against the laws and to avoid the burdens of life, and all sorts of undesirable persons. (परस्य भार्यां कन्यां वित्तं वापहरन्तं सद्योग्टहीतलिङ्गिनं गूढभारभाण्डशासनशस्त्राग्नियोगं विषहस्तं दीर्घपधिकममुद्रं चोपग्राहयेत् । p. 127.)

(6) Protection of vessels or seamen in distress. (मूढ़वाताहतां तां पितेवानुग्टह्णीयात्).

(7) Regulation of the entry and exit of foreign ships or vessels going to foreign lands (क्षतप्रवेशा: पारविषयिका: सार्थप्रमाणा वा विशेयु:).

Maritime taxes—Maritime tolls and duties were a source of income to the state. These included.

(1) Kliptas from maritime villages (वेलाकूलग्रामा: क्लृप्तं दद्युः)

(2) Nauka-hāṭakas paid by fishermen (मत्स्यवन्धका नौकहाटकं दद्युः)

(3) Harbour-dues paid by merchants (पत्तनानुवृत्तं शुल्कभागं वणिजो दद्युः)

(4) Fares for voyages, paid by merchants and passengers using royal ships (यात्रावेतनं राजनौभिस्सम्पतन्तः)

(5) Duties and taxes paid by those employed in pearl-fishery or collection of conch-shells (शङ्खमुक्ताग्राहिणो नौहाटकान्ददुः)

VI. Elephants—Constituted an important arm of the fighting force. They were used in war from time immemorial. Elephants were covered with mail and thus protected, they carried fighting-men on their back and were used in checking the advance of enemy elephants and of infantry. The Arthaśāstra contains directions for the proper feeding, training and treaṭment of elephants. Elephant-forests were kept under royal officials and elephants were preserved from hunting.

The above departments supervised the control and organisation of the army. Kauṭilya mentions single officers, while, the Greeks mention departmental boards. Perhaps, each department was controlled not by individual officers, but, was presided over by a number of ministers who held office for a limited term as directed by Kauṭilya. (बहुमुख्यमनित्यं चाधिकरणं स्थापयेत् p. 70.)

In addition to these, there were other branches of the fighting force. The chapter on **Sāṅgrāmika** gives us many more interesting details about the Auxiliary Limbs of the fighting force. These included the following sections of the army :—

(1) Guards for protecting the life of the Sovereign. (अष्टादशवर्गाणामात्मरक्षविपर्यासं-कारयेत् p. 362.)

(2) Troops of the Vardhaki and Viṣṭi, corresponding to our Sappers, Miners and Engineers. Their business was to march in advance of the army, to dig wells or to construct roads. They were led by the Praśāstā who held independent command. These were trained in the work of speedy entrenchment, in constructing camps, and in raising quick fortifications. cf.

पुरस्तादध्वन: सम्यक् प्रशास्ता ग्रहणानि च ।
यायाद्वर्धकिविष्टिभ्यामुदकानि च कारयेत् ॥

(3) Spies of various descriptions, *e.g.*

(*a*) Spies who collected informations about the enemy's strength or the disposition of his forces.

(*b*) Fighting spies (akin to the *agents provocateurs* of the German army) well-versed in Kūṭayuddha, who incited enemy forces to revolt, spread false rumours about the enemy's defeat, mixed poison in the enemy's food supply, poisoned their drinking water, set fire to enemy's camp and spread havoc and destruction, or if possible, assasinated the enemy leaders.

(4) Cooks and suppliers of food to the Army. The Arthaśāstra mentions the establishment of the Mahānasa, akin to the modern canteen arrangement.

(5) Drummers, singers and minstrels, who encouraged the troops and called upon them to fight for their king.

(6) Medical Department.—Physicians and nurses were also employed by the government, constituting something like the modern *Red Cross* or the *Red Crescent* department for the treatment of the sick and wounded.

This department was carefully organised and medical men, including nurses carried food and medicine to the fighting lines and tended the wounded. (चिकित्सकाः शस्त्रयन्त्रागदस्नेहवस्त्रहस्ताः स्त्रियश्चान्नपानरक्षिण्यः पुरुषाणां उद्धर्षणीयाः पृष्ठतस्तिष्ठेयुः Kau. p. 367.) The Mahābhārata also mentions them in many places.

Constitution of the Army.—The command of the army, in times of war, was entrusted to chosen officers, *e.g* the Nāyaka, the Senāpati and their subordinates. Strict discipline was maintained in the camp. All these military regulations will be described in detail in the chapter on war. (in the next volume)

The recruitment of the army was carried on with care. Probably, no conscription existed, though, it was the duty of all Kṣattriyas to fight. Kauṭilya prefers them to Brāhmaṇa soldiers. The personnel included the following varieties of fighters.

(1) The Maula or hereditary troops or the active houschold troops.

(2) The Bhṛtakas or mercenaries fighting for money.

(3) Śreṇībala or contingents supplied by corporations of various description. (श्रेणीबल:). These were short-service men. [ह्रस्व: प्रवास: ?]

(4) Troops furnished by the allies. (मित्रबल:)

(5) Troops furnished by wild tribes. (अटवीबल:)

XII
REGULATION OF COMMERCE AND INDUSTRY

The regulation of Commerce and Industry, attracted the special attention of the Arthaśāstra government. As it was the case in many ancient civilizations, so in India, the mind of the common peeple as well as that of the Lawgiver was dominated by an idea of 'just price'. In the social organism, all sections had a place. Each was entitled to the social benefits arising out of the labours of another. Unrestricted freedom for the individual to determine the price of his own effort, or an uncontrolled raising of prices on the part of merchants and labourers, was regarded as something going directly against all principles of justice or of reasonable regulation of the mutual interests of classes.

To add to these, the period immediately preceding the composition of the Arthaśāstra saw the evil effects of capitalism and cornering, as we know from the regulations of the Dharma-sūtras denouncing usury and the raising of prices. Consequently, society demanded the intervention of the government with the purpose of enforcing

(1) a just price in the case of merchants
(2) a just profit in the case of manufacturers.
(3) a just renumeration for labourers.

Restrictions on Commerce and Industry.—Consequent upon this, commerce and industry did not enjoy the benefits of a 'no control' or "Laissez-faire" system. Traders and manufacturers were subjected to vexatious interferences on the part of the state. One important source of interference was the active competition of the state which came to enjoy a number of monopolies, with a view to enhance its revenue. The creation of these monopolies subjected traders to a keen competition with the state. The government zealously guarded its own interests in regard to its profits, and consequently, the individual trader suffered and the scope of private enterprise was narrowed down.

Of the monopolies, as stated already the following were the more important, *e.g.*—

(1) mines and the mining industry, which was wholly a government monopoly.

(2) salt was also a government monopoly.

Next to these monopolies, the government probably enjoyed special privileges in regard to the sale of the produce of its own farms and factories. The Paṇyādhyakṣa was in charge of the sale of these and looked to their disposal prior to the sale of similar commodities of private production. As a rule, they were entrusted to royal agents and were sold to the benefit of subjects.

In regard to further restrictions on commerce,

the government was actuated by a desire to see that first of all, its own coffers were filled and secondly, the people got things cheaper and at a reasonable price.

No shop without a license.—With a view to these, the government did not allow persons to engage in any trade without its permission. Any one who desired to open a shop, had to take out a license. This put a stop to speculation in commodities of every day use, and allowed only *bona fide* traders to open a shop. And, as a result of this, greedy speculators were prevented from interfering with the normal supply and distribution of commodities.

Any one except a recógnized tradesman making purchases to the excess of his own needs, had his goods confiscated. (तेन धान्यपण्यनिचयांश्चानुज्ञाता कुर्युः । अन्यथा निचितमेषां पण्याध्यक्षो गृह्णीयात्). During the Great War, all governments were compelled to suppress such speculations and similar measures for controlling supplies and regulating prices were taken.

Regulation of profits.—Next, it regulated the profits and prices of merchants. The Arthaśāstra theory in regard to traders was that they were really thieves though not in name. Cf.

एवं चोरानचोराख्यान् वणिक्कारुकुशीलवान् ।
भिक्षुकान् कुहकांश्चान्यान्वारयेत् देशपीडनात् p. 202. ॥

As a rule, all profits were regulated in the case of merchants. In the case of articles of local produce, only 5% profit on cost was allowed, (अनुज्ञानक्रयादुपरि चैषां स्वदेशीयानां पण्यानां पञ्चकं शतमाजीवं स्थापयेत् । परदेशीयानां दशकम् p. 202) while, on those of foreign production, the profit was limited to 10% of the purchase price.

Any one taking extra-profits was fined. (ततः परमर्घं वर्धयतां क्रये विक्रये वा भावयतां पणशते पञ्चपणाद्विशतो दण्डः p. 205)

No Sale except in Markets—To ensure success in the regulation of prices and profits, the government forbade all sales except in the markets. No commodity could be sold according to the Arthaśāstra, in the place of its production. (जातिभूमिषु पण्यानामविक्रयः । खनिभ्यो धातुपण्यादानेषु षट्छतमत्ययः……etc. chapter on Śulka-vyavahāra pp. 112—113). This fact has also been attested to by the Greek historians. All commodities were examined and sealed by the local officers before being sent to the market. There, the goods were examined, their price ascertained and then the toll was taken according to the schedule given in the chapter on Śulka-vyavahāra.

Cornering Checked—Cornering was also checked and great pains taken to prevent the fluctuation of prices, owing to abnormal variations in demand and supply. The dependence of prices on demand and supply was clearly understood in those days, but the government believed in protection, and as such, took care not to allow the fluctuation of prices with abnormal demand or unusual supplies. In case of the over-supply of a particular commodity, the Paṇyādhyakṣa acted as the controller of the goods. He established the sale of that article through one single agent, (पण्यबाहुल्यात् पण्याध्यक्षः सर्वपण्यान्येकमुखानि विक्रीणीत। तेष्वविक्रीतेषु नान्ये विक्रीणीरन् p. 205) and forbade others to sell it until the stock was exhausted.

Further-more, it severely checked any tendencies towards the raising or lowering of prices, by means of cornering. (वैदेहकानां वा सम्भूय पण्यमवरुन्धतामनर्घेण विक्रीणतां क्रीणतां वा सहस्रं दण्डः p. 204). Groups or associations of merchants raising or attempting the raising of prices through combination were heavily fined.

No Adulteration of Foodstuffs.—Great care was also taken to see that the people might not suffer through the lowering of the quality of foodstuffs and other commodities. (धान्यस्नेहक्षारलवणगन्धभैषज्यद्रव्याणां समवर्णोपधाने द्वादशपणो दण्डः p. 204.) Adulteration was severely punished, as we shall see later on in the section on sanitation.

Weights and measures—The government regulated weights and measures too. Men using false weights or measures were severely punished.

For this, there were different royal officers as mentioned in the chapter on Pautavādhyakṣa.

Controlling Officials—In order to enforce all the above mentioned regulations, there were the following officers [or officials presiding over boards] :—

(1) The Śulkādhyakṣa—who ascertained the price and quality of goods and levied toll at the market-place.

(2) The Paṇyādhyakṣa—who regulated the supply, sale, and price of commodities, issued licenses to men setting up any trade, checked cornering and punished the adulteration of foodstuffs.

(3) The Saṃsthādhyakṣa—who superintended the sale of new or second-hand goods, put down the sale of goods of inferior quality, regulated their demand and punished the use of false weights and measures.

(4) The Pautavādhyakṣa—who issued standardised weights and measures which were regarded as the official standards in all transactions. (see ch. on Tulā-māna-pautavaṃ.)

(5) The Antapālas—who examined all saleable commodities at the time of their entrance into the country, ascertained prices, levied taxes on beasts of burden and examined seals.

Encouragement to Foreign Trade and Foreign Merchants.—While internal trade was subjected to all sorts of vexatious regulations, the government did its best to foster foreign trade by inviting merchants from abroad to reside in its territory or by finding out markets for the goods produced at home.

To encourage foreign merchants, they were invited, and privileges and exemptions were granted to them. (परभूमिजं पण्यमनुग्रहेणावाहयेत्। नाविकसार्थवाहेभ्यश्च परिहारमायतिक्षमं दद्यात्। अनभियोगश्चार्थेष्वागन्तूनामन्यत्र सभ्योपकारिभ्य:) Though, details about their privileges are lacking, yet they seem to have enjoyed freedom from being sued in ordinary courts, except under circumstances not clearly explained.

The existence and the settlement of foreign merchants in the country is also testified to by the Greeks who visited India. According to a fragment of Megasthenes one of the Boards of the Municipal Administration of the city of Pāṭaliputra was in charge of the property of foreigners in case of their death in India, and provided arrangements for their safety during their stay in India.

The government also made honest attempts to find out markets for Indian goods abroad, while inviting foreign merchants to settle in India. It does not seem to have been idle in its efforts for the sale of Indian goods abroad. It not only examined the possibility of sale in these markets, but calculated the cost of transportation, duties leviable at different places and all other accessory expenses. Then, it tried to further the cause of Indian merchants by encouraging them to export. (**परविषये तु पण्यप्रतिपण्ययोरर्घंमूल्यं च आगमय्य शुल्कवर्तन्यातिवाहिकगुल्मतरदेयभक्तभागव्ययशुद्धमुदयं पश्येत्। असत्युदये भाण्डनिर्वहणेन पण्यप्रतिपण्यार्घेण वा लाभं पश्येत्। ततः सारपादेन स्थलव्यवहारमध्वना क्षेमेन प्रयोजयेत्। अटव्यन्तपालपुरराष्ट्रमुख्यैश्च प्रतिसंसर्गं गच्छेदनुग्रहार्थम्** । Kau. p. 99.)

In case of no such possibilities, not even for barter, the government tried to send out a commercial expedition under a merchant who was to sell in free markets. (**आत्मनो वा भूमिमप्राप्तः सर्वदेयविशुद्धं व्यवहरेत्** ?)

XIII

REGULATION OF GUILDS AND WAGES

While trade or commerce was thus regulated, the government controlled the guilds, their profits and wages. In an earlier period, the spirit of combination of the guilds seems to have enabled them to exact as much profit as they insisted. Consequently, during the age immediately preceding this governmental intervention, the guilds were very powerful. They decided all questions affecting themselves by their own combinations. Probably as a result of this, the middle-class consumer or employer had no means of opposing them or of holding their own against this guild-tyranny.

The powerful Kauṭilya government could not brook such independence on the part of these combinations of artisans or workmen. They were not satisfied with half-measures and took necessary steps to bring them under control. With a view to the control of the guilds, Kauṭilya recommends the creation of a Board presided over by three Amātyas or Pradesṭāraḥ, to protect and regulate the earnings of guilds. (*cf.* प्रदेष्टारस्त्रयस्त्रयो वामात्याः कण्टकशोधनं [कारुरक्षणं] कुर्युः Kau. p. 200). The chapter on Kaṇṭaka-śodhanaṃ while silent as to the more important details about guilds, gives us some suggestions about their formation or working. From the evidence of an important passage, it seems that the board supervised the formation of guilds. Each individual wishing to enter a guild, seems to have paid an entrance-fee, deposited with guild-elders, who were selected on account of their capacity to control guild-men, on account of their being good capilalists, or being men of original ideas. These deposits so collected formed something like the capital of the guild, and could only be used up in times of distress. (**अर्थ्यप्रतीकाराः कारुशासितारः सन्निक्षेप्तारः स्ववित्तकारवः श्रेणीप्रमाणा निक्षेपं गृह्णीयुः। विपत्तौ श्रेणी निक्षेपं भजेत।** Kau. p. 200). Thus formed, the guilds had to work under the directions of the Board, the existence of which is clearly testified to by the Greek writers. The Board settled wages and work, together with details about the time for completing a work or about fines owing to loss of material caused during work. Failure to do the work according to the regulations meant the loss of wages as well as punishment as would appear from the following passage :—*cf*.

निर्दिष्टदेशकालकार्यं च कर्म कुर्युः। अनिर्दिष्टदेशकालकार्यापदेशं कालातिपातने पादहीनं वेतनं तद्द्विगुणश्च दण्डः। अन्यत्र भ्रेषोपनिपाताभ्यां नष्टं विनष्टं वाऽभ्याभवेयुः। कार्यस्यान्यथाकरणे वेतननाशः तद्द्विगुणश्च दण्डः Kau. p. 201.

In the days of the Arthaśāstra, numerous guilds existed. Of these, the following were the more important :—*e.g.*

(1) Guilds of weavers—*i.e.*

(*a*) weavers of cotton-cloth or coverings.

(*b*) wool-weavers and blanket-makers.

(*c*) silk-weavers.

(2) Guilds of miners—employed in extracting minerals, including those who detected ores or reduced them.

(3) Guilds of metal-manufacturers, gold and silver smiths, braziers and of the following classes :—*e.g.*

(4) Carpenters.

(5) Workers in stone or masonry.

(6) Medical men.

(7) Priests and sacrificers.

(8) Musicians, dancers, actors etc.

(9) Menials of various grades *e.g.* bath-servants, shampooers, barbers, washermen, scavengers, news-runners, servants of various grades, village servants etc.

(10) Lower artisans, like potters, washermen dyers, basket-makers, confectioners etc.

(11) Sellers and makers of cheap articles *e.g.* sellers of meat, vegetables or cooked food.

(12) Members of various kinds of service *e.g.* soldiers, troopers, lower officials, clerks, scribes and accountants.

To this number, we may add various grades

of other people whom we find already mentioned in the Buddhist works. These include workmen or labourers, whose traditional number of 18 śreṇis, we find mentioned even in the later Smṛtis.

From the point of view of modern Economic theory or classification, we may divide these guilds into the following :—*e. g.*

(1) Guilds having the character of a joint commercial undertaking [though not often permanent] with capital of their own and designated by the name of Saṅgha. These undertook to perform any piece of work. Masons or house-builders may be cited as examples.

(2) Guilds of skilled workmen, who were supplied materials by capitalists and who turned the raw material into the fabric required, and were paid according to their out-turn.

(3) Guilds of lower class artisans or traders, who could work independently of capitallistic connection and depended solely on cheap natural products and on their labour or skill. As examples, we may cite potters, garland-makers, and basket-makers.

(4) Various grades of menials and low class workmen like servants, scavengers, charioteers, grooms, barbers, washermen, cooks, agricultural labourers etc.

(5) Men of various professions and occupations, like priests, physicians, medical men, nurses, musicians, scribes, officials etc.

The Saṅghas or guilds of joint-workers enjoyed certain privileges including a few days' grace in completing their work. Generally however, they had to do their work in a specified time with the remuneration agreed upon. This was divided among themselves. (see ch. on Joint-enterprise p. 185).

Other artisans had to work according to the rates specifically laid down by the Controlling Board. If they failed, they were fined and otherwise punished, if they caused loss. In cases of non-fulfilment of work, they were liable both to fines and punishment. But, if they fulfilled their promise, payment was enforced. (see pp. 185 and 200—202).

In cases of dispute with regard to wages or work, experts mediated, (श्रद्धया रागविवादेषु वेतनं-कुशलाः कल्पयेयुः) and probably the government enforced their decision on both the parties. This may be compared with the mediation-boards often appointed by modern governments to settle strikes in our own days.

The position of artisans and skilled workmen was further strengthened by a series of regulations which made it criminal on the part of employers and capitalists to combine with a view to lower their wages. In such offences, fines to the extent of 1000 paṇas (*i.e.* the highest amercement levied) were imposed. (कारुशिल्पिनां च कर्मगुणा

पकर्षमाजीवं विक्रयं क्रयोपघातं वा सम्भूय समुत्थापयतां सहस्रं दण्डः p. 204.) The Greek accounts go farther than this and say that the artisans enjoyed the special protection of the king, and injury in life or limb to them was severely punished. According to them, death sentence was often inflicteo on culprits doing violence to them.

XIV

REGULATION OF LABOUR.

Next to the regulation of the guilds, the Arthaśâstra throws a flood of light on the conditions of labour in ancient India. Unlike most ancient civilizations where slavery was the basis of social life, that of India was characterised by the fact that here slavery never became the sole basis of Economic life. India thus stands alone and occupies an unique position. The conditions of labour were such, that, even when slavery existed, the condition of slaves was so far ameliorated as to elicit the admiration of foreign visitors, who denied the existence of slavery in India.

In India, as we have already said, free labour had an existence even in the remote past, side by side with servile labour. The Karmakara or the free labourer was free to enter into contracts as to his work and wages. (यथासम्भाषितं वेतनं लभेत) In the absence of such contracts, the renumeration of the labourer was regulated according to the principles recognised by the ancient customary law of the land. These laid down the proportion of profit between the capitalist and the worker. Of such stipulations as regards shares, we find mention of some rules in the Artha-śāstra as well as in the Epic. The Arthaśāstra generally assigns 1/10 to the labourer, when there was no stipulation as to wages. Thus, a husbandman tilling another's land was to get 1/10 of the grains, a cow-herd was to get 1/10 of the milk, and a hawker or trader in the employ of a capitalist was to receive 1/10 of the goods. (*e.g.* कर्मकालानुरूपमसम्भाषितवेतनं । कर्षकस्सस्यानां गोपालकस्सर्पिषां, वैदेहकः पण्यानामात्मना व्यवहृतानां दशभागमसम्भाषितवेतनो लभेत । Kau. p. 183.).

The Epic text is more explicit, and seems to be older. There we are told that—

ब्राह्मणाय च राज्ञे च सर्वाः परिददे प्रजाः ।
तस्य वृत्तिं प्रवक्ष्यामि यच्च तस्योपजीवनम् ॥
षण्णामेकां पिबेद्धेनुं शताच्च मिथुनं हरेत् ।
लब्धाच्च सप्तमं भागं तथा शृङ्गे कलाखुरे ॥
सस्यानां सर्वबीजानामेषा साम्वत्सरी भृतिः ।

Śānti ch. 60.

Even, in the case of artists or artisans, mechanics, physicians, priests, or various grades of workers, who expected wages on the completion of work, the same rule *i.e.* wages according to understanding, guided their relations. In cases of difference, the opinion of experts was taken. (*e.g.*, कारुशिल्पिकुशीलवचिकित्सकवाग्जीवनपरिचारकादिराशाकारिकवर्गस्तु यथाऽन्यस्तद्विधः कुर्यात् । यथा वा कुशलाः कल्पयेयुः तथा वेतनं लभेत । Kau. p. 184.)

In cases of non-payment of wages, the master, employer or the capitalist was fined ten times. On the other hand, the employee had a liability to complete the work according to terms. If he failed, he was fined and was even liable to be confined by the master (गृहीत्वा वेतनं कर्म अकुर्वतो भृतकस्य द्वादशपणो दण्डः। संरोधश्चाकरणात्। p. 184.) But, if his inability was due to illness, or distress or owing to the degrading nature of the work, he was given an exemption. In further cases of disagreement, there were other rules regulating the relation between master and servant.

There were also similar laws regulating joint-undertakings of workmen. Generally speaking, in all such joint-undertakings, the united workers had to complete the work within the specified period, though they were given seven days grace in some cases. Until completion, they could not leave the master's work or leave it undone. In that case, they were fined.

The men employed were to divide the profits equally among themselves, unless, anything was specified to the contrary (सङ्घभृतास्सम्भूयसमुत्थातारो वा यथासम्भाषितं वेतनं समं वा विभजेरन् p. 185).

Land-owners and merchants were to pay to their employees as much as the latter's share or wages proportional to work. Labourers were also bound to find substitutes, if they left their work in the middle. The principle guiding these relations always was that wages should be proportional to work. In case of desertion or negligence on the part of the workman, he was fined or warned on his first offence. Such rules also guided priests engaged in a sacrifice. The heirs of a priest dying in course of a sacrifice already begun by him along with others, got 1-5 to 3-4 of the profits, he would have earned, had he but lived and completed his work. Subject to this, the surviving priests of a sacrifice divided the profits among themselves. In the case of the death of the institutor of the sacrifice, the priests appointed were to complete the sacrifice, dividing the presents equally among themselves. In the case of sacrificing priests, they could even be dismissed if they were found to be unworthy of performing such a sacred service by reason of being drunkards, adulterers or men of heinous character.

Servile Labour :- —In addition to the regulation of the wages and work of free workmen, the Arthaśāstra government tried its best to ameliaorate the condition of unfree labourers.

The attitude of Kauṭilya in this respect was to strive for the abolition of slavery altogether. Selling of children into slaves, whether Śūdras, Vaiśyas, Kṣattriyas, or Brāhmaṇas, was strictly forbidden. Not only the seller, were he even the father of the child sold, but also those who knew of it or witnessed the purchase of it, were fined. In the case of those who were not blood-relations of the child sold, they were punishable with the highest fine or even death. Thus says Kauṭilya :—

उदरदासवर्जमप्राप्तव्यवहारं आर्यप्राणं शूद्रं विक्रयाधानं नयतस्स्वजनस्य द्वादशपणो दण्डः। वैश्यं द्विगुणः। क्षत्रियं त्रिगुणः। ब्राह्मणं चतुर्गुणः। परजनस्य पूर्वमध्यमोत्तमवधा दण्डाः। क्रेतृश्रोतॄणां च। (See ch on slavery. p. 181).

In regard to slavery, Kauṭilya's attitude stands apart as a glowing light of liberalism and humanity in a barbaric age. While his contemporary Aristotle was justifying slavery as a divine and a beneficient human institution not only sanctioned by nature, but justified by the circumstances of social existence, he denounced it and strove to abolish it characterising it as a custom which could exist only among the savage Mlecchas (म्लेच्छानामदोषः प्रजामाधातुं विक्रेतुं वा). He boldly enunciated that among Āryas [free-born ?] none should be unfree or enslaved (न त्वेवार्यस्य दासभावः). His definition of the Ārya again was not narrow. According to him, the Śūdra was equally an Ārya with members of the higher castes.

In spite of this liberal tendency on the part of the law-giver, slavery had however too deep-rooted an existence to be easily eradicated. Prior to Kautilya, none dared to abolish it. Even the Buddhists did not admit slaves into their Saṅgha. From time immemorial, there were several classes of slaves. *e.g.* (1) men captured in raids and battles. (ध्वजाहृत:) (2) men condemned for heinous offenes, this practice being general in the ancient world. (3) men who sold themselves and their children for want of maintenance. (4) children of men already slaves

Sale of Children Stopped.—To abolish slavery altogether was a very difficult task. So, the first step taken, was to stop the sale of children, which was as we have seen severely penalised. But, as this regulation could not operate against those who bartered their own personal freedom, the government tried to interfere on behalf of their children. These latter were regarded as freemen inspite of their parents selling themselves and thus the number of slaves was restricted. (आत्मविक्रयिण: प्रजामार्यां विद्यात्)

Right of Slaves.—Not satisfied with these measures, the government issued laws, which fostered the abolition of slavery by compulsory manumission. By virtue of these regulations, the following rights were conferred on all slaves, *e.g.* :—

(1) They became entitled to be freed by their masters, on payment of ransom. Any one failing to liberate such a slave, ready to pay ransom, was fined. (दासमनुरूपेण निष्क्रयेन आर्यमकुर्वंतो द्वादशपणो दण्ड:)

(2) The slave or the slave-girl was automatically freed if the master put him or her into base or ignoble work, kept him naked, or violated the slave-girl. (प्रेतविन्मूत्रोच्छिष्टग्राहिणामाहितस्य नग्नस्तापनं दण्डप्रेषणं अतिक्रमणं च स्त्रीणां मूल्यनाशकरम् । etc. p. 182).

(3) A man enslaved for some heinous offence or non-payment of fine was freed, on performing his agreement to pay or serving out his term of imprisonment. (दण्डप्रणीत: कर्मणा दण्डमुपनयेत् । p 183).

(4) A captive in battle was freed by paying half his ransom. (आर्यप्राणो ध्वजाहृत: कर्मकालानुरूपेन मूल्यार्धेन वा विमुच्येत । 183).

(5) In the case of a slave-girl used as a concubine by the master and who had become a mother, she together with her children (and other relations ?) was freed. (स्वामिनस्तस्यां दास्यां जातं समातृकमदासं विद्यात् p. 183.)

(6) The Kauṭlyian regulations conferred some further rights on the slaves, and empowered them to be capable of inheriting property and made their natural relatives their heir. This practically destroyed their character as *Res* and conferred a *persona* on them. They were also empowered to earn without prejudice to the master, or without neglecting his work. These earnings went to them and thus enabled them to buy their freedom.

(आत्माधिगतं स्वामिकर्माविरुद्धं लभेत, पित्र्यं च दायं । मूल्येन चार्यत्वं गच्छेत् । p. 182).

Again, as regards such acquisitions of the slave, these went to his natural heirs and relatives, only the escheat being reserved for the master. (दासद्रव्यस्य ज्ञातयो दायादाः तेषामभावे स्वामी p. 182).

The conferring of all these concessions on the slaves made it possible for them to buy their freedom. The condition of those who yet remained in slavery was ameliorated by the issue of other regulations which punished masters who tryrannised over slaves, put them into dirty work, violated slave-girls or injured their modesty, sent them to foreign lands, sold pregnant slave-girls, or made boys under eight years to do hard work. (*e.g.* धात्रीमाहितिकां वाकामां चाधिगच्छतः पूर्वः साहसदण्डः ; दासमूनाष्टवर्षं विबन्धुमकामं नीचे कर्मणि विदेशे दासीं वा सगर्भामप्रतिविहितगर्भभर्मण्यां विक्रयाधानं नयतः पूर्वः साहसदण्डः etc. Kau. P. 183.)

As a result of all these measurers, slavery was almost stamped out. Even those who remained slaves, enjoyed such privileges that in the eyes of the Greeks they appeared more as free-men than slaves. The Greeks whose social life was based on slavery, denied the existence of slavery in India. For this, they praised the Indians and as such declared their superiority even to the Spartans who kept foreign slaves only.

Labour Conditions—The Arthaśāstra throws a further flood of light on labour conditions in Ancient India, and from it we can glean some more facts regarding the various labouring classes, their position and economic condition. From it we know further that

(*a*) it was an accepted principle that none could be employed in dirty or killing work.

(*b*) children under eight could not be employed in hard work.

(*c*) further, more, labourers enjoyed holidays during which they abstained from work. Those who worked got extra wages and rewards.

(*d*) skiled workmen received rewards and bonuses.

(*e*) Lastly, the state facilitated wage-earning by men and women of poorer families. Widows or poor women of various castes, who did not come out of their houses, too, had chances of earning. They were supplied with materials through maid-servants under the master of the factory. Some of these widows and orphan women came to the factory, took materials and returned them. Cottege industry thus had a place in the economic development of the country. These too were subject to the same regulations as free-labourers or guildmen. (याश्चानिष्कासिन्यः प्रोषितविधवा न्यङ्गा कन्यका वाऽत्मानं बिभ्रयस्ताः स्वदासीभिरनुसार्य सोपग्रहं कर्म कारयितव्याः ।

स्वयमागच्छन्तीनां वा सूत्रशालां प्रत्यूषसि भाण्डवेतनविनिमयं कारयेत्। p. 114)

In addition to the ordinary free labourers or slaves owned by private citizens, there were the royal slaves and enslaved criminals, who were employed by the state in its farms and factories. (see ch. on Sītādhyakṣa) Old prostitutes, too were employed. Probably, the lot of these was harder.

In addition to these, there were some classes of labourers who did not receive wages in cash, but worked in lieu of food, clothing or subsistence. The position of some labouring classes *e.g.* the Ahitakas and the Grāmabhṛtakas is not clearly explained. Probably, their position was intermediate between slaves and freemen. The Grāmabhṛtakas were the servants of the village and their position was not unlike that of the serfs of Europe.

While labourers had their wages fixed and were free from the tyranny of employers, they themselves were liable to keep the terms of their contract. Reciprocity was enforced and non-performance was punished. Strikes and combinations to compel masters to submit to them were probably unknown. If these took place, they seem to have been suppressed.

The state thus seems to have intervened with the double object of enforcing the claims of both parties and it took most stringent measures to prevent classes carrying on war against each other.

We know nothing about the renumeration of these various classes of workmen. But, if we are to look to the rates of pay in the chapter on 'Payments to Servants', the wages of skilled workmen at least seem to have varied from 500 paṇas to 2000 paṇas a year.

XV

JUSTICE AND THE JUDICIARY.

In such a highly developed administrative system, judicial administration had naturally a well-recognised place The government made arrangements for the proper dispensing of justice, appointed judges in important centres, ensured the protection of life and property, as well as the trial and punishment of wrong-doers.

The king was the highest judge in his realm, but he does not seem to have always dispensed justice with his own hands. Of course, in his daily Durbar, he received all complaints of his subjects, and thereby discharged the functions of the highest Court of Appeal. This practice continued even under Mogul Emperors like Jahangir.

For the administration of justice, properly-constituted law-courts were established in important centres like Saṅgrahaṇas, Droṇamukhas, Sthānīyas, and in junctions of provinces. (जनपदसन्धिसङ्ग्रहणद्रोणमुखस्थानीयेषु व्यावहारिकानर्थान् कुर्युः: p. 147.)

There were two sets of courts *e.g.*

(1) Courts presided over by the Dharmasthas, accompanied by the Amātyas

(2) Those presided over by Pradesṭārah or Amātyas only.

In the first set of courts, the Dharmasthas were the real judges, while the Amātyas were probably royal delegates to watch over the procedure. The Dharmasthas represented men of character and well-versed in the secred law, who settled disputes arising out of the violation of traditional customs and principles. They seem to have exclusive jurisdiction over the following eighteen* titles or divisions of Law :—

(1) Disputes regarding non-performance or non-validity of agreements (व्यवहार:)

(2) Law of marriage ; marital status and woman's property, (विवाहधर्म:, स्त्रीधनम्) including the chastisement of women leaving their husbands' protection.

(3) Law of divorce and re-marriage.

(4) Inheritance and division of property among sons and heirs (दायक्रम:, अंशविभाग:) ; law of sonship. (पुत्रविभाग:)

(5) Household or real property. (गृहवास्तुकम्)

(6) Sale of household-property. (वास्तुविक्रय:)

(7) Non-performance of agreements (समयस्यानपाकर्म).

(8) Law of debt. (ऋणादानम्).

(9) Law of deposit and mortgage (औपनिधिकम्).

(10) Law of slavery and servants (दासकल्प:, कर्मकरकल्प:).

---

* Probably, this division of the old law into the eighteen branches was due to the codifiers of the Pre-Kauṭilyan period.

(11) Joint-undertakings (सम्भूयसमुत्थानम्).

(12) Resission of sale (विक्रीतानुशय:).

(13) Sale without ownership (अस्वामिविक्रय:).

(14) Law of violence and crime (साहसम्).

(15) Assult, hurt, or battery (दण्डपारुष्यम्).

(16) Defamation (वाक्पारुष्यम्).

(17) Law of dice-playing.

(18) Miscellaneous (प्रकीर्णकानि).

In these courts, the Dharmasthas probably took the leading and active part. They examined witnesses, cross-examined them, enquired into their character, and the Lekhakas took down the evidence.

The Law of evidence was sufficiently well-developed and tallied substantially in principle with the old Dharmasūtra laws or embodied those principles developed in the older Arthaśāstra schools. As a rule, Brahmins, Śrotiyas, the king, those interested in the suit, low-class criminals (see second half of the chapter on ऋणादानम् p. 175 and 176) were rejected as witnesses. The rest, who appeared to have been of good birth and purity were sworn in and the old procedure of oaths was followed. Their evidence was taken and the evidence of both parties was weighed. Either the opinion of the majority or that of the trustworthy was taken into account to determine the facts of the case.

As regards procedure, we have little of details. As a rule, the judge cross-examined the parties (a principle which lasted till the end of Hindu independence) and the answers were taken down by the Lekhaka. Oaths were taken, but of ordeals we have but the least evidence. Time or postponement was granted and probably representatives or sureties were accepted. In cases of theft or in certain criminal offences, judicial torture was applied to make the suspect confess. (pp. 218—20) But, this was only done when his guilt was almost apparent. [owing to strong circumstantial evidence]. (आप्तदोषं कर्म कारयेत्). But, Kauṭilya's own views were against the application of torture and he exempts women and the weak or aged from torture

Cross-examination was carried on before witnesses and both the parties. As a rule, in criminal cases, no suspect could be apprehended except within three days from the commission of the crime. The suspect or accused was sent to the lock-up (चारक), and in the next day he was brought up for trial. The judge questioned him and enquired of him the following :—

(1) his name, family, caste, profession or occupation,

(2) the work he did or his occupation during the time when the crime was committed,

(3) his friends or accomplices if any, motives, explanations as regards his presence there, and other facts touching the circumstances of the crime.

When his answers tallied with those of reliable witnesses for the defence, he was acquitted. When the guilt was apparent, he was made to confess by judicial torture.

In criminal cases, the presumption of law was to recognize the accused as free from guilt unless it was fully proved. There was no presumption of gullt, unless proved by circumstances. Kauṭilya to his own credit cites the example of Māṇḍavya, as an instance of the miscarriage of justice through too much faith in circumstantial evidence and in confessional due to torture.

Impartial judicial administration was one of the ideals of Kauṭilya. It was the king's duty as the Dharma-pravartaka to uphold justice and to punish the guilty, without consideration of position, kinship or anything. The king in his state was the sole authority who wielded the rod of chastisement, and was the only person who could use violence in checking violence on the part of the individuals. Impartiallty was the first and the foremost consideration, and as Kauṭilya thinks, it not only ennobled the king during this existence but led to a brighter existence after this life. cf.

राज्ञः स्वधर्मः स्वर्गाय प्रजा धर्मेण रक्षितुः ।
अरक्षितुर्वा क्षेप्तुर्वा मिथ्यादण्डमतोऽन्यथा ॥
दण्डो हि केवलो लोकं परं चेमं च रक्षति ।
राज्ञा पुत्रे च शत्रौ च यथादोषं समं धृतः ॥

Next to being impartial, the king was bound to use his discretion and reason. In adjudicating, he was to consider Dharma, Vyavahāra, and Saṃsthā, but in interpreting the laws, he was bound to follow the dictates of reason and equity (or न्याय ।) cf.

अनुशासद्धि धर्मेण व्यवहारेण संस्थया ।
न्यायेन च चतुर्थेन चतुरन्तां महीं जयेत् ॥

In cases where custom was in disagreement with the text of the Dharmaśāstras, or where the Śāstric rule was at variance with practice, he was to uphold the righteous custom by using his reason. Furthermore, in interpreting the Śāstras, the king was to be guided more by the dictates of reason and equity (धर्मन्याय). In such cases of disputed interpretation, the dictates of righteous conscience alone were to be the highest text of the Śruti and the written injunction must be regarded as lost. Cf.

संस्थाया धर्मशास्त्रेण शास्त्रं वा व्यावहारिकम् ।
यस्मिन्नर्थे विरुध्येत धर्मेणार्थं विनिश्चयेत् ॥
शास्त्रं विप्रतिपद्येत धर्मन्यायेन केनचित् ।
न्यायस्तत्र प्रमाणं स्यात् तत्र पाठो हि नश्यति ॥

To maintain the impartial administration of justice, the judges themselves were under a liability not to violate justice by their own misconduct. In such cases, they themselves were punished. Thus, in the chapter on the 'Protection of Departments of Government' (सर्वाधिकरणरक्षणम्), we are told that an offending judge was liable to be tried by a superior court, presided over by the Samāhartā and composed of a number of Pradesṭāraḥ. This court was not unlike the Adminstrative Courts applying the Droit Administratif in France and in some countries of the Continent. The offences which could bring censure or punishment on a judge were the following :—

(1) If the judge was found to have chastised, or rebuked one of the parties without any reason ;

(2) If he put unnecessary questions, without putting those necessary ;

(3) If he gave hints to witnesses, granted undue advantages to either party, gave more time than necessary, or otherwise tampered with the normal course of justice. (p. 222—223) ;

The punishments for such offences varied from fines of the lowest amercement to the highest one. On repeating the same offence, the offender was fined twice the amount or dismissed [transferred ?] from office (पुनरपराधे द्विगुणं, स्थानादव्यपरोपणं च). Similarly, unjust sentence [lower or heavier than that laid down for the offence] being inflicted, judges were punished.

Scribes, too, were liable to be punished if they neglected to put down the evidence correctly or tampered with it intentionally

In criminal cases, men were put in lock-ups during the trial. Here, too, if the officer in charge ill-treated the accused, law inflicted punishment upon the guilty officer. The punishable offences on account of which charges could be preferred against these prison officers were—

(1) The putting of undue pressure on prisoners, by inflicting illegal torture.

(2) Making them suffer hardships in regard to food, clothing or bed.

(3) Rape on female prisoners.

(4) Transferring of prisoners from one prison to another. (compare a similar provision of the Habeas Corpus Act.)

XVI

THE NEW TRIBUNALS.

In addition to these properly constituted courts under the Dharmasthas, there were other tribunals, which arose with the vesting of criminal and administrative jurisdictions in Amātyas and Pradeṣṭāraḥ who presided over the departments of administration. They administred not the old [traditional or] customary laws, but, took cognizance of offences created by regal ordinances. They performed at the same time multifarious duties vested in them by royal prerogative, like the English High Commission court or the court of Star Chamber during the sixteenth and seventeenth centuries. Their duties included the following :—

(1) Regulation of guilds, artisans' wages, and the sale of goods. They punished all who violated the rules and ordinances issued by the government in regard to these matters.

(2) They detected through spies, criminals or those with criminal tendencies, and either caught them red-handed, or apprehended them while making plans. They also held post-mortem examinations and applied judicial torture to make suspects confess.

(3) They tried guilty officials or judges under the government, and suppressed tendencies

towards dishonesty or the taking of illegal gratifications by government servants.

(4) They administered the criminal law and took cognizance of offences under the New Criminal Code with special reference to

(a) offences of violence or outrage for which the punishment of death with or without torture was prescribed ;

(b) offences of Treason and those against the Royal person and family, or the security of the state ;

(c) heinous offences, like breaking of dams, poisoning, incendiarism, theft of arms and weapons, dishonesty in dice-playing, forgery, and certain kinds of theft ;

(d) the law of adultery, forced violation of women not laid down in the old law, rape of various descriptions ;

(e) the crime of Aticāra, which included offences arising out of the violation of of sacred social rules, caste laws, moral conventions or injury to Brāhmaṇas or their immunities.

(5) Took steps to ameliorate the condition of the people in times of fire, flood, famines, pestilence, or depredations caused by wild animals.

Constitution of the Courts—Not only summary procedure and heavy punishment characterised these courts, but, the composition of these Kaṇṭaka-śodhana courts seems to have been different from those presided over by the Dharmasthas. Thus,

(a) The guild-court was presided over by three Amātyas or Pradeṣṭāraḥ.

(b) The court for preserving the purity of officials and the departments of administration was presided over by the Samāhartā and the Pradeṣṭaraḥ. (समाहर्तृप्रदेष्टारः पूर्वमध्यक्षाणामध्यक्षपुरुषाणां च नियमनं कुर्युः)

(c) The other courts were presided over in many cases by the departmental heads. Probably, all the courts especially the criminal courts worked with a summary procedure. The Judges were vested with criminal jurisdiction, and interpreted the laws themselves. In their character, their working and in some of their functions, these may be fabourably compared wtih the High Commission Court or the Court of Star Chamber in Medieval England. (16th and 17th cen.)

The causes of their origin were many. Not to speak of the growth of arbitrary royal power, their creation was justified by the complex social and political needs of the day. Thus, the tendency towords centralisation led to the growth of innumerable departments, and the preservation of the purity of the officials required the creation of courts for trying offending officials. Similarly, the New Criminal Code necessitated the creation of new tribunals, in as much as, their functions could not be entrusted to the old Dharmastha Judges. To these' prerogative tribunals' were entrusted cases of treason, arson, incendiarism, and many other offences, which hardly existed in the older codes, and which in the past were punished only by the dictates of public opinion. Similarly, to repress social laxity due to the monastic upheaval, to punish adultery and to check abuses in sexual relations not contemplated in the old codes, the judges were empowered to try all cases of Kanyāprakarma. Again, to check irreverence to religion, violation of social conventions, violation of caste-laws, or to check prohibited sexual relations, the offences classed under Aticāra or violations were entrusted to them. The courts were thus not merely instances or instruments of Royal tyranny, but, fulfiilled great purposes by suppressing many offences, which were either not recognized by the older codes, or were created by virtue of the changed circumstances.

The nature of the laws administered by the courts and their functions would illustrate these above remarks. As regards the duties of the Guild-Commissioners or the Superintendent of

Sale, we have already said something. To give a clearer idea, we mention the other important tribunals and the sections of offences triable by them.

Court for Sarvadhikarana-raksana :— Offences triable by the Sarvādhikaraṇa-rakṣaṇaṃ included the following :—

(1) sale of goods from Royal mines, farms, commercial godowns or store-houses by government officials, or by outsiders, either by day or by night ;

(2) forgery of royal seals, writs or edicts or those issued by officials, heads of department, or by the king himself ;

(3) misconduct of judges, or their undue favours shown or bestowed on any of the parties ; (p. 222.)

(4) misconduct of court-scribes or Lekhakas, for tampering with records, depositions or court-proceedings ;

(5) misconduct of prison officials in aiding and abetting the escape of prisoners from lock-ups ;

(6) tyranny over prisoners and rape on a female in prison or lock-up ;

(7) the abetment of other people in aiding the escape of prisoners from prisons ;

(8) bribery of government officials.

The Criminal Courts—tried various offences both trivial or of a serious nature, which were punishable with fines, mutilations or death in some cases. The chief offences triable may be classified under the following heads :—

(*a*) **Inhumanity or Irreligion**

(1) murder of or violence to parents, brothers, and preceptors or bodily injury to them ;

(2) violation of the purity of a Brāhmaṇa's kitchen ;

(3) insult or violence to Brāhmaṇas or Gurus ;

(4) impersonation of Śūdras as Brāhmaṇas ;

(5) sale of human flesh (**मानुषमांसविक्रय:**) ;

(6) theft of images of gods, etc. ;

(*b*) **Crimes of Violence**—punishable with mutilations or death with or without torture included :—

(1) pick-poketting and thefts of various descriptions ;

(2) thefts of goods, or animals and of valuable jewels ;

(3) murder doing quarrel ;

(4) causing abortion by beating or by violence ;

(3) trespass into houses with violence ;

(4) breaking of dams or public reservoirs ;

(5) poisoning ;

(6) poisoning of husbands by women ;

(7) incendiarism ;

(8) destruction of the virility of a man or the cutting off of a man's tongue.

(*c*) **Treason and Traitorous Dealings**.

(1) treason of various descriptions, including waging war, incitement of enemies or correspondence with them, or the pollution of the Harem ;

(2) forgery of royal edicts or tampering with their text ;

(3) slander or defamation of the king ;

(4) theft of arms and weapons belonging to the state ;

(5) disclosure of royal secrets.

(*d*) **Kanyaprakarma** :—Offences against women triable in these courts included the following : —

(1) violation of the modesty of minor women of the same caste ;

(2) abduction, and adultery with women, either unmarried or living with their husbands ;

(3) adultery with women of higher and lower castes ;

(4) misconduct of higher caste women with slaves or lower-caste people ;

(5) theft of girls ;

(6) violation of the daughters of harlots ;

(7) outrage on slave-girls ;

(8) abduction of women whose husbands are absent ;

(9) rape on women in distress.

(*e*) **Offences of Aticara** included the following miscellaneous items :—

(1) Forcing a Brahmin to eat forbidden food.

(2) Eating of unclean food by a Brahmin.

(3) Entrance into others' houses at day and at night.

(4) Failure on the part of responsible police officers to prevent theft and loss to people under their jurisdiction.

(5) Injury to houses, by rashly driving carriages.

(6) Injury to individuals or to animals, or by letting loose animals.

(7) Employment of animals to fight each other.

(8) Using cows or sacred animals to draw carts.

(9) Cruelty to animals of various descriptions.

(10) Causing death or injury by rash-driving.

(11) Witch-craft and causing injury thereby.

(12) Holding sexual relation within forbidden degrees or sexual relation with nearer kins-women.

(13) Violation of high-caste women by Śūdras and slaves.

(14) Holding intercourse with women of lowest classes,

(15) Violation of nuns.

(16) Forcible violation of courtesans.

(17) Holding unnatural intercourse with men or women.

(18) Holding sexual intercouse with animals or with images.

(19) Injury to trees or sacred places.

(20) Violence or cruelty to big animals.

Not only were these cases summarily tried, but the offences were taken cognizance of by the officers who seem to have had inquisitional authority. The punishments inflicted were severe. Not to speak of whipping, flogging shaving of the head, branding, fines, banishment and other minor punishments, they included horrible penalties ranging from mutilations to death with horrible tortures, and comprised various forms of cruel death :—*e.g.*

Punishments ; **Mutilations**—these included the following :—

Cutting off of fingers or the right hand, for pickpocketing or theft.

Cutting off of the nose, for theft.

Cutting off of one hand, for false dice-players.

Cutting off of the nose and ears, for abetting in theft and adultery.

Cutting off of one hand and leg, for kicking preceptors or for using royal coaches.

Blinding by poisonous ointments, for Śūdras pretending to be Brahmins or for slander of the king.

Cutting off of one hand or foot, for freeing culprits, forgery or sale of human flesh.

Cutting off of the offending limb of an adulterer.

Cutting off of the tongue, for slandering preceptors, parents, and the king and for defiling a Brahmin's kitchen.

Forms of death with torture included the following :—

Death with torture for murder in a quarrel.

Death by impaling for theft of royal animals.

Death by burning hands and skin for treason.

Death by drowning, for breaking dams or reservoirs, for poisoning or for women who administered poison.

Death by tearing off of the limbs of criminals by bulls, for women who poison or set fire to houses.

Death by burning for incendiarism.

Reduction to slavery was also a punishment inflicted on women or men in cases of adultery or similar serious offences. In addition to these, there were offences for which the culprit was simply put to death without any torture being applied.

The severity of the Criminal law was testified to by the evidence of Greek writers. But, as a rule, it was mitigated in practice by various causes and circumstances. Kauṭilya's reforming spirit led him to lay down fines and ransoms in lieu of mutilations or for the death penalty in ordinary cases, and this brought a considerable income to the royal coffers. Punishments for treason were however never commuted and even the Brahmin was not allowed to enjoy his exemptions. He was put to death by drowning. (ब्राह्मणं तमप: प्रवेशयेत्)

In other offences, the Brahmin was immune from the punishment of death. The sentence on a Brahmin offender of any description was pronounced, but at the same time, his priviledged character was noted and he was branded or imprisoned. Thus, in case of theft, the figure of a dog was branded on his forehead, in murder the figure of a human trunk, in adultery the figure of the *mons veneris* was put down, and in wine-drinking, the mark of a vinter's flag was branded on his fore-head. In some cases, the alternative was to banish him from the kingdom or to confine him in the mines. *

This severity of the Kauṭilyan criminal law

---

*For the immunities of Brāhmaṇas in this respect, see Kau. VI. 2. page 220.

सर्वापराधेष्वपीडनीयो ब्राह्मण:, तस्याभिशस्ताङ्को ललाटे स्याद्व्यवहारपतनाय ।

स्तेये श्वा । मनुष्यवधे कबन्ध: । गुरुतल्पे भगम् । सुरापाने मद्यध्वज: ।

ब्राह्मणं पापकर्माणमुद्घुष्याङ्ककृतव्रणम् ।

कुर्यान्निर्विषयं राजा वासयेदाकरेषु वा ॥

has been noticed by many modern writers, and they have been cited to prove the high-handed and tyrannical form of government. But, admitting all this, we must note that India under the Mauryas was no exception to an almost universal rule in the past. It was not the only country where a drastic criminal code operated and inflicted horrible punishments on the people.

Almost all the civilizations of antiquity or of the Middle ages were distinguished by the severity of their criminal codes. In Persia, in ancient Greece, in ancient Judah, in China and in Babylonia, drastic and inhuman punishments were inflicted. The Roman law of the earliest period was far from humane, and even during the enlighted age of codification under the Christian Emperors, adultery, rape, murder, or burglary continued to be severly punished (see Gibbons' Decline and Fall of Rome. ch. XLIV). Mutilations existed in almost all countries. Everywhere, as in India, the offending limb was made to suffer or was cut off. Mutilations and also death with torture existed in the Code of England, and even when these fell into disfavour, the English Criminal Code remained terribly severe. It inflicted the death penalty for offences, for which, insignificant punishments or nothing such are awarded in our own days. Even up to 1830, when Sir Robert Peel reformed the Criminal Code of England, there were in the Statute-book

200 offences for which the sentence of death could be lawfully inflicted. Thus, even in the Eighteenth and early Nineteenth century, death was the penalty for offences like pick-pocketing to the extent of a few shillings, for a theft of 5*s*. from a shop, for begging in uniform in the case of sailors, for cutting off trees in certain localities, for killing games in certain areas, for forgery, and for various other minor offences. (see in this connection, the history of the Criminal Law Reform, Walpole, History of England Vol. II pp. 132—146).

One more point is to be noticed in connection with these horrible sentences. In India, although the criminal code was terribly severe comparcd with that our modern days, these sentences were hardly executed and were more often commuted by payment of fines. Such indeed is the evidence of the Chinese travellers who visited India during the classical period and lived here for years. Indeed, one of them, Fa-Hian has praised Indians for the absence of Judicial torture, mutilations and excessive capital punishments in their country.

XVII

ERADICATION OF SOCIAL EVILS.

The Kaṇṭka-śodhana Commissioners were also responsible for other duties. As has been already said, their criminal jurisdiction was extensive and ther duties multiferious in as much as they had to detect and suppress crimes. With this object in view, they employed emmissaries, who put on various garbs, *e.g.*, those of Siddhas, or ascetics, bards, buffoons, magcians, astrologers, mad, deaf or dumb men, artisans, craftmen, dancers, actors, hotel-keepers, or brothel-keepers, and thereby mixed freely with all classes of the people, especially the vulgar sections. Gaining their confidence, they detected the bribery of officials in league with them, and aprehended makers of counterfiet coins, poisoners, and criminals of various descriptions.

Some of them pretended to be endowed with higher spiritual powers and gave out their power of enabling people to win over the affections of women by their mantras or amulets, or of enabling thieves and house-breakers to open house-doors at night by the muttering of spells. They freely mixed with these people and caught hold of them in the commission of crimes. The chapter on Siddha-Vyañjanair-mānavakaprakāśanam gives details as to their methods of capturing these criminals. With all their arts and artifices, they also detected youths of criminal tendencies and apprehended them before they entered on a career of crime. Adulterers were also similarly detected and punished.

In cases of murder or sucide, they took hold of the dead body and after examination, ascertained the circumstances of death and tried to find out a clue to the real cause of death Murderers were punished, while in cases of suicide, the dead man's body was exposed on the public thoroughfare. The treatment of the bodies of those who destroyed themselves, were subjected to insults and indignities, and it is curious to note, that in Medieval Europe too, the bodies of men who committed suicide were similary treated. Burial or cremation was denied to them and they were exposed on public thorough-fares, or cross-roads or were thrown into jungles. *In the case of women who committed suicide, their bodies were also similarly treated. cf.

घातयेत् स्त्री वा स्वयमात्मानं पापेन मोहिता ॥
रज्जुना राजमार्गे तां चण्डालेनापकर्षयेत् ।

---

* It is difficult to explain the reasons underlying such treatment to the bodies of suicides. It may be, that the object was to check suicide, which was deseribed as a pious act by some of the heretical teachers. In the case of women, the object was to check laxity or weakness on their part.

न श्मशानविधिस्तेषां न सम्बन्धिक्रियास्तथा ॥
बन्धुस्तेषां तु यः कुर्यात् प्रेतकार्यक्रियाविधिम् ।
तद्गतिं स चरेत्पश्चात् स्वजनाद्वा प्रमुच्यते ॥

(Kau. P. 217).

The Kaṇṭaka-śodhana-commissioners also co-operated in putting down enemies to public health and prosperity, and in adjusting the claims of labour. In matters of public health, while, the town governors enforced cleanliness, or the Sūnādhyakṣa ensured the supply of fresh meat, the Saṃsthādhyakṣa helped the public cause by punishing dishonest tradesmen who adulterated food-stuffs. For the first offence, a fine of 12 paṇas was levied. In subsequent offences, it was enhanced. (धान्यस्नेहक्षारलवणगन्धभैषज्यद्रव्याणां समवर्णोपधाने द्वादशपणो दण्डः P. 204. Kau. IV. ch. 2).

The control of supplies to the market and the regulation of the price of articles have already been described in detail. The purchase price of tradesmen was taken into consideration and the profit being calculated, the market price was laid down leaving a reasonable margin for middlemen or retailers. In the eyes of modern free-traders, these may appear to have been something barbarous or primitive. But, undoubtedly these protected the cause of the ordinary customers and consumers. The necessity of such governmental interventions is becoming apparent every day.

The theorists of our own day are always inclined to bind the hands of the state in matters of taxation, but, they allow the capitalist to exploit or mercilessly run down the ordinary consumer at will. The evils of such practices are however being felt every day, and in the late war, all governments were compelled by circumstances to control the price of articles of consumption and issued laws to that effect. Very recently, the French Government went so far as to entertain seriously the proposal of centralising the traffic in food-stuffs in its own hands and the proposal is still before them.

As stated already, the Kaṇṭaka-śodhana officers were also vested with authority to regulate the claims of labour. Modern governments have recognized the claims of labour, only after centuries of struggle and not till the labouring sections (acquiring strength through associations) were able to have their claims recognized by putting pressure on employers. But, even now, they fail to handle the problem to the benefit of the other sections or to the welfare of the state taken as a whole. Now-a-days, labour unions and associations have been recognized and they satisfy their claims by paralysing industries or causing sabotage and strikes. But, under the Kauṭilyian government, the central authority regulated wages, after considering the claims of labourers and the convenience of the public.

They thus considered the claims of both parties, and instead of allowing a perpetual conflict of social sections tried to adjust the respective claims of classes. The Fascist labour charter issued by Mussolini or the contemplated prohibition of general strikes in England amply illustrate the mentality of European statesmen who are now alive to the dangers of a perpetual labour revolt.

As stated already, there existed in India laws which prevented masters from lowering wages (see IV. ch. 2, p. 204), and the employment of arbitration through experts or Kuśalas. These show how the Arthaśāstra theorists recognized the claims of labour and did not allow themselves merely to be goaded by capitalistic principles. In their eyes, the labouring section was as much important as the capitalistic one.

XVIII

EMERGENCY MEASURES.

Not satisfied with devising means for the good administration of the country in ordinary times, the government held itself ready with emergency measures for the protection of the people from catastrophes due to famines, flood, or pestilence. These were also entrusted to the officers in charge of Kaṇṭaka-śodhana.

Kauṭilya mentions eight extra-ordinary calamities befalling a kingdom, *e.g.*, fire, flood, pestilence, famine, rats and other impediments to agriculture, ferocious animals and demons. In our own days, the terrible nature of such divine visitations is still recognized, though the rationalism of modern times makes men scoff at the existence of demons or other supernatural beings. In those days however, such ideas and beliefs dominated the minds of men and the author of the Arthaśāstra was no exception.* He believed moreover like his contem-

---

*His views are set forth not only in the chapter on the calamities but also in Chapter VII of the IXth book. Thus he says—

दैवादग्निरुदकं व्याधिः प्रमारो विद्रवो दुर्भिक्षमासुरी सृष्टिः इत्यापदः। तासां दैवतब्राह्मणप्रणिपाततः सिद्धिः।

अतिवृष्टिरवृष्टिर्वा सृष्टिर्वा याऽऽसुरी भवेत्।

तस्यामाथर्वणं कर्म सिद्धारम्भाश्च सिद्धयः॥

poraries in the efficacy of prayers, incantations, magical rites and charms, and advocates in more than one place, their application to undo the evils arising from such catastrophes.

For the prevention of out-breaks of fire, Kauṭilya lays down a member of preventive measures. In crowded areas, workers with fire were segregated, the hours of fire-kindling in dry seasons were limited and moreover, men were called upon always to provide themselves with water-pots, ladders and other primitive instruments which could enable them to put down fires. *The Milinda Pañha refers to this as a practice which really existed in the East *i. e.*, in Magadha. (M. P. II. 2. 3-15). The possession of such was made compulsory and those who did not keep these were punished. Similarly, those living on the side of rivers were compelled to provide themselves with boats and rafts. Neighbours were bound to help men in distress on rivers or during fires, and if they failed they were punished. In times of pestilence, doctors and physicians were employed by the state. Mungooses and dogs were let loose to put down rats, and hunters were employed by the king, to put down the depredation of tigers.

†For an understanding of the popular mentality and the beliefs in the days of Kauṭilya, see my paper on 'Religion and Belief in the Arthaśāstra' in the proceedings volume of the second Oriental Conference held in Calcutta.

In addition to these human measures, magical rites and prayers were resorted to in times of distress. Thus, we hear of the worship of Fire, of Śacīnātha, and the river deity Gaṅgā. There were also prayers for rain, the ceremony of Mahākaccha-vardhanaṃ, penances, and other rites by the Siddha-tāpasāḥ. Even the worship of rats, of the spirit of mountains, and of Caityas by men versed in Atharvaṇa rites were performed.

The active measures for relief in times of famine are worthy of our attention. They include almost all those sagacious measures, which modern governments would have recourse to in time of national distress They are the following :—

(1) Distribution of seeds and corn among distressed agriculturists. (राजा बीज-भक्तोपग्रहं कृत्वा अनुग्रहं कुर्यात्)

(2) Distribution of food from the royal stock or doling out of food-stuffs. [to labourers in relief-works ?] (भक्तसं-विभागम्)

(3) Seeking assistance or protection of allies [by asking food supplies or maintaining some of the distressed.] (मित्राणि वा व्यपाश्रयेत)

In connection with such allies, we must bear in mind that Kauṭilya in describing the phsicaly requisites of good kingdoms, describes them as capable of helping others in distress. (परधारणस्वापदि)

(4) Tapping the resources and hoarded stocks of the rich, by commandering them in the public interest or by imposing on them heavy taxes. (कर्शनं वमनं वा कुर्यात्)

(5) Emigration to another land or removal of the population to more prosperous regions. (निष्पन्नसस्यं अन्यविषयं वा सजनपदो यायात्)

(6) Encouragement of agriculture, the introduction of new plants or supplying of food by hunting or fishing. (धान्यशाकफलमूलावापान् सेतुषु कुर्वीत। मृगपशुपक्षिव्यालमत्स्यारम्भान् वा)।

We may compare these with the measures of modern governments and thereby show the greatness of the author of the Arthaśāstra who clearly anticipated all possible measures which could be adopted in more enlightened ages. Agricultural aids, grants and loans are now common in agricultural countries and our present rulers pride upon their Takkavi grants, remissions of taxes and relief works. But, in India they are no innovations and existed more than 2200 years ago.

Emigration is encouraged by all modern states with surplus populations, and this is known to all students of modern British or Continental History. The introduction of easily-grown plants to supply wants of foodstuffs is familiar to modern statesmen, and as an example we may point out the introduction of Indian corn by Sir Robert Peel to ward off the calamities of the Irish Potato Blight of 1843-44.

Karśaṇa and Vamana, ought to draw our attention still further. These scent like high-handed emergency measures, on the part of governments imbued with the duty of preservation of the peoples' life at any cost. Though condemning the tenets of socialism, all modern governments did during the war tap the hoards of the rich in foodstuffs and useful materials. Excessive collection of foodstuffs was regarded as a national crime, as well as the waste of foodstuffs.*

These theories and measures show the greatness of the eminent Arthaśāstra writer. In that remote age, he enjoined upon kings the duty of saving the people (तेभ्यो जनपदं रक्षेत। सर्वत्र चोपहतान् पितेवानुगृह्णीयात्।) and to act towards

*Most of the readers are aware of the conviction of Miss Marie Corelli or of a German princess for keeping a stock of sugar and wasting bread to feed a monkey respectively.

them as if they were the fathers of the people they ruled.*

His sagacity is further exemplified, by his strong injunction to keep a stock of half the grain-collections (*i.e.* paid in kind) in the royal graneries for time of distress.† (ततोऽर्धं रक्षेत् आपदर्थंजानपदानाम्)

* For these, see my paper on the 'Governmental Ideals in Ancient India' read before the second Oriental Conference and published in the Calcutta Review (1923). I have shown the influence of Kauṭilya on Aśoka and his paternal idea of Monarchy.

† For royal granaries for emergency, see the Indian Antiquary 1896 p. 261.

32

XIX

PROVINCIAL AND LOCAL GOVERNMENT.

We pass on next to a consideration of the Kauṭilyian directions as to the carrying on of the administration of the provinces. As is well-known to all students of Indian history, the process of Imperialism gradually enlarged the territorial limits of the Magadhan state and thereby added to the burdens of the government. Under the Śaisunāgas, and Nandas, that Empire had become too extensive to be ruled by one Central Executive body. Consequently, the outlying provinces had to be constituted into separate yet subordinate administrative units under princes of the royal blood or trust-worthy governors.

We have already given some hints as to the machinery for provincial government. Probably, in regard to these, Kauṭilya gives us little of practical details but makes suggestions as to the government of provinces in a growing Empire. This, according to Kauṭilya, comprised in its simplest from the following officials.

(*a*) First of all, there was the Samāhartā who was the highest official in charge of revenue-collection and Police.

(*b*) Under him, were the four Sthānikas in charge of the four janapada-areas into which the state was to be divided.

(*c*) The lowest officials were the numerous Gopas, in charge of five or ten villages.

The Gopas were thus the lowest representatives of state authority in fiscal and police matters in the provinces. They watched the conduct of subjects, directed the activity of spies, kept the most detailed census of occupations, income and expenditure of men, and their stock of wealth in moveables and land. The spies watched the conduct of men, officials and subjects, detected criminal tendencies, and supplied informations to the central authority on all important matters Then, there were the Pradeṣṭāraḥ who were travelling officials with magisterial functions, and these supervised the work of the lowest officials and of the Sthānikas.

Kauṭilya describes all these in general terms and does not give us any specific details of what really existed. We have however reasons for believing that the system of provincial government described by him was a reality and the system bears a close resemblence to that described in the Aśokan edicts. The empire of that monarch was divided into provinces and subdivisions. Probably, the four greater divisions were the vice-royalties with their capitals at Taxila, Ujjain, Tosali and Suvarnagiri under royal princes (Kumāras), Mahāmātras or Ayaputas (Ārya-putras). There were below them the Prādeśikas.

The orders of the central government were communicated to the provincial governors by edicts and royal rescripts of which we have some surviving specimens in those of Aśoka to the rulers of Tosali and Kausāmbī. Their opinion was similarly invited and in the chapter on 'Deliberations' (मन्त्राधिकार:), we hear of the consultation with an absent minister by letter. Later authorities give us details about sending such royal orders to provincials, but, the Arthaśāstra is silent.

The direct control or participation of state officials was also felt in town administration. In towns, there were the Nāgarakas, whose duties were multifarious (समाहर्तृवन्नागरको नगरं चिन्तयेत्) and included the following important items :— *e. g.*

(1) They had to keep the peace of the city, watch over the where-abouts and conduct of new-comers, to take charge of foreigners and to register the names of hotel-keepers or brothel-keepers.

(2) They were also to keep a census of inhabitants, their income and expenditure.

(3) They had to ensure the good sanitary condition of towns, To do this, they punished offenders, who committed nuisance on public thorough-fares, kept dead animals or dead bodies, or otherwise violated the sanitary regulations.

(4) They had also to protect the people from the ravages of fire. Men were segregated, especially those like smiths who had to work with fire. People were also compelled to keep water-pots, axes, ladders and other instruments for quelling fire. (अग्निजीविन एकस्थान् वासयेत् । पादः पञ्चघटीनां कुम्भद्रोणीनिश्रेणी-परशुशूर्पाङ्कुशकचग्रहणीदृतीनामकरणे । Kau. p. 155.)

(5) They had to guard the city and prevent men from moving about at night except in cases of emergency when permission was given.

(6) They kept the drains and waterways in proper order, and made a daily inspection of the same, as well as of the fortifications, walls and passages of the city. (नित्यमुदकस्थानमार्गभूमिच्छन्नपथवप्र-प्राकाररक्षावेक्षणम्)

(7) They had also to take care of foreigners or outsiders in distress or in weak bodily condition.

(8) They also took charge of lost articles.

(नष्टप्रस्मृतापसृतानां च रक्षणम्)

There were other duties of the Nāgaraka. The sounding of trumpets at intervals during night, was done by his officials. The guards of the city had to be kept under control. The Nāgaraka and his officials were also responsible for the loss suffered by merchants or inhabitants.

He was assisted by other officials but we have little details about them. These guarded the city-gates and did various other duties. The officials under the Toll-superintendent or the Controller of Merchandise, examined goods coming to the city, ascertained their quality or price, levied duty and had dishonest tradesmen trying to evade payment, fined.

Many more scattered details about the arrangement or administration of towns may be gathered from the Arthaśāstra. They occur in the chapters on Durga-niveśa or other sections. From these, we can form an idea of the towns and of town-life of these days. The town in those days was a walled-up and well-fortified settlement, with facilities for trade and commerce, and was not only the centre of culture but the home of the rich. The different castes and occupations which were all organised in guilds, occupied different localities. Towns were also the seats of judicial tribunals.

The direct control of the government however did not go beyond these. The guilds and the city-elders retained many powers. In later times, the Nāgaraka's place was taken by the Sarvārtha-cintaka and not long afterwards many towns had autonomous administration under municipalities. These arose either out of the guilds or were established by royal charter. Even, in the Maurya period, we find the city-elders of Taxila taking a prominent part.*

* Further details will be out of place here. An account of town-life written by me appeared in the literary supplement of a prominent periodical. This has been incorporated in a volume in which a picture of social life in the Maurya and Pre-Maurya age has been attempted.

XX

RURAL AUTONOMY

While an effective control was kept on towns, villages were free from the active jurisdiction of royal officials. They were rather autonomous bodies and were administered by local men. Descended from the village-communities of the Vedic period, which were controlled by the Grāmaṇī, they were in the days of Kauṭilya, (as throughout the whole of Hindu period) the self-sufficient molecules, which constituted the body-politic. They were not only self-sufficient units economically, but politically, they were self-governing.

Various causes and circumstances enabled those village communities to retain their existence inspite of the powerful tide of Imperialism. In this respect, they resemble the Russian Mir which survived inspite of the growth of the most powerful autocracy in Russia.

The Kauṭilyan state allowed these communities freedom from central control and as we shall see very soon helped them in their healthy existence. Rather than trying to destroy the spirit of self-government, the advocates of Indian imperialism did everything possible for the continuance of it. Kauṭilya himself, a believer in the efficiency and benefit of a strong centralised monarchy, went so far as to promulgate laws for active co-operation in village-life and penalised irresponsible or shortsighted lack of co-operation on the part of way-ward individuals.

Under such a system, villages continued to exist as self-sufficient little republics, which remained the basis of higher political existence. They survived successive turmoils or changes of fortune, and continued to maintain the prosperity of the people, inspite of the change of dynastics or the rise and fall of empires.

The village was regarded as a co-operative social unit, and its head was the [elected ?] Grāmika. From the evidence of one passage, this man seems to have been vested with minor magisterial authority and was empowered to expel thieves, criminals, adulterers and other undesirable persons.* He was assisted by a number of officials [probably ?] elected by the people, who were probably maintained by grants of land.† Men of the locality, had to follow

---

* ग्रामिकस्य ग्रामादस्तेनपारदारिकं निरस्यतः चतुर्विंशतिपणो दण्डः । Kau. III. 11. p. 172.

† The names of the officials who formed the "Pañca" is given in the commentary of Nīlakaṇṭha on Sabhā. ch V. In that chapter, which is a dialogue between Yudhisṭhira and Nārada, the latter asks the Pāṇḍava whether the "five" were actively ministering to the welfare of the village. According to Nīlakaṇṭha, the five were the Samāhartā, Samvihdātā, Gaṇaka, Lekhaka and Sākṣī.

the Grāmika in his tours of inspection, and if they refused to do that they were fined. Probably, the inhabitants were liable to do this duty by turn. (ग्रामार्थेन ग्रामिकं व्रजन्तं उपवासाः पर्यायेणानुगच्छेयुरननु गच्छन्तः पणार्द्धपणिकं योजनं दद्युः ।)

Many more were the active social duties and functions relating to the village which were entrusted to the village-elders. Thus,

(*a*) these village-elders preserved the property of minors, and of gods. (बालद्रव्यं ग्रामवृद्धा वर्धयेयुराव्यवहारप्रापणात् देवद्रव्यं च । II ch. I P. 48.)

(*b*) they decided boundary-disputes. (क्षेत्रविवादं सामन्तग्रामवृद्धा कुर्युः III 9. p. 169.)

(*c*) they administered the property of gods or those dedicated to the public use. (सेतुरूपपुण्यस्थानचैत्यदेवायतनानि ··· स्वाम्यभावे ग्रामाः पुण्यशीला वा प्रतिकुर्युः ।—Kau. III ch. II P. 171).

Not only were these duties delegated to village-people, but co-operation among them in works of public utility was enforced by law. Even such co-operation in amusement was enforced and we hear of such things even in Prekṣās or Pravahaṇas. (*e.g.* theatrical entertainments or moving pageants).

Village people were thus always compelled to follow the orders of a man who was working for the common good. (प्रेक्षायामनंशदः सस्वजनो न प्रेक्षेत । प्रच्छन्नश्रवणेक्षणे च सर्वहिते च कर्मणि निग्रहेण द्विगुणमंशं दद्यात् । सर्वहितमेकस्य ब्रुवतः कुर्युराज्ञाम् । अकरणे द्वादशपणो दण्डः । etc.) Similarly, co-operation in other public works was enforced namely, in building of temples or holy places, public halls or resting places and the creation of dams. (पुण्यस्थानारामाणां च सम्भूय सेतुबन्धादप्रकामतः कर्मकरबलीवर्दाः कर्म-कुर्युः । व्ययकर्मणि च भागी स्यात् । न चांशं लभेत ।) That these were actually done by villagers, we know from the Jātakas.

In newly settled villages, the prosperity of the community was ensured by establishing village officials or medical men by grants of land. Cultivators were given grants of land, and loans of money and corn. Water-supply was ensured by erecting dams or constructing reservoirs, either by the state or by helping such co-operative undertakings on the part of the villagers.

(Kau. pp. 45—49.)

The village-common was safe-guarded, and encroachment on it was punished. (स्तम्भैः समन्ततो ग्रामाद्धनुश्शतापकृष्टमुपशालं कुर्यात् etc. p. 172). Bulls dedicated to the village-gods were preserved from molestation. Villages were also saved from the activity of exploiters or of heretical sects and congregations.*

Such were the principles which actuated the great author of the Arthaśāstra, and the result was that village-life thrived and the prosperity of the country was ensured in spite of disasters to the central government.

The self-governing village remained a feature of Hindu political lite. Guilds and industrial units too were allowed to remain almost autonomous. In the absence of a central representative body, they ensured the continuance of a popular government and withstood the ills of tyranny or of foreign invasions.

---

* These are laid dawn in Ch. 1 of Book II. As Kauṭilya says,—'वानप्रस्थादन्य: प्रव्रजितभाव: सजातादन्य: सङ्घ: सामुत्थायकादन्य: समयानुबन्धो ना नास्य जनपदमुपनिवेशेत।

Again. नटनर्तनगायनवादकवाग्जीवनकुशीलवा वा न कर्मविघ्नं कुर्युः।

परचक्राटवीग्रस्तं व्याधिदुर्भिक्षपीडितम्।
देशं परिहरेद्राजा (रक्षेत् ?) व्ययक्रीडाश्च वारयेत्॥
दण्डविष्टिकराबाधै: रक्षेदुपहतां कृषिम्।
स्तेनव्यालविषग्राहै: व्याधिभिश्च पशुव्रजान्॥
वल्लभै: कार्मिकैस्तेनैरन्तपालैश्च पीडितम्।
शोधयेत् पशुसङ्घैश्च क्षीयमाणं वणिक्पथम्॥
एवं द्रव्यं द्विपवनं सेतुबन्धमथाकरान्।
रक्षेत पूर्वकृतान राजा नवांश्चाभिप्रवर्तयेत्॥ Kau. p. 49.

XXI

SANITATION AND PUBLIC WORKS

Sanitation also attracted the attention of the goverment. Even in those early days, the state seemes to have made provisions for preserving the health of its subjects. In ordinary times, physicians and medical men were stationed in all centres of life. The chapter on janapada-nivesa contains a reference to medical-officers in villages, and these seem to have been maintained by grants of land enjoyable by them. (गोपस्थानिकानीकस्थचिकित्सकाश्वदमकजङ्घारिकेभ्यश्च विक्रयाधानवर्जम्—Kau. p. 46). In towns, such duties were entrusted to medical men under the Nāgaraka, who was bound to look after the health of citizens and take care of men suffering from diseases or in bad state of heath. (see ch on Nāgaraka. p. 144, also pp. 199). Similar attention seems to have been paid to diseased animals, though we have no details in the Artha-śāstra. Hospitals however do not find mention in the work of Kauṭilya.

While this was the arrangement in ordinary times, vigorous steps were taken to combat out-breaks of pestilence or epidemic. As stated already, medical men were employed and medicines were distributed. (See sec. XVIII. p 245).

For ensuring the good health of the country, great attention was paid to sanitary arrangements as well as to the prevention of adulteration of food-stuffs. Royal officials supervised the cleaning of village-roads or sewers and stringent regulations were promulgated punishing offenders who caused nuisance or injury to public health. In towns, the drains and sewers were regularly examined, while the city-magistrates punished men who committed nuisance on thoroughfares, kept refuse matters in house-fronts, deposited carcases of animals on public roads, or cremated the dead in inhabited quarters. (For details, see chapter on Nāgaraka)

As stated already, (see. section on commerce p. 197) food-adulteration was severely punished. The sale of meat as well as of cooked food was also carefully supervised and this work of supervision was entrusted to the Sūnādhyakṣa. The appointment of this special officer was due to the fact that meat-eating was then in great vogue in ancient India. The sale of bad meat, adulterated meat or the meat of diseased or dead animals was severely punished.

The public works department was also very active in the interest of the public. The creation of dams and water reservoirs, the making and repair of roads and the erection of public buildings were in their hands. This has already been noticed, but we find no more details till we come to the days of Aśoka whose edicts mention the construction of roads, serais, hospitals for men and animals and other useful public works. The existence of an extensive canal system has been noticed by the Greeks, who also mention the existence of a great trank road from Pāṭaliputra to the extreme west, with posts denoting the distance at intervals. The Arthaśāstra gives us little details in regard to these, but, seems to entrust these duties to the Sannidhātā.*

*This last officer was also entrusted with the duty of making weather-observations, which according to the evidence of two chapters, seem to have been regularly taken. The chapter on the Sannidhātā mentions the measurement of rainfall (कोष्ठागारे वर्षमानरत्निमुखं कुण्डं स्थापयेत्), while the chapter on the Sītādhyakṣa refers to the classification of lands according to the average annual rainfall. Astronomical observations also seem to have been made for agricultural or religious purposes.

XXII

SOCIAL SERVICE AND POOR RELIEF.

Following the time-honoured traditions of the past, the government looked upon the lives of the people as sacred, and did its best to ensure their preservation and maintenance. It was the king's duty to preserve the life of all without means, and as such all without means of livelihood became charges of the king. As stated already, the king had to feed the weak and indigent, the widow without children and orphans without any one to look after them. As *parens patriae*, the king took charge of the property of minors or widows and this duty was often delegated to village-elders.

As in England during the Middle ages, poor relief was entrusted to the king and entailed considerable expenditure. This was already recognized by the lawgivers of the Dharma-sūtras and in some of these works, we find repeated injunctions for the establishment of alms-houses and infirmaries. The Jātaka evidence points to the existence of these institutions.

The Kauṭilyan government recognized this, but it refused to be encumbered with the maintenance of women or children left destitute by men who had fallen victims to the monastic propaganda, or who out of laziness refused to work for their own living. The government believed in social coopration and enforced social duties on its subjects. Any dereliction of such duties was penalised. As such, punishments were inflicted on men forsaking wife and children, on husbands refusing to maintain wives or on brothers with means, refusing to take care of minor brothers and sisters. (अपत्यदारं मातापितरौ भ्रातॄनप्राप्तव्यवहारान् भगिनीः कन्या विधवाश्चाबिभ्रतः शक्तिमतो द्वादशपणो दण्डः। अन्यत्र पतितेभ्यः अन्यत्र मातुः। p. 48).

With the same object in view, it checked the monastic propaganda. Men were allowed to take to orders, only when they were too old to procreate, or when they had made full arrangements for the maintenance of their family. On the contrary, men who left wife and children to join any of the medicant orders, were punished. It was also penalised to persuade or seduce women to join orders. (लुप्तव्यवायः प्रव्रजेदापृच्छ्य धर्मस्थान्। अन्यथा नियम्येत। पुत्रदारमप्रतिविधाय प्रव्रजतः पूर्वः साहस दण्डः। स्त्रियं च प्रव्राजयतः। Kau. p. 48) Not only was such mendicancy made penal, but effective steps were taken to prevent indiscriminate mendicancy* Men or women, suspected of having

---

* It may be unpalatable to many, but the evils of this monastic propaganda can hardly be minimised. The pessimistic teachings of that gloomy age made men forget their social duties and in many cases obliterated the natural social

recently joined any of the orders, were apprehended by the police or by the officers of the Nāvadhyakṣa at the ferries (See ch. on Nāvadhyakṣa) Members of the non-brahmanical monastic orders were also excluded from villages and were not allowed to have Saṅghas or Ārāmas in villages. (वानप्रस्थादन्य: प्रव्रजितभाव: सजातादन्य: सङ्घ: सामुत्थायकादन्य: समयानुबन्धो वा नास्य जनपदमुपनिवेशेत। न च तत्रारामविहारार्था: शाला: स्यु:। Kau. p. 48).

More stringent measures were taken against beggars. Like the old English practice of meting out flogging or hard labour to the able-bodied beggar, tramp and vagabond, beggars were punished with beating by means of iron-rods

---

instincts of men and women. Under the influence of the teaching, that the world is a place of sorrow, husbands left their wives, wives forsook their lords and refused the overtures of love or affection. Social abuses also crept in and morals were jeopardised. Domestic ties were often broken and women or children were made homeless. The Therigāthā gives us instances of all these. We find instances of women refusing to marry or rear children, or of being repeatedly left destitute owing to the desertion of successive husbands. Of shocking social abuses, we have the revolting story of a man's marriage with his own daughter. Both had left their home, the father forsaking the child in its infancy. Both had joined the Saṅgha. After a time, their aversion to life passed away and without knowing each other they cast glances of love on each other and retuned home in a condition of ncestuous union.

(भिक्षुकानामयःशूलेन यावतः पणानभिदेयुः तावन्तः शिफा-प्रहारा दण्डाः p. 202).*

---

* In England, Poor Relief came to be recognized as a function of the government, owing to the teachings of the Church. But gradually, the number of beggars became so great, that, by the time of Edward III, steps had to be taken against vagabond mendicity. For some time (Richard II), the issue of licenses to the really needy was resorted to, but, as this was of no avail, penal laws were passed against 'valiant and sturdy' beggars inflicting punishments ranging from whipping to hanging. Indiscriminate almsgivers were also punished with fines ten times the amount paid. (See Eng. Cons. History by Tasswell Langmead. pp. 383-385). The law of Holland was equally severe.

XXIII

PRESERVATION OF SOCIAL ORDER ; RELIGION.

Neither Kauṭilya nor the other theorists of the Arthaśāstra school seems to have advocated regal interference in religious matters. Such a thing was opposed to Indian sentiment and tradition, and there was hardly any scope for interference on the part of the king. However priest-ridden or subjected to successive spiritual upheavals, India had been in the past, she never came under the influence of the dogma that the state has a spiritual character in addition to the political one. Owing to the absence of such teachings, regal interferences in matters spiritual never took place in India, as in the countries of western Asia or Europe which were dominated by the intolerent teachings of semitic religions.

In spite of this, there were decided attempts at such interferences during the Maurya period and this can hardly be denied. Of course, we have no evidence to prove, that, as in the west, any Indian king ventured to lay down the creed of his subjects, or to persecute those who differed in their tenets from those laid down by the state. But, we have evidence that indirectly, the king could meddle in the affairs of people, so far as they related to some aspects of social or religious life. Such an interference was made possible by the circumstances peculiar to the age and was probably forced on kings by the active propaganda of some of the sects who tried to undermine or subvert the social order which existed in those days.

According to the accepted Indian theory, the Hindu king was vested with the duty of maintaining the social order and of protecting all in the performance of their religious rites. As the majority of Indians in those days believed in the religion and teachings of the Vedas, it was the primary duty of the king to see that the votaries of the orthodox religion were not molested in the profession of their faith nor hindered in the performance of its rites. Probably, the activity of the heretical orders made the king alive to the consequences of such propaganda and he had to interfere on behalf of the orthodox section following the traditional teachings. That this was done in the Maurya age, there is no denying. The Arthaśāstra furnishes clear evidence to this. And, we find in it, the following measures aimed against heretical orders. *e.g.*

(*a*) members of heretic sects were not allowed to organise Saṅghas in newly-settled villages (Kau. p. 48. see previous section). They were not allowed to live in towns (new ?) and were compelled to live near the cremation-ground.*

(*b*) as already stated, indiscriminate mendicancy was checked and penalised, especially the enticement of women to join the orders. †

(*c*) Wanderers belonging to heretical sects were not allowed to enjoy the alms and profits arising out of ceremonies like Śrāddhas and to feed such men (Vrsata-pravrajitān—Sākya-jivakādin) was penalised ‡ (sec. pp. 199 on Prakīrṇaka).

Furthermore, the government seems to have proceeded to maintain and safe-guard the social privileges of the Brāhmaṇa. As stated already, insults to him or bodily violence were severely punished. Any one forcing him to eat unclean food was punished. Any one defiling his kitchen was penalised. Moreover, if śūdras pretended to be brahmins, they were made to suffer punishment and torture.§

---

* सामुत्थायकादन्यः सङ्घः नास्य जनपदमुपनिवेशेत ।

† अपत्यदारं अप्रतिविधाय प्रव्रजतः पूर्वः साहसदण्डः । स्त्रियं च प्रव्राजयतः ।

‡ शाक्याजीवकादीन् वृषलप्रव्रजितान् देवपितृकार्येषु भोजयतः शत्यो दण्डः । (p. 199. ch. on Praktrṇaka.)

§ शूद्रो येनाङ्गेन ब्राह्मणमभिहन्यात् तदस्य छेदयेत् । p. 195 ; ब्राह्मणं अपेय-

The existing social order was enforced. The purity of blood of the higher castes was maintained and *mesalliances* of the nature of pratiloma sexual union whether voluntary or not was severaly punished In doing this, the old tradition was merely continued and there was no innovation (Āpastamba denounces such pratiloma unions ; see his chapter on marriage.)*

At the same time, a new official the Devatā·dhyakṣa was appointed [by the early Mauryas ?] and probably, he had charge of sacred places and temples. No more details about his functions are known except that in times of financial stress, he played upon the fears and superstitions of the people and made them pay in the name of gods and these filled the royal coffers (Kau. p. 244. ch. on Koṣābhisaṃharaṇaṃ).

मभोज्यं वा संग्रासयत: उत्तमो दण्ड: ; शूद्रस्य ब्राह्मणवादिन: योगाञ्जनेनान्धत्वं अष्टशतो वा दण्ड: (p. 225) ; ब्राह्मणमहानसावलेहिनश्च जिह्वां उत्पाटयेत्, pp. 228.

* ब्राह्मण्यां शूद्र: कटाग्निना दह्येत, राजभार्यागमने कुम्भीपात: । सकामाया: दासपरिचारकभुक्ताया: वध: । स्वयं प्रकृता राजदास्यं गच्छेत् ।
These laws shocking and severe as thay are, are perhaps as horrible as the lynching of Negores in America.

XXIV

ON THE KAUTILYIAN CIVIL LAW.

Before we conclnde this account of public administration, we must say something on the ordinary civil law as it appears in the Arthaśāstra. Next to the Dharmasūtras, the work of Kauṭilya comprises the earliest codification which has come down to us. Whether owing to subsequent development or due to their modification in the hands of Arthaśāstra writers, the Kauṭilyian laws form an important chapter in the history of Hindu jurisprudence.

The Arthaśāstra chapters on Dharmasthīya show the evolution of legal schools with their juristical expounders who discuss important principles relating to inheritence, woman's property, the laws of divorce and remarriage and the other important topics of civil law, which we have already mentioned in previous sections. The importance of these laws consists in proving that the early legal system of India was marked by a spirit of rationalism, and this was probably due to the interference of the king who accepting the equitable principles advocated by the jurists of the day, modified thereby the laws to suit the requirements of society and went so far as to suppress unreasonable customs or repealed them. As such, the laws had a just consideration of the rights of women and of children born in a family. Many of the Kauṭilyian laws show clearly, that, as yet reactionary movements had not influenced society, and we hardly find any trace of the later maxims which vest absolute rights in fathers or deny real property to women. Division of property was on a rational basis and distribution tended on lines of equality since society expected provisions for all [not excluding varieties of illegitimate children], and in this the king cast his influence. The daughter's claims to mother's property was recognized and divorce or the re-marriage of young widows was not looked with disfavour.

Local custom, if reasonable, received recognition in all matters and in points of dispute equitable principles were applied. The law of real property had developed and the principle of pre-emption was recognized in many cases. Torts arising out of injury caused by neighbours were recognized subjects of dispute. The principle of co-operation in village life was recognized and enforced by the government as pointed out in a previous section. Usury was regulated by the government and excessive interest checked. In the law of debt, we find the mutual liability of the husband or wife laid down. Again, in the same connection, we find the liability of heirs defined and the circumstances of the liability of the husband for wife's debts laid down. The laws of ownership by prescriptive right, of Associations and Corporations, as well as that of joint-enterprise were developed with changing circumstances, and these being recognised by the king, equitable maxims were applied in interpreting them. The law of slavery as well as that relating to the work and wages of labourers was a sound one, and the chapters relating to them are bound to remain glorious landmarks in Hindu legal history. The traditional laws relating to defamation, adultery, violence, robbery, injury or assult, seem to have been but little advanced, and probably, these were being supplanted by the regal laws which we have already discussed. The definition of Sāhasa is however interesting, while in connection with Vākpāruṣya, the laws indicate the growing empire, the rulers of which penalised the ridicule of provincials like men of Prārjunaka and Gāndhāra. The chapter on Daṇḍapāruṣya shows the evolution of penal laws against Śūdras injuring or insulting Brāhmaṇas and gives us the important Kauṭilyian maxim of criminal law, that the offender cannot go without punishment (नास्त्यपकारिणो मोक्षः). The same chapter gives us an insight to the humane ideals of the day which penalised injury or violence to animals and even to trees. The law of dice-play or miscellaneous offences contain nothing more important.

The laws of evidence and procedure were being developed gradually. The progress was on the lines which we find in the Dhamasūtras and practically the same procedure was followed in taking evidence, or swearing in witnesses or for determining their veracity. As yet, however, there was no use of ordeals.*

---

* In regard to these laws, some of the items mentioned above require explanation, although it will be rather out of place to enter into a detailed discussion about the various branches or the maxims underlying them. The Arthaśāstra-laws regarding inheritance, marriage, woman's property and other allied topics, though they are more important to the student of Hindu Jurisprudence, are hardly less so to the historian, in as much as they unfold to us the prevailing social ideas and the aims of the government in regard to them. As such, they show a liberal spirit or a tendency to equitable adjustment of rival claims, which a later reaction blunted and nullified.

As instances of such, we find Kauṭilya advocating an equal division of property by a father among his children (see p. 161), and making compensatory provisions for minors and unmarried daughters. The daughters' right to inherit property, both real and personal is also vindicated (see p. 160), while their preference in regard to their mothers' strīdhana is clearly recognized (see p. 162). In regard to the remarriage of women, Kauṭilya is very sympathetic and lays down the maxim, *e.g*, तीर्थोंपरोधो हि स्त्रीणां धर्मवधः. In matters of divorce, he carries on the older tradition and mentions the conditions of nullification of marriages in the four oridinary forms which are distinguished from the Dharma-vivāhas in which there was no legal separation at all. In regard to strīdhana, he carefully safeguards woman's rights, though exceptions are made in cases of treason. As regards the transfer of house-property, he recognizes the pre-emption of kinsmen or neighbours (pp. 168). In the law of debt, the liability of sons and heirs are defined, while the creditors' right of imprisoning the debtor is mitigated in some cases (p. 175). In the laws relating to contract or joint-enterprise, reasonable maxims are discernible, while in matters relating to labour or wages, one is bound to mark the spirit of enlightenment. As to the influence of these Kauṭilyian laws on later law-givers, I have discussed the topic in connection with my compilation of the laws of Kātyāyana, published by the Calcutta University.

In course of time, however, the reactionary movement became stronger and the Arthaśāstra laws were at a discount, as is proved by the statement in Yāgñavalkya smṛti to that effect.

BOOK V.

RETROSPECT AND CRITICISM

I

CHARACTER OF THE ADMINISTRATION

Any one who has studied in detail the administrative system of the Arthaśāstra, can not but fail to mark the wide scope of governmental authority, the extreme policy of interference in the various aspects of life and the almost paternal care which, the government bestowed on its subjects. Unlike most of the states of Europe in the eighteenth or the early nineteenth century, the functions of the governing authority were not merely reduced to those of police and protection from high-handedness. The comprehensive code of laws with stringent sanction, the vast array of officials and the almost unlimited resources of the crown, were all employed in the furtherance of a great goal in view, namely, the realisation of the prosperity of the diverse classes and sections of people and consequently of the country as a whole. The co-operation of all sections was a primary desideratum and their energies were directed by the central adminstrative body which adjusted their shares of profits and thereby made their efforts directed towards the fruition of the great ideal.

The government was not satisfied with the exercise of a mere political authority, but openy participated in the national activity to further material progress. To ensure the common good, which was based on an identification of the interests of the ruler and the ruled, the Central Authority appropriated many of the natural sources of wealth and added to its margin of resources by exploiting such sources of income, whether natural or derivable from nature through the agency of human labour. These gave rise to monopolies in certain resources, which in addition to the produce of crown lands or royal manufactories, swelled the revenue derivable from land-tax and the customary dues of the crown.

This vast income was spent not for the luxury of the king but mainly to the benefit of the people, and we find all sections of the people, all industries and all occupations cared for. The chief duties of the Government fall into the two following heads *e.g.* :—

(1) Maintenance of the social order and the protection of life and property

(2) Active help to all classes and sections for the realisation of their material aims of life.

The measures for the preservation of peace or the defence of the country hardly require any detailed discussion and we pass on to the active duties of the king. In some previous section (see pp 107-8) we have already summed up the duties of the king as conceived by the author of the Arthaśāstra. Of these however some items require amplification with a view to prove the extent of active help which the community expected and received from the head of the body-politic.

As we have said, the king was bound to protect his subjects. Pālana was his highest duty and as such, he stood to his subjects in the relation of a natural guardian and saviour irrespective of caste and creed. As the *parens patriae* of his subjects, naturally the maintenance of the sick, aged, indigent, and the orphan, came under his actives protection (**वालवृद्धव्याधितव्यसनानाथांश्च राजा विभृयात्** Bk. II. ch. 1). Women without children and those with infants were maintained by him (**स्त्रियमप्रजातां प्रजातायाश्च पुत्रान्** Bk. II. ch. I). Similarly, the property of orphans came under the jurisdiction of the king. (though its active management was often left in the hands of the village-elders. *e.g.* **वालद्रव्यं वर्धयेयुराव्यवहारप्रापणात् ग्रामवृद्धा:** P. 48.) Pensions to the servants of the state and the maintenance of their widows and orphans, have already been mentioned. The extraordinary measures in times of emergencies like famine and floods have already been detailed and these show the fatherly care bestowed by the king.

This was not all. The king was not only to save the life of his people in distress, but to contribute actively to the promotion of the industries and arts, which were the foundations of life. His activities led to the furtherance of social solidarity. We have dealt with these in their proper places, yet we give a summary of all such measures for the convenience of the readers, though this involves a repetition distasteful to many.

First of all, agriculture and the section of population engaged in it attracted the attention of the king. Royal bounty was lavished on agriculture and the agriculturist class. As laid down in the chapter on Janapada-nivesa, poor agriculturists were given land from the crown domains, seed corn was advanced to them, they were exempted from taxation for certain periods and in times of distress, they were maintained with paternal care (अनुग्रहपरिहारौ चेभ्यः कोशवृद्धिकरौ दद्यात्। निवेशसमकालं यथागतकं वा परिहारं दद्यात्। निवृत्तपरिहारान् पितेवानुगृह्णीयात्। Kau. p. 47.) Furthermore, the king did much to help agriculturists by giving irrigational facilities. (सहोदकमाहार्योदकं वा सेतुं बन्धयेत्) In some cases, the state subsidised the erection of dams or reservoirs by the co-operation of villagers, and in such cases, the people got help from the king and were exempted from taxation for a term of years. (Bk. III. ch. 9. p. 170.—तटाकसेतुबन्धानां नवप्रवर्तने पाञ्चवर्षिकः परिहारः—भग्नोत्सृष्टानां चातुर्वर्षिकः etc.)

The highly developed irrigational works, and their preservation and superintendence is testified to by the Greek writers.

In addition to these, they enjoyed other facilities which saved them from other troubles. Laws protected husbandmen from being arrested for debt during harvest. (अग्राह्या कर्मकालेषु कर्षकाः III. 4. p. 175). Moreover, if evicted by owners of their land after five years' enjoyment, they received compensation for the improvements done by them. (अनादेयमकृषतोऽन्यः पञ्चवर्षाण्युपभुज्य प्रयास-निष्क्रयेण दद्यात् p. 171.)

In the interest of cattle-rearing, which was then an important occupation of the poorer classes, the pastures were maintained intact by the promulgation of royal laws. The government farms supplied models, and bulls and horses belonging to the king were lent to the people for crossing purposes. (पौरजानपदस्यार्थेन वृषा वड़वास्वायोज्याः II. 30). At the same time, a series of laws prevented cruel sports like bull-fighting or the slaughter of the kine (यूथवृषं वृषेणावपातयतः पूर्वः साहसदण्डः… ; also वत्सो वृषो धेनुश्चैषामवध्याः ch. on Sūnādhyakṣa). Castration was discouraged and the killing of the female or the calf of all cattle forbidden. (योनिबालवधं पुंस्त्वोपघातं च प्रतिषेधयेत्) The slaughter of all animals for flesh was prohibited for 15 days during Cāturmāsya, and for four days on the occasion of the full moon. (चातुर्मास्येष्वर्धमासिकमघातं पौर्णमासीषु चातुरात्रिकम् Bk. XIV, I.) These laws were clearly the forerunners of those which Aśoka promulgated in the interests of the brute creation after his conversion to the pacific teachings of Buddhism.

To further the interest of traders, encouragement and bounties were made to them. Foreign merchants were invited and privileges were granted to them. Markets for the sale of indigenous products were found out. But, at the same time, the trading community was prevented from exploiting the consumers by the undue raising of prices.

Crafts-men and artisans had their work and wages regulated and their interests safeguarded. These have been described already. The interests of the labouring classes both free and unfree were safe-guarded. There were laws, as pointed out already, preventing rich people to lower wages. Artisans were thus free to enter into contracts as regards wages and work and in cases of dispute, commissioners and experts settled them.

Lastly, the cause of education was encouraged. Grants and pensions were made to those learned in the sacred lore, (आचार्या विद्यावन्तश्च पूजावेतनानि लभेरन्). as well as to the expounders of useful sciences and skilled craftsmen. (शिल्पवन्त: etc. Bk. II. ch. III.)

In addition to active help, the Śrotriyas enjoyed their time-honoured privileges, both legal and fiscal. They enjoyed freedom from punishments like death or other corporeal sufferings. They could not be made witnesses and their property had no prescription. Properties of Śrotriyas dying without heirs passed to their relations and not to the king.

Moreover, poorer yet useful sections like them had freedom from taxation. Toll or duty was not leved on goods brought for sacrifices or sacraments. Ferry-dues were not exacted from them, while they enjoyed the free use of salt from the royal stock.

It would appear from the above, that, more attentian was paid to the advancement of the material basis of existence than to mere preservation of social order. No important art or industry was excepted from the paternal care of the government and none of the diverse social sections could complain of want of protection or encouragement. The laws maintained the respective privileges of all and saved them from the tyranny of more powerful sections. Clearly, the business of the Government was to look to the welfare of the whole social group, rather than to that of favoured sections. As such, the government favoured neither the priest-hood nor the capitalist nor was overawed by the pretensions of the labouring sections but, did its best for all. Of course, equality of opportunity was not an accepted principle in those days, but, the government did not hesitate to offer rational or equitable opportunities to the diverse sections on whose co-operation, public welfare depended. There was, indeed, much that is liable to criticism by a modern advocate of equality, but we must bear in mind, that, with the peculiar ideas and beliefs dominating the minds of men in those days, "equality never became a political necessity" with Indian thinkers.

Social happiness was the supreme ideal. With that end in view, the governmental measures were applied to eliminate sectional tyranny or the loss of economic opportunity. Diversities and inequalities were allowed to subsist and attempt was never made to level distinctions or differences. In the midst of these, ample room was found for cooperation and progress. With a composite social structure, with all its cultural or occupational differences not easily to be obliterated, this was all they could look to and strove for.

The concentration of power was remarkable and it appears the greater when we look to the emergency authority claimed by the government. Yet, it was amply compensated by the intensive social service and the enormous benefits conferred by the state on the community enjoying its protection.

Recently, some Indian writers have attempted to describe this system as State Socialism, which is supposed to be an ideal existence in which the state is to control the instruments of production and is to be vested with the task of equal distribution. Whether such a system will ever be practicable, still remains an open question and our modern thinkers with the exception of the extreme champions of socialism, are not as yet unanimous as to whether it would be feasible to eliminate individual effort and supplant it by the activity of the state. In spite of this, however there have been experiments in the nationalisation of certain industries, and the claims of all to equal opportunities have been recognized.

In the system described in the Arthaśāstra, we find the operation of some principles advocated by modern socialists, namely, the recognition of sanctity of the lives of subjects and the claim to rational opportunity on the part of all. Moreover, some of the greater sources of natural wealth were undoubtedly controlled by the king. But, with all this, there was hardly any recognition of equality or any deliberate attempt to kill private enterprise. The existence of monopolies, moreover, hardly prove, a socialistic structure organisation, or purpose, since, such things exist even in many primitive or despotic systems.

Moreover, in the Arthaśāstra, the state is not a *res publica* but, is masked by the omnipotence of the king.

In our opinion, it would be injudicious to apply any such name borrowed from modern western terminology. All that we can do is to describe the Arthaśāstra government as a peculiar lype of administrative paternallism which regulated the relation of classes and spent its resources for the welfare of the community. Western analogies hardly hold good and fail to designate the system, in which peculiar Indian ideas predominated.

Note. Before we pass on to other topics, we ought to discuss a point about which doubts have been raised by many scholars, namely, whether the system described in the Arthaśāstra was merely a philosopher's ideal or was something which existed in reality. In answering this, we must be rather cautions and well-guarded, since, we have no realistic account of the Maurya administration except that which we find from the Greeks. Yet, from the meagre evidences furnished by the latter and by our literature, we may hold the conclusion that the system of the Arthaśāstra was subastantially in existence. From the Greeks, we know that the Boards of Pāṭaliputra regulated the work and wages of artisans, issued weights and measures, took charge of foreigners and looked to the sanitation of the city. The system of roads and canals is confirmed by the same foreigners. The control of the market is also proved by their testimony. The existence of the Adhyakṣas of factories, is proved by the evidence of the Vātsyāyana Kāmasūtra (ch. on Pāradārika). The activity of the Devatādhyakṣa may be presumed from Patañjali who speaks of the earning of money by the Mauryas by selling images. Fire-regulations compelling citizens to keep waterpots, ladders and other implements for extinguishing fire, are confirmed by the evidence of the Milinda Pañha, while the activity of spies is detailed by innumerable Indian writers. In fact, one of the commentators quotes a large passage from the present Kauṭilīya. (see com. on ślokas on espionage. VII. Manu). Other confirmations come from the evidence of Daṇḍi or that of the later Smṛti works. This point will be discussed in detail in an appendix to the next volume.

II

GRADUAL EVOLUTION OF THE SYSTEM

The administrative system thus described in the Arthaśāstra, with its policy of extreme interference and protection of classes and industries, was not the work of a single day or of a single genius. As I have attempted to show else-where,* it owed its development to a long course of gradual social and political evolution. Its germs lay in the social and political concepts of the Vedic period. In that early period, the state was conceived as being more social than political, and the duties which the community expected from the head of the state comprised not only those of protection and police, but also of active furtherance of the material foundations of human existence.† As stated already (p. 53), this is apparent from the Coronation Hymn in the Vājasaneyī Samhitā, which reminded the king of his duty to maintain social order and of preserving life by encouraging agriculture and by finding sustenance for the people.

---

* See my Economic Life and Progress in Ancient India, Vol. I. 278—284.

† It was pointed out earlier, by Mr K. P. Jayaswal M. A. Bar.-at-Law, in the Modern Review (1913).

There the king is addressed as follows :--

इयं ते राट् । यन्तासि यमनो ध्रुवोऽसि धरुणः ।
कृष्यै त्वा । क्षेमाय त्वा । रय्यै त्वा पोषाय त्वा ।

Vāj. Sam. IX 22.

These remained no mere ideals, but seem to have been actually translated into practice, as would appear from the praise of a Kauravya, uttered in honour of king Parīkṣit (A. V. XX. 127). Similar stories are common in the Brāhmaṇas and the Upaniṣads. In the Chāndogya Upaniṣad, (IVth prapāṭhaka, part I. 1). a king, Jānaśruti Pautrāyana, is described as a giver and a feeder of his people, in as much as, he had established poor-houses throughout the realm. One of the Dharmasūtra-writers, Āpastamba, reminds kings of the duty of establishing poor-houses and resting-houses, with directions as to their construction. Other Dharmasūtra writers are unanimous in enjoining upon kings the duty of maintaining the poor, the aged, the infirm, the widow and the orphan and in exempting Śrotriyas, minors and females from taxation (see Vaśiṣṭha XIX. 35 ; Gau. X 9-12). That these were translated into practice, appears from the evidence of the Jātakas, where we find kings taking the keenest possible interest in the material progress of their subjects, and doing their best to save them in times of distress.

While these were the active duties of kings

society called upon them to step in and take proper measures in order to prevent the exploitation of one section of the people by another. The laws against excessive usury or raising of prices in the Dharmasūtras show clearly that society expected such regulations on the part of the king.

On similar grounds, royal intervention was expected by the people in various other matters. The dishonest tradesman's cornering or undue raising of prices led to royal intervention. The Agghakāraka of the Jātakas, is clearly the first step in that direction and clearly he is the forerunner of the Paṇyādhyakṣa, the Saṃsthādhyakṣa or other officials of the Arthaśāstra who regulated the supplies of markets, prices and profits.

The necessity for labour regulations came from the conflict of capitalists and labourers. While the former tried to reduce the profits of the latter, the latter seem to have raised their demands higher, and this clearly contributed to the interference of the state with a view to the convenience of the community. Society seems to have devoted its attention to the adjustment of the relative shares of the employer and the labourer, and this is proved by the passage of the Mahābhārata which has already been cited in this book. (see p. 208.)

While interference was growing every day, the resources at the king's disposal were augmented by various causes and circumstances. Already, towards the close of the period, the picture of which we have in the Jātakas and the Dharmasūtras, the king's revenue came to comprise incomes from various sources. Primarily, a share of the produce of fields went to him, in lieu of his protection. In the Jātakas, we find the Droṇamāpaka exacting this in the name of the king. According to Vaśiṣṭha, it was 1/6, but according to Gautama it varied from 1/10 to 1/6 (see Va. I, Āpas. II. 10. Gau.—X. 24). The king came to enjoy also a tax on cattle and gold amounting to 1/50 of the value of the stock. (Ch. 67 of the Sāti-parva mentions this. See also Gau. X. 25.) Gradually, a toll on merchandise was paid to him while owners of ships and carts made him some gifts. Gifts of merchandise by merchants or presents at a lower price than in the market, swelled his coffers. In addition to these, we know from the Jātakas, that tolls came to be exacted at the gates of the city (Mahāunmagga Jātaka), and an excise-duty was levied on wines and liquors (chāṭikahāpaṇa). As the lord of his subjects and their protector, the king became entitled to treasure-troves, lost articles, shares of booty gained in war, the escheat of property without heir, and also to the free services of artisans once a month. Even in the Jātakas which do not mention forced labour, the people are depicted as helping in a king's hunting expedition.

Occasional taxes also came to be levid. The Jātakas give us instances of such. Thus, in some of them, we hear of the payment of "Khīrapaṇa" by the people to the king, on the birth of a royal prince. It is not difficult to see how this once voluntary gift hardened into a tax like the Utsaṅga which is mentioned in the Arthaśāstra. Constant warfare, too, enabled the king to demand contributions for maintenance and this was transformed into a tax like the Senābhakta.

Perhaps the most important cause and circumstance which added considerably to the royal prerogatives and resources, as we have said already, was the imperialistic movement and the series of conquests which followed it. Great sources of income, and vast natural resources were placed at the disposal of the Magadhan ruler. Thus, with the conquest of the smaller states, the intervening forest-areas became the king's property. The mighty conqueror came to exercise jurisdiction over rivers and waters, and these became sources of income. Mines, which came to be regarded as treasure-troves passed to the king. Once vested with supreme authority, kings were enabled to claim extraordinary revenues in times of emergencies, as detailed in the section on the "Collection of Additional Revenue." They claimed also summary fiscal powers in times of need and even had the land of subjects tilled by royal officials, on the failure of tenants to pay their dues in proper time. (see ch. on Kosābhisaṃharaṇam.)

The advance of royal power and prerogatives was further fostered by other circumstances. The lax social discipline consequent upon the pessimistic teachings of some of the Parivrājaka teachers had a disastrous consequence. Men left their wives and children. Wives left the protection of husbands. Marriage was looked upon as a burden by women. The consequences were serious. Poverty and indigence became greater. The state was faced with the problem of maintaining the destitute and as a result of this, the Mauryan rulers interfered with the activity of the monkish orders. Indiscriminate mendicancy was forbidden and men were punished for leaving wives and children destitute and joining the order. To put an end to these the government promulgated stringent laws which forbade men not to join orders without providing for wife and children. The monastic propaganda was excluded from villages. The government, seemingly, was empowered by circumstances to interfere even in religious matters.

III

KAUTILYIAN IDEAL.

The system thus described should thus be regarded as being something of natural evolution. Its intimate connection with Kauṭilya was due not to his creation of the whole system but to the fact that he believed in it and proved to be its sincerest and ablest advocate. Power had accumlated in royal hands and the king's functions had become more and more elaborate with the lapse of centuries. The process of conquest had strenthened the king's authority and the growth of mighty empires proved the death-knell to democratic life and republican activity. The policy of "Blood and Iron" had already been inaugurated. the spy system had been elaborated even in the sixth century B. C. and a century later the empire was an acomplished fact.

On the fall of the Nandas—if we are to believe in tradition—it devolved upon Kauṭilya to look to the organisation of their vast empire, to infuse life into it, and to give it a higher meaning and purpose. This he did with all his genius and his fine understanding of men and matters. A believer in the political and economic principles of the Arthaśāstra teachers, he proceeded to define the relation of the ruler and the ruled and to allocate to them their respective duties and obligations. In doing this, again, he was actuated by the best of motives and guided himself with the noblest teachings of Indian social dicipline. He believed in monarchy, since, it appeared to him as the best and the most stable form of goverment and, since, in it there was no element of turbulence or eternal war which characterised the clan-oligarchies which even then subsisted in many localities. Goverment by the will of the majority to the extinction of the just claims of minorities, or the eternal strife of sections did not appeal to him.

Hereditary monarchy was his ideal and he regarded it as the most beneficent human institution that could come into existence. In his eyes it was neither divine nor irresponsible. A champion of monarchy, he never approved the exercise of powers except for the common good. The king, according to him, was to be the custodian of national resources and of public rights and was to live only for the prosperity and happiness of his snbjects. Nowhere in his work, does Kauṭilya soar so high in his idealism as when he identifies

---

* In the chapter on Saṅgha-vrtta, he describes the evils of envy and of perpetual intrigue which subsist in republics. Again, in the chapter on the "calamities befalling a kingdom" (Bk. VIII ch 2), he discusses the evils and the disastrous consequences of Vairājyas or Dvairājyas.

the monarch with his people or dreams the prospect of a truly "national king" who was to merge even his identity with the people he was to rule, by adopting their manners, customs and language. (अविश्वास्यो हि प्रकृतिविरुद्धाचारस्य । तस्मात् समानशीलभाषावेशाचारतामुपगच्छेत् see p. 407.)

With all his belief in monarchy, Kauṭilya advocatd the fatherly protection of his subjects on the part of the king, as has been detailed already. His social out-look, too, was wide. A Brāhmaṇa and a conservative by training and tradition, it was reserved for him to advocate the emancipation of the slave, the mitigation of judicial torture, the remission of heavy taxation and similar other measures of liberalism and humanity. His sympathy for the masses, his reasonable championship of the claims of woman whose rights he recognized and whom he tried to save from the tyranny of socity, his admission of the aborigines to royal protection — all hold him up as a humane and far-sighted advocate of benevolent government. He was averse to oligarchy and republicanism, yet, he never strove to trample under foot the autonomous government of the rural centres of life. Harmony between king and people was his highest aim and far from believing in autocracy, he reckoned the loyalty of subjects as the highest asset of a ruler. His statecraft became unpopular in a later age, his imperialism became the subject of scoff and ridicule, and men denounced him for his advocacy of fraud and deception in outwitting an enemy. Yet, a careful enquiry convinces us that these were due to the unscruplous age in which he lived and not the outcome of his own innate crookedness.*

* We reserve a fuller discussion about Kauṭilya's services or his guiding principles in politics for the next volume But, for the present, it may be stated, that, he occupies a unique place among the Arthaśāstra thinkers. With his predecessors, politics had degenerated into the art of kingcraft, the main objective of which was to strengthen the regal power, at the cost of rivals or by deceiving the people. The welfare of the people or the good government of the country was no consideration of theirs. With Kauṭilya, however, these unmoral principles were exchanged for other ones which identified royalty with the people. Any one who studies the Kauṭilīya cannot fail to mark this. Kauṭilya's liberalism is clearly apparent from his dissertations on royalty, his acceptance of the injunctions of religion and reason, his belief in the sound education of princes, his sympathy for the masses and his identification of the interests of the ruler with those of the ruled. His teachings thus mark a new era in politics and political thought.

IV

CONSOLIDATION OF GOVERNMENTAL AUTHORITY

We have discussed in detail the administrative system and the principles of good government as conceived and laid down by the great author of the Arthaśāstra. We now proceed to a discussion of the further measures, which according Kauṭilya, are to be undertaken by a prince to consolidate his sovereign authority and the prosperity of his kingdom.

The first duty on the part of a king is to discipline himself, so that he would be able to see his objective clearly, and devote his energies properly. His control of the senses was a primary necessity, since, it would help him in protecting his self from greed, lust or intemperence. (Ch. on Indriya-jaya pp. 7– 9).

His next duty is to ensure proper deliberation, and the understanding of the situation. Consequently, he should try to deliberate cool-headedly and accept the opinion of the largest possible number of advisers. As Kauṭilya himself says, if wanting in the power of deliberation, he should collect wise men around him, (**मन्त्रशक्तिहीनः प्राज्ञपुरुषोपचयं विद्यावृद्धसंयोगं वा कुर्वीत। तथा हि सच्छ्रेयः प्राप्नोति** VII. 14. p. 304) and take their opinion.

After this, he should proceed to ensure the loyalty of his subjects, and eradicate internal discontent. Kauṭilya more than once emphasises, that, loyalty of the subjects is the greatest of all assets a king could possess. (अनुरागे सार्वगुण्यम् p. 273. VII. 5). He should, therefore, take the best precautions against popular discontent, (प्रकृतीनां क्षयलोभविरागकारणानि नोत्पादयेत्) and if there were signs of such, he should immediately remedy it. (उत्पन्नानि सद्यः वा प्रतिकुर्वीत) Bk. VII ch. V). The causes of popular discontent are detailed in the fifth chapter of the seventh book. They may be summarised as comprising tyranny over the good, leniency to the wicked, injustice, indulging in unpopular measures, withholding of justice to the aggrieved, over-greediness, insults to the eminent, erroneous or impolitic actions and indolence. All these are to be avoided and no time is to be wasted in applying the remedies demanded by the situation. Indolence, according to Kauṭilya, and waste of energy are the worst vices and are sure to lead to destruction. Next, irresolution, inactivity and trusting to fate are to be given up. (दैवप्रमाणो मानुषहीनो निरारम्भो विपन्नकर्मारम्भो वाऽवसीदति। यत्किञ्चनकारी न किञ्चिदासादयति स चैषां पापिष्ठतमो भवति। VII ch. II p. 295.)

The king should therefore free himself from the influence of wine, women, or addicion to diceplay or other vices, since, these dissipate energy and bring in irresolution.

The eradication of internal enemies is of highest importance to a prince. Of two kinds of enemies, *i.e.* foreign (बाह्य) and internal (आभ्यन्तर), Kauṭilya fears the former most. He compares it to a lurking snake. (अहिभयादभ्यन्तरः कोपो बाह्यकोपात्पापीयान्) See VIII. 2 ; IX 3 ; IX 5.) Of such internal troubles, he recognizes the following four important varieties. *e. g.*

(*a*) of external origin and internal abetment

(*b*) of internal origin and external abetment

(*c*) of external origin and external abetment

(*d*) of internal origin and internal abetment. (Bk. IX. ch. 5.)

Kauṭilya always harps on the seriousness of discontent, intrigues and propaganda and explains the remedies to be applied. These are described in detail in three chapters (*e.g.*, 3, 4, 5,) of the IXth. Book. According to him, the four recognized means of averting evil *e.g.* Sāma, Dāna, Bheda and Danda are applicable according to circumstances. With the details we are not at present concerned, but, this may be said that the consideration of the nature of these together with the remedies suggested show him to be a statesman of remarkable fore-sight. The maxim laid down by him is that in purely internal intrigue, a king should not apply punishment to the masses, since, that will not only not produce the desired result, but produce something otherwise more serious. (दण्डो हि महाजने क्षेप्तुमशक्यः p. 352.)

After all this, the king should devote his energies to the acquisition of real strength based on the development of the economic resources of his kingdom. He should devote its efforts to the development of his territory, its defensive fortifications, its irrigational works supporting agriculture, roads of traffic facilitating trade, mines bringing in gold, silver and precious metals, timber-forests, elephant-forests, and pasture lands. (Bk. VII ch 14 on Hīnaśaktrpūraṇam p. 305).* In the absence of such resources, he should strive to acquire such necessaries from his friends, allies or relatives. These will surely put him in a secure footing and lead to his success in life and bring in the prosperity of his subjects.

Then, if he happens to be destitute of an army, he should try to recruit one by enlisting brave men, members of (fighting) corporations, [desperados] wild tribes, mlecchas, and also enlist intelligent spies in his service.

---

* प्रभवहीनः प्रकृतियोगक्षेमसिद्धौ यतेत । जनपदः सर्वकर्मणां योनिः । सेतुबन्धः सस्यानां, वणिक्पथः परातिसन्धानस्य योनिः । खनिः सङ्ग्रामोपकरणानां योनिः ; द्रव्यवनं दुर्गकर्मणां यानरथयोश्च । हस्तिवनं हस्तिनाम् । गवाश्वरथोष्ट्राणां च व्रजः ।

In regard to foreign policy, he should as a rule strive to be at peace with neighbouring kings and secure powerful allies. He should not ruin himself by coming into conflict with powerful enemies. But, if attacked, he should strive to strengthen himself by the forces of his allies or adopt the policy of the weak towards the strong, and thus avert all dangers. These methods will not only ensure his safety, but at the same time enable his elements to prosper,* and will thereby raise hlm to the highest place among kings.

Thus strengthened, a king must follow the principles of diplomacy. Thereby safeguarded and if his energies are well-directed, proper methods are sure to make him a conqueror of the world, though his territory or resources be initially very small.

The principles of a wise foreign policy and of a successful diplomacy, leading to the consolidation of an empire, we shall discuss in the next volume.

---

* अरिवर्जाः प्रकृतयः सप्तैताः सगुणोदयाः ।
उक्ताः प्रत्यङ्गभूतास्ताः प्रकृता राजसम्पदः ॥
सम्पादयत्यसम्पन्नाः प्रकृतीरात्मवान्नृपः ।
विवृद्धाश्चानुरक्ताश्च प्रकृतीर्हन्त्यनात्मवान् ॥
आत्मवांस्त्वल्पदेशोऽपि युक्तः प्रकृतिसम्पदा ।
नयज्ञः पृथिवीं कृत्स्नां जयत्येव न हीयते ॥

Kau. Bk. VI. p. 257.

APPENDIX

A

ECONOMIC PRINCIPLES OF KAUTILYA

Economic theories in the proper sense of the expression were not developed in India. As elsewhere in this world, economic phenomena were noticed and certain conclusions were drawn with a view to their application in connection with the enrichment of the community or of the head of the state. The method of enquiry of the Ancients were hardly scientific and they failed to go to the root-causes or to enquire into the natural laws which govern production or distribution.

In spite of these deficiencies, however, proper attention was paid to the arts and industries which were supposed to bring in wealth, and the science or art of economic welfare was not neglected in India. Vārttā was a recognized branch of study and innumerable treatises seem to have been written on the various branches of it. The Arthaśāstra school laid great emphasis on the art of attaining material welfare, since, with them it was the basic objective of man on which the attainment of the rest depended.* Vārttā was regarded as a

* अर्थ एव प्रधानः ; अर्थमूलौ धर्मकामौ । Kau. p. 12.

branch of study which brought prosperity to all, especially to the head of the state, by enabling him to have prosperity at home and power abroad.* The aims and objectives of the teachers of this school were similar to those of the Kameralists in whom there was a peculiar "combination of ideas political, juristic, technical and economic". Kauṭilya, too, gives a high place to this science, since it was instrumental in bringing in wealth, thus enabling kings to gain their ends.

Like most of the ancients, Kauṭilya does not define wealth. From a perusal of his work, however, we may draw certain inferences in regard to his ideas, and these seem to make us hold the conclusion that in his eyes 'anything which was of utility or service to man by satisfying his needs and wants' could be regarded as wealth. Thus, he attaches importance to everything, e.g., to the produce of fields, gold and silver, the wild products of forests and even the labour of artisans. Crude and undefined as his ideas were, they were certainly far in advance of Medieval thinkers, who attached sole importance to the precious metals. Of course, he regarded the precious metals as the best and highest form of wealth, yet in his eyes, these were not the only wealth. That such were his ideas, would appear from his dissertations on

* कृषिपाशुपाल्ये वणिज्या च वार्त्ता। धान्यपशुहिरण्यकुप्यविष्टिप्रदानादौपकारिकी। तया स्वपक्षं परपक्षं च वशीकरोति कोशदण्डाभ्याम्। Kau. p. 8.

the importance of mines* as well as from his views regarding the comparative valuability of mines to agricultural land.†

In regard to his ideas of value or price, Kauṭilya is not far in advance of his contemporaries. The idea of a just price or of just remuneration dominates his policy as well as measures, as we shall see presently. He seems to have been not unacquainted with the law of variation of price with demand and supply. In one place, he speaks of the rise of prices with too many purchasers (क्रेतृसंघर्षे मूल्यवृद्धिः—Kau. p. 110), and in another place, he takes precautions against the fall in the price of articles with too much supply (पण्यबाहुल्यात्).

The natural laws of demand and supply, however, made no influence on him. In the highly protective and artificial system of the day, such variations were not regarded as the outcome of natural laws, but as menaces to social prosperity and attempts were made to check such variations. Thus, as we have pointed out already, interest was regulated, as well as the price and profits de-

---

* cf. Kau. p. 85.

आकरप्रभवः कोशः कोशाद्दण्डः प्रजायते ।
पृथिवी कोशदण्डाभ्यां प्राप्यते कोशभूषणा ॥

† खनिधान्यभोगयोः खनिभोगः कोशकरः । धान्यभोगः कोशकोष्ठागारकरः । धान्यमूला हि दुर्गादीनां कर्मणामारम्भः महाविषयविक्रयो वा खनिभोगः श्रेयान् । Kau. p. 294. Owing to the same reasons, Kauṭilya prefers the South, since, here—कम्बलाजिनाश्वपण्यवर्जाः शङ्खवज्रमणिमुक्ताः सुवर्णाश्च प्रभूततरा दक्षिणापथे । p. 298.

manded by merchants.* Freedom of trade was restricted in all possible ways, since, indiscriminate speculation interfered with the normal supply of markets and penalised the consumers.

On similar principles, the government put down cornering or attempts to lower or enhance the price of articles through combination. Merchants, as we have stated already, were regarded as thieves, though not in name, since, they robbed people by their combinations.†

Protection was carried on in various ways. Weights and measures were regulated, while the amount of compensation owing to the handling of goods in retailing was laid down. In the case of artisans, the quality of their work was laid down, wastage of materials during work was regulated and their wages were fixed down. Details are meagre, and so, we cannot form an idea as to whether interference was carried to that extent as we find in the Colbertian system.

In regard to the industries and manufactures, the ideas of the Arthaśāstra thinkers do not show the one-sided views or the narrow perspective of Medieval European writers. All industries and

---

*अनुज्ञातक्रयादुपरि स्वदेशीयाणां पण्यानां पञ्चकं शतं आजीवं स्थापयेत। परदेशीयानां दशकं। अतः परं अर्घं वर्धयतां क्रये विक्रये वा भावयतां पणशते पञ्चपणाद्द्विशतो दण्डः। p. 204-5.

† Kauṭilya describes profitiering in this way—*e.g.* वैदेहकास्तु सम्भूय पण्यानां उत्कर्षापकर्षं कुर्वाणाः पणे पणशतं कुम्भे कुम्भशतं" इत्याजीवन्ति—Kau. p. 331.

In another passage, they are described as अचोरश्चोरः।

occupations, including agriculture and mining, were highly patronised and handicraft works were encouraged. We find neither a preference given to foreign commerce as with the Mercantilists, nor a supreme position accorded to agriculture as in the economic thought of the Physiocrats. The ideas of the Arthaśāstra thinkers were thus more comprehensive and in some respects more advanced. This appears the more so when we bear in mind that India was mainly an agricultural country.

Trade was regarded as profitable and encouraged, though traders were looked down upon with suspicion. Exchange of commodities was associated with the idea of enrichment through the deception of others.* Some passages seem to hint at prosperity due to the gain of precious metals and gems through trade, and show ideas not dissimilar to those of the Mercantilists. (See p. 298). But, gain of gold and silver was not the sole end or aim of trade. Intercourse with foreign countries was looked upon as a source of gain to the mother country in diverse ways and so foreign merchandise and merchants were invited and encouraged.

This importance attached to foreign imports shows clearly that the Arthaśāstra thinkers did not believe in an isolated self-sufficient economic existence. We have shown already, that Kauṭilya

* वणिक्पथः परातिसन्धानस्य योनिः । p. 305.

attaches great importance to the production of all possible necessaries of life at home. The conditions of an ideal Janapada, according to him, are laid down in the chapter on Prakṛti-sampat, and these include the capacity of the country to maintain a large population, with space for their increasing requirements. The existence of good boundaries, water-ways and road-communications, provision with pasture, valuable mines, wealth in cattle, freedom from detriments to material progress, fertility of the soil, absence of dependence entirely on rain and the existence of a labouring population are the other important requisites.*

The mention of these requisite qualities show Kauṭilya's belief in self-sufficiency, yet he is not blind to the conditions of nature. As such, he lays down a capacity for maintaining other countries in distress (**परधारणश्चापदि**) as one of the requisites of an ideal Janapada. Perhaps, his belief in this was actuated by the development of Indian foreign trade and the growth of the inter-world commerce with the Hellenic and Mediterranean countries which was so profitable to India. The same idea of mutual help of communities in distress is found from his directions to avert famines.

---

* स्थानवान् आत्मधारणः परधारणश्चापदि स्वारक्षःस्वाजीवः···शक्यसामन्तः··· कान्तः सीताखनिद्रव्यहस्तिवनवान् गव्यः पशुमान् अदेवमातृको वारिस्थलपथाभ्यामुपेतः सारचित्रबहुपण्यो दण्डकरसहः कर्मशीलकर्षको बालिश्यस्वाम्यवरवर्णप्रायो भक्तशुचि मनुष्य इति जनपदसम्पत्। Kau. p. 256.

Like many of the Medieval thinkers, Kauṭilya believed in an increasing population, since, their activity was bound to bring wealth and prosperity to the king and kingdom. In the respect, his ideas are similar to those of many Mercantilists and Kameralists.

As to the economic functions of the state, we have discussed all possible points of interest to us. Clearly, according to Kauṭilya, the fruition of material aims of life was the primary condition of existence or of social happiness. It was the duty of the king to help the individual as much as was possible, through the resources at his disposal. The king was to help individuals and industries as well as the various industrial sections, equitably and rationally. As such, the prosperity of the community contributed to the prosperity of the king, while the distress of the latter led to their poverty. A well-filled treasury was a prime requisite for the progress of a prosperous kingdom (कोषपूर्वाः सर्वारम्भाः), since, upon it depended the army, and upon the army the safety and prosperity of the people. The king's poverty, according to Kauṭilya, led to the economic ruin of the country and he was sure to devour up his people. (अल्पकोषो हि राजा पौरजानपदानेव ग्रसते*)

---

* This seems to be the converse of the Physiocratic motto '*poor peasant, poor king, and poor king, poor peasant.*'

APPENDIX

B

ADDITIONS AND CORRECTIONS

Page 6, l. 13. Regarding Kātyāyana's indebtedness to Kauṭilya, see the introduction to *Katyayana-mata-sangraha*, where I have quoted passages from Kātyāyana and Kauṭilīya which show similarity in language and ideas.

Line 15. Kulluka. This is an error and should be Medhātithi, who in his commentary on verse 154, ch. VII. of the Manusaṃhitā, quotes practically the whole of the chapter on Gūḍhapuruṣotpattiḥ. (Kau. pp. 18—19).

Page 52. For the Jewish king's duties, see the Mosaic laws in the Old Testament. and note the *Jubilee* which used to take place every fifty years.

For Hammurabi's doings, see Maspero, *Struggle of Nations* pp. 40 C to 44. Hammurabi repeatedly speaks of his services through his efforts for irrigation and the "mounds of grain" which were stored for the people. The same also appears from the history of Egypt.

Page 52. For the Taikwa reforms of Japan, see MacLaren's *History of Japan during the Meiji Era*, chapter on the origin of Feudalism.

Pages 80-81. See any Constitutional History of England.

In regard to the Hereditary Revenues of the British Crown, see Walpole's History of England Vol. II pp. 88—90.

P. 268-271.—In regard to social order and interference in ecclesiastical matters, there are other instances of such, in the Arthaśāstra. In the sixteenth chapter of the third book (p. 191.), there is express provision for punishing men in holy orders for serious offences. In minor crimes, such offenders were allowed to do penance or pray for the king in lieu of fines. In serious offences, their immunities were cancelled. cf. the verse—

प्रव्रज्यासु यथाचारान् राजा दण्डेन वारयेत् ।
धर्मोह्यधर्मोपहतः शास्तारं हन्त्युपेक्षितः ॥

Note on the active social service of ancient governments For tendencies to restrict slave-trade, see Civilization of Babylonia and Assyria—Jastrow, pp. 314. For an attempt to regulate relation between merchants and retailers, see the same book p. 298. The Roman system of distribution of land and corn among the people is too wellknown to be described in detail. The Peruvian Incas too maintained a paternal government, which kept grain reserves for the people and constantly relieved poverty by grants from the royal coffers. For details, see Prescot's Conquest of Peru, chapters II to IV.

APPENDIX

C

KAUTILYIAN GFNERAL MAXIMS

मनुष्याणां वृत्तिरर्थः [मनुष्यवती भूमिरित्यर्थः । तस्याः] पृथिव्या लाभपालनोपायः शास्त्रमर्थशास्त्रम् ।

आन्वीक्षकी त्रयी वार्त्ता दण्डनीतिश्चेति विद्याः ।

ताभिर्धर्मार्थौ यद्विद्यात् तद्विद्यानां विद्यात्वम् ।

कृषिपाशुपाल्ये वणिज्या च वार्त्ता ; तया स्वपक्षं परपक्षं च वशीकरोति कोशदण्डाभ्याम् । (I. iv.)

आन्वीक्षकीत्रयीवार्त्तानां योगक्षेमसाधनो दण्डः । तस्य नीतिर्दण्डनीतिः । अलब्धलाभार्था लब्धपरिरक्षणी रक्षितविवर्धनी, वृद्धस्य तीर्थेषु प्रतिपादनी च । तस्यामायत्ता लोकयात्रा । (I. iv).

विनयोमूलो दण्डः प्राणभृतां योगक्षेमावहः ।

कृतकः स्वाभाविकश्च विनयः ।

श्रुताद्धि प्रज्ञोपजायते । प्रज्ञया योगः । योगादात्मवत्तेति विद्यासामर्थ्यम् । (I. v).

विद्याविनयहेतुरिन्द्रियजयः कार्यः । कृत्स्नं हि शास्त्रमिन्द्रियजयः । (I. vii)

अविद्याविनयः पुरुषव्यसनहेतुः । अविनीतो हि व्यसनदोषान् न पश्यति । तस्मादरिषड्वर्गत्यागेनेन्द्रियजयं कुर्वीत । कोपजस्त्रिवर्गः कामजश्चतुर्वर्गः । तयोः कोपो गरीयान् ।

प्रायशश्च कोपवशा राजानः प्रकृतिकोपैर्हताः श्रूयन्ते। काम-वशाः क्षयव्ययनिमित्तमतिव्याधिभिः। (Ix. iii)

वश्येन्द्रियः परस्त्रीद्रव्यहिंसाश्च वर्जयेत्। स्वप्नलौल्यमनृतमुद्धतवेशत्वमनर्थसंयोगं च। अधर्मसंयुक्तमनर्थसंयुक्तं च व्यवहारम्। (I. vii).

अर्थो धर्मः काम इत्यर्थत्रिवर्गः। तस्य पूर्वः पूर्वः श्रेयानुपसम्प्राप्तुम्। अनर्थोऽधर्मः शोक इत्यनर्थत्रिवर्गः। स्वतः परतो वा भयोत्पत्तिरनर्थः। तस्य पूर्वः पूर्वः श्रेयान् प्रतिकर्त्तुम्। क्षयस्थानवृद्धीनां चोत्तरोत्तरं लिप्सेत। प्रातिलोम्येन वा क्षयादीनामायत्यां विशेषं पश्येत् (IX. vii)।

धर्मार्थाविरोधेन कामं सेवेत। न निःसुखः स्यात्। समं त्रिवर्गमन्योन्यानुबन्धम्। एको ह्यत्यासेवितो धर्मार्थकामाना[मा त्मान]मितरौ च पीड़यति। अर्थ एव प्रधानः। अर्थमूलौ धर्मकामौ। (I. vii).

लोकयात्रार्थी नित्यमुद्यतदण्डः स्यात्।

सुविज्ञातप्रणीतो हि दण्डः प्रजाःधर्मार्थकामैर्योजयति।

अप्रणीतो हि मात्स्यन्यायमुद्भावयति। बलीयानबलं हि ग्रसते दण्डधराभावे। तेन गुप्तः प्रभवतीति। (I. iv)

दण्डमूलास्तिस्रो विद्याः। क्षयः स्थानं वृद्धिरित्युदयाः। तस्य मानुषं नयापनयौ दैवमयानायौ।

दैवमानुषं हि कर्म लोकमर्वात। अदृष्टकारितं दैवं तस्मिन्नष्टेन फलेन योगोऽयः।

दैवप्रमाणो मानुषहीनो निरारम्भो विपन्नकर्मारम्भो वाऽव-

सीदति। यत्किञ्चनकारी न किञ्चिदासादयति, स चैषां पापिष्ठतमो भवति। (VII. xi.)

पुरुषवद्धिराज्यम्। अपुरुषागौर्वन्ध्येव किं दुहीत।

(VII. xi)

स्वाम्यमात्यजनपददुर्गकोशदण्डमित्राणि प्रकृतयः। (VI i)

[राजा राज्यमिति प्रकृतिसंक्षेपः] VIII. ii.

मन्त्रिपुरोहितादिभृत्यवर्गमध्यक्षप्रचारं पुरुषद्रव्यप्रकृतिव्यसनप्रतिकारमेधनं राजैव करोति। स्वयं यच्छीलः तच्छीलाः प्रकृतयो भवन्ति। तत्कूटस्थानीयो हि स्वामी। VIII. i.

कृतस्वपक्षपरपक्षोपग्रहं कार्यारम्भान् चिन्तयेत्।

मन्त्रपूर्वाः सर्वारम्भाः। उच्छिन्देत मन्त्रभेदी।

कर्मणामारम्भोपायः, पुरुषद्रव्यसम्पत्, देशकालविभागः, विनिपातप्रतीकारः कार्यसिद्धिरिति पञ्चाङ्गो मन्त्रः।

अवाप्तार्थः कालं नातिक्रमयेत्।

रक्षितो राजा राज्यं रक्षति आसन्नेभ्यः परेभ्यश्च। पूर्वं दारेभ्यः पुत्रेभ्यश्च। कर्कटकसधर्माणो हि जनकभक्षाः राजपुत्राः। (I. xvii)

राजानमुत्तिष्ठमानमनूत्तिष्ठन्ते भृत्याः।

प्रमादयन्तमनुप्रमादयन्ति। कर्माणि चास्य भक्षयन्ति, द्विषद्भिश्चातिसन्धीयते। तस्मादुत्थानमात्मनः कुर्वीत। (I. xix)

सहायसाध्यं राजत्वम्। प्रत्यक्षपरोक्षानुमेया हि राजवृत्तिः। स्वयंदृष्टं हि प्रत्यक्षम्। परोपदिष्टं हि परोक्षम्। (I. ix)

मन्त्रशक्तिहीनः प्राज्ञपुरुषोपचयं विद्यावृद्धसंयोगं वा कुर्वीत। तथा हि सद्यःश्रेयः प्राप्नोति। (VII. xiv).

अमात्यपूर्वाः सर्वारम्भाः। जनपदमूलाः दुर्गकोशदण्डाः सेतुर्वातारम्भाः। लम्भपालनो हि दण्डः कोशस्य। दुर्गाभावे कोशः परेषाम्। दण्डाभावे ध्रुवं कोशविनाशः। VIII. i.)

कोशदण्डशक्तिमात्मसंस्थां कुर्वीत। (VIII. ii.)

अमात्यसम्पदोपेताः सर्वाध्यक्षाः शक्तितो कर्मसु नियोज्याः। कर्मसु चैषां नित्यं परीक्षां कारयेत्। चित्तानित्यत्वान्मनुष्याणाम्। अश्वसधर्माणो हि मनुष्या नियुक्ताः कर्मसु विकुर्वते।

बहुमुख्यं चानित्यं चाधिकरणं कुर्यात्। (II. ix.)

कोशपूर्वाः सर्वारम्भाः। कोशमूलो दण्डः। तस्मात् पूर्वं कोशमवेक्षेत। अल्पकोषो हि राजा पौरजानपदानेव ग्रसते।

उपस्थानगतः कार्यार्थिनामद्वारासङ्गं कारयेत्। दुर्दर्शो हि राजा कार्याकार्यविपर्यासमासन्नैः कार्यते। तेन प्रकृतिकोपमरिवशं वा गच्छेत्। (I. xix.)

प्रभवहीनः प्रकृतियोगक्षेमसिद्धौ यतेत। जनपदः सर्वकर्मणां योनिः। ततः प्रभवः। तस्य स्थानमापदि आत्मनश्च दुर्गम्। सेतुबन्धः सस्यानां योनिः। वणिक्पथः परातिसन्धानस्य योनिः। खनिः संग्रामोपकरणानां योनिः। द्रव्यवनं दुर्गकर्मणां, यानरथयोश्च। हस्तिवनं हस्तिनाम्। गवाश्वखरोष्ट्राणां च व्रजः। (VII. xiv.)

अहिभयादभ्यन्तरः कोपो बाह्यकोपात् पापीयान् (VII.xi.)

प्रकृतीनां क्षयलोभविरागकारणानि नोत्पादयेत्। उत्पन्नानि वा सद्यः प्रतिकुर्वीत।

सर्वत्रचोपहतान् पितेवानुगृह्णीयात्। अनुरागे सार्वगुण्यम्।

INDEX